T0305511

Organizations and Activism

Series Editors: **Daniel King**, Nottingham Trent University and **Martin Parker**, University of Bristol

---

Organizations and Activism publishes books that explore how politics happens within and because of organizations, how activism is organized, and how activists change organizations.

Forthcoming in the series:

Sociocracy at Work:
Possibilities and Limitations of an Alternative Democratic Model of Organization
Martyn Griffin, **Daniel King**,
Ted Jennifer Rau and **Jerry Koch Gonzalez**

Organizing Food, Faith and Freedom:
Imagining Alternatives
Ozan Alakavuklar

Organizing for Change:
Social Change Organizations and Social Change Makers
By **Silke Roth** and **Clare Saunders**

Food Politics, Activism and Alternative Consumer Cooperatives
By **Beyza Oba** and **Zeynep Özsoy**

Find out more at
bristoluniversitypress.co.uk/organizations-and-activism

Organizations and Activism

Series Editors: **Daniel King**, Nottingham Trent University and **Martin Parker**, University of Bristol

Find out more at
bristoluniversitypress.co.uk/organizations-and-activism

CO-OPERATION AND CO-OPERATIVES IN 21ST-CENTURY EUROPE

Edited by
Julian Manley, Anthony Webster
and Olga Kuznetsova

BRISTOL
UNIVERSITY
PRESS

First published in Great Britain in 2023 by

Bristol University Press
University of Bristol
1–9 Old Park Hill
Bristol
BS2 8BB
UK
t: +44 (0)117 374 6645
e: bup-info@bristol.ac.uk

Details of international sales and distribution partners are available at bristoluniversitypress.co.uk

© Bristol University Press 2023

British Library Cataloguing in Publication Data
A catalogue record for this book is available from the British Library

ISBN 978-1-5292-2641-6 hardcover
ISBN 978-1-5292-2642-3 ePub
ISBN 978-1-5292-2643-0 ePdf

The right of Julian Manley, Anthony Webster and Olga Kuznetsova to be identified as editors of this
work has been asserted by them in accordance with the Copyright, Designs and Patents Act 1988.

Cover design: blu inc
Front cover image: Getty Images/Eastimages
Bristol University Press uses environmentally responsible print partners.
Printed and bound in Great Britain by CPI Group (UK) Ltd, Croydon, CR0 4YY

FSC
www.fsc.org
MIX
Paper | Supporting
responsible forestry
FSC® C013604

To AK – my loyal co-everything
To NK – a source of creativity
– Olga Kuznetsova

To the Director Members of the Preston
Cooperative Education Centre
– Julian Manley

With thanks to members of CoRNet for
their support during this project, and to the
Co-operative College UK
– Anthony Webster

Contents

Series Editors' Preface

Daniel King and Martin Parker

Organizing is politics made durable. From co-operatives to corporations, Occupy to Meta, states and NGOs, organizations shape our lives. They shape the possible futures of governance, policy making and social change, and hence are central to understanding how human beings can deal with the challenges that face us, whether that be pandemics, populism or climate change. This book series publishes work that explore how politics happens within and because of organizations and organizing. We want to explore how activism is organized and how activists change organizations. We are also interested in the forms of resistance to activism, in the ways that powerful interests contest and reframe demands for change. These are questions of huge relevance to scholars in sociology, politics, geography, management and beyond, and are becoming ever more important as demands for impact and engagement change the way that academics imagine their work. They are also important to anyone who wants to understand more about the theory and practice of organizing, not just the abstracted ideologies of capitalism taught in business schools.

Our books offer critical examinations of organizations as sites of or targets for activism, and we will also assume that our authors, and hopefully our readers, are themselves agents of change. Titles may focus on specific industries or fields, or they may be arranged around particular themes or challenges. Our topics might include the alternative economy; surveillance, whistleblowing and human rights; digital politics; religious groups; social movements; NGOs; feminism and anarchist organization; action research and co-production; activism and the neoliberal university, and any other subjects that are relevant and topical.

'Organizations and Activism' is also a multidisciplinary series. Contributions from all and any relevant academic fields will be welcomed. The series is international in outlook, and proposals from outside the English-speaking global north are particularly welcome.

This book, the fourth in our series so far, is the first to directly address one of the oldest forms of business-based activism – cooperative organizing. In the UK, The Rochdale Society of Equitable Pioneers, founded in 1844, is usually cited as the first example of an organization which was owned and controlled by workers. Beginnings are always tricky though. According to the International Cooperative Alliance, the earliest record of a co-operative comes from Fenwick in Scotland where, 'in March 14, 1761, in a barely furnished cottage local weavers manhandled a sack of oatmeal into John Walker's whitewashed front room and began selling the contents at a discount, forming the Fenwick Weavers' Society'.[1] There's a romance and drama to this sort of origin story, as if something were conjured into existence that didn't exist before. But was cooperation new? Did it begin then?

A co-operative, as a noun, is an organization that institutionalises cooperation, as a verb. It celebrates the theory and practice of interdependence and pitches them against countervailing powers which demand separation and competition. No wonder we have an origin story for co-operatives which begins in the most industrialised country in the world at the beginning of a revolution which tore workers from common lands and made them compete for wages. Yet now, after centuries of individualist ideology, we often need to be reminded that the practice of capitalism, like almost all human practices, actually relies on co-ordination, on common understandings and efforts, on a general intellect. In fact, the institutionalisation of cooperation is an intensification of everyday mutual aid, not a radical departure from something that went before. It certainly pushes back against hierarchy, against the unequal distribution of the surplus produced by collective activity, but it reflects the ways that all of us commonly behave with our family and friends, and often enough with our neighbours and workmates.

For some, co-operatives might sound a bit dated, as if they were an institution from the 1960s associated with dried beans and earnest people in sandals. A hippy utopia. This book places the co-operative at the centre of contemporary political struggles, in part because of its connections to ideas about Community Wealth Building from Jackson Mississippi to Preston Lancashire, or Cleveland Ohio to Hamburg Germany. Embedding cooperative ownership and control as part of a wider political strategy, whether involving municipal governance, energy generation, transport or the local public house is an extraordinarily powerful way to produce an economy that spreads wealth rather than concentrating it. Yet as the chapters in this book make clear, this isn't just about economics, as if the economy were what Marx called 'a hidden abode', a room of dirty secrets in which we all act selfishly.

One of the wider implications of a cooperative economy would be that the distinction between economics and politics, or economy and culture, would no longer make much sense. The very idea of a 'business school' implies that business is, and perhaps should, be different to everyday life. For years, those business school professors interested in corporate social responsibility have been writing about culture and values, and most lately about corporate purpose. Yet they rarely try to unsettle assumptions about the ownership and control of work organizations, refusing to question the financial rents owed to shareholders, or the salaries and entitlements of managers. In a different economy, the values of our 'private' lives would be carried into the practices of our public lives, with no need for 'business ethics', as a state of exception in which everyday ethics no longer apply. Cooperation, in other words, dissolves separation, and demands forms of schooling which demonstrate in theory and practice that we rely on each other in the most profound ways. Not just co-operatives then, but a cooperative economy supported by cooperative education. A worthy aim for any business activist.

We hope you enjoy this book. If you want to discuss a proposal yourself, then email the series editors. We look forward to hearing from you.

Note

[1] www.ica.coop/en/cooperatives/history-cooperative-movement#:~:text=In%201 844%20a%20group%20of,known%20as%20the%20Rochdale%20Pioneers [Accessed on April 2023].

List of Figures and Tables

Figure

Tables

List of Abbreviations

ABCD	asset-based community development
AOM	Academy of Management
BBLC	blockchain-based limited liability company
Brexit	withdrawal of the UK from the European Union
CBS	community benefit society
CCIN	Co-operative Council Innovation Network
CEO	chief executive officer
CERN	Co-operative Early Researchers Network
CFDT	Confédération Française Démocratique du Travail
CGSCOP	Confédération Générale des SCOP (General Confederation of Productive Workers' Co-operative Societies)
CHE	Co-operative Higher Education
CIC	community interest company
CICOPA	Comité International des Coopératives de Production et Artisanales
CIO	charitable incorporated organization
COALA	Coalition of Automated Legal Application
CoRNet	Cooperative Researchers Network (formerly CERN)
CPF	Co-operative Productive Federation
CPR	common pool resources
CSFO	community-supported farming organizations
CSR	corporate social responsibility
CU	Co-operative Union
CWB	community wealth building
CWS	Co-operative Wholesale Society
DAO	decentralized autonomous organization
DIY	do it yourself
EU	European Union
FED	Fagor Electrodomesticos (Mondragon)
HEC	Higher Education Co-operative
HRM	human resource management
ICA	International Cooperative Alliance

ILO	International Labour Organization
JICA	Japanese International Cooperation Agency
LAT	Leicester Ageing Together
LBS	London Graduate School of Business
LFA	Leicestershire Footpath Association
LRO	Labour Representation Organization
LVC	Leicester Vaughan College
MBA	Master of Business Administration
MFI	micro finance institutions
MLIT	Ministry of Land, Infrastructure, Transport and Tourism (Japan)
NC	New Cooperativism
PCC	Preston City Council
PCDN	Preston Co-operative Development Network
PCEC	Preston Cooperative Education Centre
PM	Preston Model
PRME	Principles for Responsible Management Education
S&S	Star & Shadow Cinema Co-op
SACMI	Società Anonima Cooperativa Meccanici Imola
SCWS	Scottish Co-operative Wholesale Society
SEs	social enterprises
SMEs	small to medium enterprises
STUC	Scottish Trades Union Congress
UK	United Kingdom
UN	United Nations
US	United States
WISCP	West Indian Senior Citizens Project

Notes on the Contributors

François Deblangy is a PhD student at the department of British Studies of the University of Rouen-Normandy. His research work explores the social and political history of industrial democracy in Great Britain since the 1960s. He is currently writing a thesis about the British worker co-operative movement and is the author of a recently published research article on this topic, 'From workshop democracy to democratic workshop: A historical sketch of production co-operation in Great Britain' (2022).

Temidayo Eseonu completed her PhD in Politics at the University of Manchester where she researched racial equity in public service delivery. Her current research interests include racial justice, deliberative and participatory democratic governance, and research methods which centre the experiential knowledge of racially minoritized communities. She is author of the article 'Co-creation as a social innovation process to include "hard-to-reach" groups in public service delivery' (2021).

Andrei Kuznetsov is Professor of International Corporate Social Responsibility at Lancashire School of Business and Enterprise and Deputy Director of the Lancashire Institute for Economic and Business Research. Andrei has doctorates in Economics and in Social Sciences. Prior to joining academia in the UK, he conducted research at the European University Institute (Florence, Italy) and KU Leuven (Belgium). Andrei's research interests include CSR, cross-cultural management, corporate governance, responsible business practices in international business contexts, institutional analysis. Andrei has published in leading international journals, including *Journal of International Business Studies*, *Journal of Comparative Economics* and *Journal of Small Business Management*. His published articles include 'Building professional discourse in emerging markets: Language, context and the challenge of sensemaking' (2014) and 'Threats to security of property rights in a transition economy: An empirical perspective' (2013).

Olga Kuznetsova has worked in academia for over 30 years, of which more than 20 years at Manchester Metropolitan University (UK), where currently she is Visiting Research Fellow at the Institute of Place Management and Centre for Policy Modelling. Olga's research centres on transitioning societies, especially the economic agents' responses to changing institutional and business environments. Her current research portfolio includes also co-operative studies and hybrid organizations. Olga has published in leading international journals, including *Journal of International Business Studies*, *Journal of Comparative Economics* and *Europe-Asia Studies*. Her published articles include 'And then there were none: What a UCU archive tells us about employee relations in marketising universities' (2020) and 'Contextual constraints and knowledge relevance: Challenges facing knowledge gatekeepers in emerging economies' (2016).

Kiri Langmead works at Edinburgh Napier University. Her research includes ethnographic and action research with Worker Co-operatives in the UK, with a specific focus on practices of participatory decision-making and non-hierarchical HRM. Recent publications include 'Can management ever be responsible? Alternative organizing and the three irresponsibilities of management' (2020) and 'Realizing the critical performative potential of responsible organizational research through participant action research' (2020).

Julian Manley, University of Central Lancashire, applies psychosocial and Deleuzian approaches to studies in co-operation. His central research interests are based around the study of human relations in different contexts. He is one of the designers and theorists behind the Preston Model of community wealth building. His work in human relations includes pioneering studies using social dreaming as a method to understand the hidden dynamics that influence different collectives, such as groups, teams and organizations. He has a long-standing relationship with the co-operative movement in Mondragón and is a founder member of three co-operatives that form part of the co-operative ecosystem in Preston, UK. Recent publications include *The Preston Model and Community Wealth Building: Creating a Socio-Economic Democracy for the Future* (2021) and 'A socio-economic system for affect: Dreaming of co-operative relationships and affect in Bermuda, Preston and Mondragón' (2020).

Morshed Mannan is a Max Weber Fellow at the European University Institute in Florence, researching blockchain governance and platform co-operatives. He is part of the European Research Council project 'BlockchainGov' and is a Research Affiliate at The New School. His most recent publications include 'The alegality of blockchain technology' (2022) and 'Solidarity in the sharing economy: The role of platform cooperatives at the base of the pyramid' (2021).

Malcolm Noble is a practitioner and researcher of Co-operative Higher Education, working in and writing about both institutional formations and classroom pedagogies. In 2017 he helped found Leicester Vaughan College, and is an active member of the project to establish a Co-operative University in the UK, as a radical alternative to the managerial university. Publications include *Reclaiming the University for the Public Good: Experiments and Futures in Co-operative Higher Education* (2019).

Ioannis Prinos, University of Central Lancashire, is seeking to combine empirical research and social theory in understanding the socio-dynamics of unequal power relations and their consequences in terms of poverty, marginalization, democracy and inequality. His research is centred around the ways alternative paradigms of economic organization focusing on co-operation, economic democracy, public-private sector partnerships and the pursuit of social value such as community wealth building, can help alleviate these issues. Currently, he is working on assessing the overall impact of the Preston Model and the impact of community wealth building initiatives on health and wellbeing. His articles include 'The Preston Model: Economic democracy, cooperation and paradoxes in organisational and social identification' (2022) and 'The Preston Model and co-operative development: A glimpse of transformation through an alternative model of social and economic organisation' (2021).

Hiroshi Sakai is Professor of Literature at Hokusei Gakuen University in Sapporo, Japan. He teaches contemporary sociology and journalism ethics. He worked as a journalist for a Japanese newspaper for 30 years. After the Great Earthquake in 2011, he moved to the university. His research interests include community regeneration through co-operation, the nature of the press in areas affected by catastrophes, and freedom of expression in wartime. His publications include *Pacific War of Journalists* (1990), *Justice of Reporters, Justice of Citizens* (2013) and *The Era of Journalism Crisis* (2015).

David Stewart is Senior Lecturer in History at the University of Central Lancashire, Preston, UK. His research interests traverse modern Scottish political history, the history of deindustrialization and labour and co-operative movement history. His publications include *The Path to Devolution and Change: A Political History of Scotland under Margaret Thatcher, 1979–1990* (2009) and *The Hidden Alternative: Co-operative Values, Past, Present and Future* (2012).

Christo Wallers is a post-doctoral researcher working with the Digital Cultures Research Centre at the University of West of England. He recently completed his PhD on DIY Cinema in the UK, historically situating and theorizing a culture of resistant screening practices celebrating democracy, community and rights to the city. He is a co-founder of Star & Shadow Cinema Co-op in Newcastle upon Tyne. He also co-founded Filmbee Co-op, an artist-run film lab housed within Star & Shadow. His collaborative 16 mm films and performances have been screened internationally in formal and informal contexts. He is an active member of Kino Climates network of alternative cinemas and recently launched a zine, Filmo#, to share reflections on film exhibition culture. Publication include 'Star & Shadow and before: Radical screening culture in Newcastle upon Tyne' (2020).

Anthony Webster is Professor in History at Northumbria University, a former trustee of the Co-operative College and now a trustee of the Co-operative Heritage Trust. He has published extensively on the co-operative movement, and his jointly authored book *Building Co-operation* was used as the main historical source for the Kelly and Myners Reviews into the problems of the Co-operative Bank and Co-operative Group in 2013/14. Recent academic publications include *The Hidden Alternative: Co-operative Values, Past, Present and Future* (2011) and 'Building the wholesale: The development of the English CWS and British co-operative business 1863–1890' (2012).

Acknowledgements

The Editors would like to thank their respective universities for providing them with the space and support for compiling this edition and the publishers for their continuous advice and rigorous attention to detail. We would like to thank the anonymous reviewers to the original proposal and subsequent manuscript review. We would also like to warmly thank Gillian Lonergan for indexing the work.

Foreword

Sonja Novkovic
International Centre for Co-operative Management
Saint Mary's University, Canada

An increased interest in cooperative organization in the last couple of decades is attributed to a large extent to the undisputable failures of neoliberalism as well as new forms of capitalist exploitation of labour and resources, such as platform capitalism's manipulation of gig workers, or extraction and commodification of the commons. Rising discontent with existing economic systems, policies and their outcomes reflected in social inequities and ecological disasters have given rise to the search for an economic paradigm accompanied by an enterprise model fit for humans and the planet.

In the search for a new economic paradigm, cooperative enterprise has a lot to offer. Rooted in economic democracy and built on ethical values, the cooperative model provides an alternative to the supremacy of capital and individual ownership of equity as the foundation of a presumably efficient and well functioning capitalist market economy. In the neoclassical model, capital and labour mobility is required for efficient functioning of respective capital and labour markets. The 'externality' produced by this quest for efficiency, however, includes a rupture in communities, since labour is not a commodity and cannot be separated from the human being and their social relations. Further to negative community impact, voiding economic transactions of social and ecological concerns has resulted in broad-based discontent, giving rise to multiple social movements and actions of civil society attempting to change the course. Therefore, the 'new economics' now sought by many theorists and practitioners ought to be concerned with its impact on the planet and on human beings and their communities. It ought to internalize human rights and enhance human dignity. In the same vein, a model which understands work as the foundation of human expression and personal development, rather than merely an input in production, is resonating with current generations. Interest in social solidarity enterprises such as co-operatives has re-ignited from these movements.

The cooperative model can be thought of as a benchmark for enterprises in the social solidarity economy espousing ethical values. It is an association, jointly owned and controlled by members who join the enterprise for its use value as consumers, workers, producers, or supporters of its purpose. Democratically governed, it is people (instead of capital) centred, but not anthropocentric. The special value of the model is that it provides a blueprint for economic democracy, and serves as a yardstick for other types of social enterprises, given a clear definition, values and principles in the *ICA Statement on the Cooperative Identity* (ICA, 1995). One can argue that interpretations of the *ICA Statement* may vary, particularly when raising concerns about its focus being only on members, and ignoring the natural environment and the broader community. The *ICA Guidance Notes on the Cooperative Identity* (ICA, 2015) assist in the interpretation of the Cooperative Principles, placing the seventh principle (*Concern for community*) in the framework of economic, social and ecological sustainability. Humanistic theories of the cooperative enterprise also interpret it as a social-ecological economic model, applying ethical values to both human relationships, and relationships of humanity with non-human world (Novkovic, 2021; Novkovic et al, 2023).

While not a panacea, democratic cooperative organizing contributes to radical imagination so desperately needed after decades of polarized propaganda claiming two as the only options – either neoliberal efficiency, or state-centrism. Co-operatives have always been thought of as part of the 'third way', but in the context of early 21st century they also counterbalance stakeholder capitalism and social business as spillovers of neoliberalism into the 'social' sphere. Commodification of the commons and of social needs (such as shelter, healthcare, or education) has given new meaning to co-operation as an agency for decommodification.

However, incumbent co-operatives need to partner with universities and other educational institutions to create capacity for appropriate cooperative (management) education, since the collective, associative, self-help nature of cooperative enterprise is often misinterpreted due to more recent promotion of social business, stakeholder capitalism and impact investment as solutions for sustainable futures. While all these emerging enterprise forms may provide a welcome diversity, they often prove not to change the essence of economic activity, staying true to the neoliberal tradition looking for the highest return on investment instead of repurposing the enterprise (Wilson, 2014; Bakan, 2020).

The cooperative character, its meaning, its potential to create, rebuild, strengthen or support communities is dealt with in this collection of diverse chapters, which together weave a rich tapestry that reflects the cooperative spirit. This is a story about the building blocks of the Community Wealth Building venture and its collective nature fitting for a commons, such as the Preston project. Ultimately, it is a story about cooperative networks and ecosystems transferable beyond local boundaries. The volume starts from the foundations (cooperative development), flows through the glue that holds them together (cooperative education) and ends in the superstructure of the Preston community, with the underlying supporting public institutions.

Besides the growing interest in the cooperative enterprise as a building block of community wealth, attention is being given to the ecosystems that sustain it. Like this volume, many look to Mondragon's cooperative network for inspiration. Mondragon's laser focus on jobs creation and preservation is difficult to emulate without an ecosystem to support it. However, the systems in the Mondragon complex have also evolved as workers uncovered unmet needs besides meaningful work, as well as business opportunities and innovations which contribute to jobs creation. About a quarter of Mondragon's co-operatives are multi-stakeholder, with different types of members contributing to governance – from consumers, to service users and providers, to Mondragon's primary co-operatives as members. Multi-stakeholder democratic governance is mixing meaningful jobs with meaningful stakeholder participation in their continued quest for social transformation through work. Mondragon also creates complex networks with external ecosystems for diverse purpose and projects, from research and knowledge hubs to innovation and sustainability.

The Preston Model, on the other hand, is building a broad support network contributing to community wealth creation within the community actors. Community wealth maintained by meaningful employment of its citizens seems to be the formula for success. This book talks about the challenges but also successes of these joint efforts between policy makers, educational institutions and co-operatives on the ground. Due importance is given to education as the vehicle for transformation, connecting individual building blocks of co-operation to community wealth building, thereby creating a cooperative economy. But the role that 'new municipalism' plays in (re)localizing the economy cannot be overstated. Importantly, all actors are adopting a cooperative ethos and thereby changing the nature of exchanges between them, from market to values driven; from transactional to relational. At issue, as pointed out in the book, is the longevity of these relationships and autonomy of individual enterprises. They may look for inspiration in the multi-stakeholder model in years to come.

Another challenge briefly tackled in this volume which will resonate for current and future generations is co-operativism driven by technology. Some form of hybridization of the model seems inevitable, although there are different kinds of platform collectives, cooperative or otherwise, with diverse members and visions, which are already difficult to categorize. The challenge for cooperative platforms posed by the nature of communication among members is one of building a lasting community. While technology facilitates quick connections, it is an impediment to meaningful and complex relationships afforded by physical gathering places. A community-owned football club, or a pub, enhance communities by the nature of collective and direct, local, engagement. Bonds are built by physical presence and shared experiences which spill over to other aspects of one's life. Building meaningful social relations in a virtual environment is work in progress and the meaning of 'community wealth building' in this context will continue to occupy spaces of research and practice for some time.

This book exposes many important issues and questions of interest to co-operatives anywhere. It is a welcome addition, presenting the radical imagination of new generations of co-operators. It also points to the shift in policy frameworks and identifies the cooperative values at its core, zeroing in on a story of a collective effort to rebuild the community spirit that is a common thread in this volume.

References

Bakan, J. (2020) *The New Corporation: How 'Good' Corporations Are Bad for Democracy*. London: Allen Lane.

ICA (1995) 'Statement on the cooperative identity'. Available from www.ica.coop/en/cooperatives/cooperative-identity [Accessed on 10 June 2023].

ICA (2015) 'Guidance notes on the cooperative principles'. Available from www.ica.coop/en/media/library/research-and-reviews/guidance-notes-cooperative-principles [Accessed on 10 June 2023].

Novkovic, S. (2021) 'Cooperative identity as a yardstick for transformative change', *Annals of Public and Cooperative Economics*. DOI: 10.1111/apce.12362

Novkovic, S., Miner, K. and McMahon, C. (eds) (2023) *Humanistic Governance in Democratic Organizations: The Cooperative Difference*. Basingstoke: Palgrave Macmillan.

Wilson, J. (2014) *Jeffrey Sachs: The Strange Case of Dr. Shock and Mr. Aid*. London: Verso.

1

Introduction: European Co-operativism in a Changing World

Julian Manley, Anthony Webster and Olga Kuznetsova

Background to the book

The background to this book is an almost overwhelming and growing list of international tensions of various kinds: a pandemic, the climate emergency, the struggle for social justice as manifested in the Black Lives Matter movement, an alarming rise of extremist right-wing political positions, the politics of austerity, wage stagnation, growing inequalities, the refugee crises and, at the time of writing, the 'cost of living' crisis in Europe; all, combined with and partly as a result of the Russian military conflict with Ukraine, are causing serious social and economic uncertainties that bring into question previously held socio-economic expectations of citizens in 21st-century Europe. The present volume cannot hope to pretend to offer solutions to these multiple challenges, but nevertheless intends to present the reader with a consideration of the potential of co-operatives and co-operation as a means of reconstructing some of the damaged aspirations of the 20th century, as the 21st gets underway.

It is a premise of this book to argue that co-operatives *per se* are an important and globally relevant organizational form for business. They are an economic force with a wide-ranging social and economic imprint. In Europe alone, agricultural co-operatives process 60 per cent of all agricultural produce and there are 4,000 co-operative banks with 50 million members and a market share of 20 per cent (Dilger et al, 2017; Gouveia, 2012; World Coop Monitor, nd). The UK co-operative sector alone showed a £39.7

billion turnover in 2021, employed 250,128 people and had 13.9 million members (Co-op Economy, 2021). Over time, co-operatives have credibly established a reputation of organizations being most resilient to calamities and highly productive in pooling resources to achieve both economic and social value-driven outcomes (Roelants, 2013). Despite these facts, business and management literature often give the impression that co-operatives exist on the periphery of the modern economy and, as a result, the contribution of co-operatives to the GDP and their wide-ranging social imprint does not translate into a matching societal recognition (Develtere et al, 2008). One of the explanations for this apparent contradiction could be that modern capitalism has been hesitant to fully embrace the cooperative model as a legitimate part of its operational system. In other words, perhaps this is an example of an ideological rather than economic rejection. Neither has the system given much attention to learning from the successes of co-operatives in building organizational resilience, enhancing a capacity for tackling employment issues and contributing to wellbeing of different communities.

In the light of these paradoxes, much of this volume will make sense to scholarly discussions that take an interest in cooperative successes and the potential for their development in the 21st century. In particular, the chapter contributions investigate and clarify the cooperative values of collaboration and co-governance (Emerson et al, 2012; Engler and Engler, 2022; Novkovic et al, 2023). Although we discuss co-operatives as legal entities, we are also concerned with the idea of co-operation as a principle of workplace organization and life in general. In doing so, there is an emphasis on cooperative principles and values as conceptual frameworks that should underpin any organizational structure. These principles are those publicly enshrined as the seven international principles that speak to processes of democracy and human relationships, which resonate with Parker et al's (2014) principles for 'alternatives': autonomy, solidarity and responsibility, which are ways of being rather than organizational principles. They speak to 'affect' in organizational and community life, leading to working with trust and engagement and sharing decision-making in ways that move away from hierarchical structures of governance (Jussila et al, 2012; Manley and Aiken, 2020).

It is in this context that the chapters in this edition offer a critical look at cooperativism in the 21st century in a collection of case studies that demonstrate different aspects of cooperative development in Europe, concluding with one example from Japan that shows the influence of a European perspective that potentially transcends cultural and geographical boundaries. The book as a whole also reveals where and why co-operatives have not, as yet, become active and influential agents of change and a driving force behind a new paradigm of development. Such analysis of cooperativism is very important, but rare. The literature suggests that cooperative-themed publications are carried out mainly among parties who may share a strong belief in the supposed moral superiority of the cooperative form of organization and this may create a picture of a cooperative movement that is largely insulated from an external critical reference. To praise co-operation and its historical achievements, which are remarkable indeed, might not be enough to explain the immediate 21st-century relevance of the cooperative enterprise.

In line with such thinking, the discussions in these chapters are centred on co-operatives as an organizational format and a model of enterprise with a potential to reconnect organizations and institutions with public purpose, enrich the dominant business mentality with humanistic values, enact market plurality, advance participatory economy and enhance polycentricity of decision-making and governance. Here we explore the extent to which the cooperative organization has significant operational capabilities in contemporary capitalism and can even act as a catalyst for paradigmatic changes in business culture and mentality currently entrenched in market orthodoxy. As such, this book ultimately questions the adequacy of the capitalist system as we know it, a subject of growing concern and debate in recent literature on the future of economic and social systems (Wilkinson and Pickett, 2009, 2018; Adler, 2014, 2019; Klein, 2014; Piketty, 2014; Mason, 2016; Monbiot, 2016; Raworth, 2017; Trebeck and Williams, 2019; Varoufakis, 2017). The authors of the present edition contribute to the argument that scenarios and value benchmarks for future societal development should explicitly include learning from the experience of cooperative economy (Novkovic and Webb, 2014; Webster et al, 2016; Manley and Whyman, 2021; Novkovic et al, 2023).

The historical roots of European co-operation

In the UK, ideas about the need for alternatives to the exploitative system of industrial capitalism emerged in the early 19th century, especially through the work and writings of Robert Owen and later Christian Socialists such as E.V. Neale and Thomas Hughes (Hughes and Neale, 1915). For them, the emphasis was upon co-operatives becoming self-sufficient communes of people living outside mainstream capitalist society, a utopian objective never realized in a sustainable way. Ultimately, however, it was the practical adaptation to problems of food quality and supply arising from rapid industrialization and urbanization, which gave rise to the Rochdale Pioneers co-operative, established in 1844. This provided a model of local retail co-operation which addressed consumer needs so successfully that the model was copied across the UK and Europe. In Germany, the pressing need for capital by small farmers and artisans gave rise, through the ideas of Raiffeisen and Schultze-Delitzsch, to the Credit Union movement, under which problems of capital shortage, or lack of short-term credit could be addressed through co-operatives organized by the artisans or farmers themselves (MacPherson, 1999). In Denmark, the creation of farmer co-operatives in the 1860s and 1870s was transformational for the nation. The creamery co-operatives dramatically improved the quality of Danish butter, enabling it to dominate the European market by 1900 (Henriksen, 1999; Henriksen and O'Rourke, 2005; Henriksen et al, 2011). Attempts were made to copy this system in Ireland but with limited success (Henriksen et al, 2015).

Worker co-operatives sprang up across the continent, in response to unemployment, poor wages and bad working conditions. While co-operatives were and are certainly ubiquitous across the continent, they became especially well-established in France and Italy (Pérotin, 2012). Emilia-Romagna and Trentino in northern Italy became exceptional in the importance of co-operation to their local economies (Zamagni, 2012; OECD, 2014; NSP, 2016). A recent study by Costa and colleagues (2022) provides evidence of the Italian co-operatives' impressive contribution to regional prosperity and shows a positive association between the size of the regional cooperative movement and the resilience of regional economic systems.

In the Basque Country, Spain, the most remarkable development was the establishment of the Mondragon Corporation of co-operatives from the early 1940s, in the unpromising context of the Franco regime, becoming eventually one of the most successful cooperative organizations in the world (Molina and Walton, 2011). Mondragón is an example of another important European cooperative phenomenon, the emergence of a regional concentration of co-operatives, in which inter-cooperative trade and other links between co-operatives create what might be described as a local cooperative economy. This ecosystem of co-operatives has provided much of the inspiration for the development of Community Wealth Building (CWB) initiatives in Europe and the UK, which is why this book frequently references the Preston Model, one of the most significant and sustainable recent examples of CWB that incorporates cooperativism, whether as a value base for business or indeed in the actual development of cooperative businesses. Although the Preston Model is partly influenced by the cooperative experiments in Cleveland, Ohio, the latter is significantly influenced, in turn, by the Mondragón experience. In a sense 'all roads to a cooperative ecosystem lead to Mondragón'. Therefore, CWB is approached in this volume from a cooperative perspective and emphasizes how the cooperative business of the future may be based on inter-co-operation between cooperative businesses rather than the cooperative business as a stand-alone enterprise, called 'radical' municipalism by Thompson (2023). A different take on this is provided by Novkovic and colleagues (2023), where networking of co-operatives is viewed as important but not necessarily linked to 'municipalism': 'Importantly, members' and stakeholders' continuous involvement and engagement with the organization provides a normative framework for "best practice" in cooperative governance, but it needs to be amplified by the organization's embeddedness in society and the natural environment' (Novkovic et al, 2023, p 29).

The ideological shift to 'neo-liberalism' at the end of the 20th century was accompanied by deep scepticism about co-operatives and other mutual forms, especially in the USA and UK, which were increasingly seen as an adjunct of socialism, and intrinsically inferior to the market-driven efficiency of investor-led capitalist companies. At best, co-operatives were time-limited 'stop-gaps' to provide much need services until such time as capitalist provision 'caught up' and displaced the co-operatives. The truth is, more often than not, the reasons for cooperative failure were similar to other failing companies – poor management (Fanasch and Frick, 2018). A wave of demutualizations duly followed during the 1990s, especially in the UK, where Tony Blair's New Labour policies encouraged 'social enterprises' that failed to embrace cooperative and community participation in the economy (Huckfield, 2021). The transition from communism in Eastern Europe did nothing to encourage co-operatives. Ideologically, coops were considered immature and a traditional form, not fully compatible with the socialist/communist mode of ownership of the means of production, useful, perhaps, as a step on the way to the fulfilment of these aspirations. There was, therefore, a great deal of suspicion and prejudice against co-operatives in these countries.

In the 21st century, one of the key criticisms of the neoliberal status quo targets its primary focus on market supremacy, inadequate attention to market failures, narrow view of macro-stability and its limited conception of the goals and instruments of development (Stiglitz, 2002). New thinking about development argues that GDP growth is not an end in itself and highlights the importance of social aspects in economic progress such as inclusivity; finding a balance between market, state and community and achieving a more egalitarian distribution of market rewards (Alkire et al, 2016; Lewin et al, 2022). This is the situation that we find ourselves in as the starting point for the chapter contributions in this book.

Motivation and context today

The origins of this volume, therefore, lie in the deepening problems experienced by co-operatives since the 1980s, a watershed decade in global social and economic policy. For 30 years after the Second World War most countries of Western Europe had followed policies which tempered the market by state intervention and the provision of a welfare safety net but Thatcherism became a dominant feature of the 1980s, with profound effects in Europe as well as in the UK. State intervention was curtailed, publicly owned industries and assets privatized, efforts made to restrict public expenditure and shrink the state and deregulation implemented especially in banking and finance. Significantly, among free market proponents, one model of commercial organization was believed to be the most efficient in meeting the economic demands of society – the investor-led company committed principally to delivery of shareholder value. Market orthodoxy was explicitly founded on the idea of 'natural competition' between individuals with little place for collaboration and co–operation (McLachlan, 2020).

In this context, according to the dominant neoliberal canon, cooperative companies were seen as impractical and utopic in their foundation on collaborative and shared governance (Heras-Saizarbitoria, 2014). Co-operatives were regarded as being unable to make rapid decisions and adjustments to the market due to the slow consultative process of cooperative governance (Basterretxea et al, 2020). Additionally, it has been suggested that co-operatives are only truly effective at smaller scales, precisely due to the cooperative dependence on fostering good relationships in the workforce. If true, the smaller scale of co-operatives would make it difficult for them to expand into the international market, and it is sometimes claimed that when they do expand, cooperative principles fall away and are replaced with the unadulterated values of the marketplace (Errasti et al, 2003; Flecha and Ngai, 2014). Such criticisms would seem to indicate that co-operatives are an inferior organizational format in the market context. These are themes that this book considers.

Although, we do not specifically address a presumed cooperative weakness related to company size, we do claim, with reference to the Mondragón experience, that co-operatives have capabilities and coping mechanisms to overcome this challenge through the principle of co-operation between co-operatives. It is worth noting that even during the period of retreat in the 1980s and 1990s, co-operation across Europe was more robust than neoliberals had assumed. Even in consumer co-operation, there were bright spots, notably in the Nordic countries (Norway, Sweden, Finland, Denmark), where skilful policies were adopted in response to growing competition (Ekberg, 2012; 2017). Finland, for example, was (and remains) arguably the most cooperative country in the world, with over 80 per cent of the population being a member of at least one co-operative, and co-operatives supplying 45 per cent of the nation's goods, as well as the largest bank in the country being a co-operative (Pellervo, 2022). Also, in the Basque Country, Spain, co-operation thrived in the 1980s and 1990s, growing in terms of employment and sales (Molina and Walton, 2011; Mondragón, 2022), and even the failure of the large *Fagor Electrodomésticos* coop can be viewed as a systemic success, at least socially, since none of the workers became unemployed, being moved to other co-operatives within the network, retrained or awarded generous early retirement packages (see Chapter 12 in this volume).

Despite all the difficulties, the global movement, represented by the International Cooperative Alliance ICA, also reformed itself, especially by updating its Statement of Cooperative Identity in 1995. It developed a clearer definition of what a co-operative is and the values of co-operation. This has provided a basis for other international bodies such as the UN and the International Labour Organization (ILO) to promote co-operatives (ICA, 2020).

However, it was in the first decade of the 21st century – where our book begins – that a new interest in co-operation began to gather momentum, confirming the insights of Väinö Tanner, the president of ICA in 1937, who argued that the virtues and relevance of the cooperative movement become even more obvious when the forces of the liberal economy are unleashed (Tanner, 1937). It is in the present century that we are beginning to witness growing concerns in societies, which had embraced neoliberal principles, about the economic rewards not being widely shared and many voices not being heard, leading to interest in other normatively preferred and different forms of economic organization and governance, which can counteract the neoliberal order with alternative and more sophisticated economic strategies and forms of commercial organization. The catastrophic financial crisis of 2008 rocked some of the 'certainties' underpinning the neoliberal consensus. Since then, there has been an uneasy return to the same previously held consensus, but with less certainty than before. The gap that has emerged between certainty and uncertainty is the potential gap for cooperative development.

In the more advanced European economies, including Britain, Germany and France, new opportunities created by borderless work, accelerating automation and the outsourcing of services has led to chronic insecurity at work, with a growing number of people being corralled into temporary and/or part-time work often riddled with legal insecurities of the 'gig' economy. In today's circumstances, neoliberal policies continue to ignore, but no longer unchallenged, the need for market plurality while struggling to meet the high expectations of spreading prosperity. It is becoming more and more obvious that a future of prosperity and wellbeing requires a much wider variety of resilient models of societal organization and opportunities for co-operation. This was confirmed by the onset of the COVID-19 pandemic which necessitated the exploration of alternative sources of resilience and co-operation in times of crisis. Not surprisingly calls for an alternative to the neoliberal paradigm have intensified. Such is the current state of flux and uncertainty in contemporary Europe that solutions are no longer givens. Certainly, economic and political shocks that rattled the status quo in Europe and beyond and exposed the vulnerabilities of the neoliberal ideology have created a historical opportunity for non-mainstream models of business organization such as co-operatives to move out of the shadow and present themselves to the public and policy makers as a viable model of business capable of providing some answers both to the challenges of the moment and long term. There is apparent 'social thirst' for some new form of social and economic structures to emerge from the ruins of a post-COVID-19 society (Blakeley, 2020; Parker, 2020; Lewin et al, 2022), despite the marked resistance to recent new municipalist efforts in Europe (Davies, 2023). This is the premise of the current edition.

The Cooperative Research Network of activist scholars

Many of our author contributors are active in their communities, as well as being scholars in their academic institutions. This book treads the line between research and practical pragmatic activism and aims at facilitating a conversation between academic theory and reflection and application in multiple contexts of social organization. The objective is to provide an up-to-date picture of what European co-operatives in the 21st century are about, what makes them relevant for anybody looking for solutions to the crises we face. Understandably, no one volume can create a complete picture, including this one. What makes this edition distinctive is that many research topics were selected by or in collaboration with early career researchers, people who make part of a generation that belongs as much to tomorrow as to today. This generation's vision of the potential of co-operatives and their role in society will shape the society to come and determine whether the cooperative movement will be seen as an example that may lead to the emergence of new forms of business organization characterized by inclusion, equality and democracy.

Many of the conversations continued in the chapters in this book can be linked to the establishment, early in 2018, of a network intending to bring together researchers of co-operatives and the social economy. Originally called CERN (Co-operative Early Researchers Network), the network aimed at early career researchers and research students to share ideas, help the researchers develop themselves and to work closely with the co-operative movement (Webster and Kuznetsova, 2018). CERN was also designed to overcome scholarly isolation, especially given the decline of the study co-operatives in UK Business Schools (Kalmi, 2007; also see Chapter 8).

CERN emerged at the behest of the Cooperative College UK, which wanted to bolster its connections with research and higher education, at a time when it was being incorporated as a charitable trust. Following in the wake of the Co-operative Bank crisis in 2013, its associated scandals (see Chapter 8 in this book) and the severe impact these had on the Co-operative Group, the reputation of British co-operation plunged. This was after over a decade of reform of the Group and commercial recovery that had given rise to hopes for a new renaissance of British co-operation (Wilson et al, 2013). The Co-operative College UK was determined to stimulate interest in the latest cooperative research among scholars and practitioners alike.

CERN was born therefore at a time when the movement was at a low ebb, and there was a need to revitalize cooperation as an idea; as a commercial strategy, which might be restored to a significant position in the British economy, and as a socio-political movement to address poverty, inequality and disempowerment. Shortly, it became clear that the network would benefit from the inclusion of experienced and established academics, to provide expertise and guidance for those relatively new to their careers, and the network relaunched itself as the Cooperative Research Network (CoRNet). The remit of CoRNet is to provide a supportive academic environment and bridge the gap between academia and cooperative practice, to encourage the interest in cooperative economy among HE educators. The members of CoRNet (about 60 being currently active) are committed to raising international awareness of cooperative research, to which this volume is a testimony.

Purpose and aims

The different research areas addressed in this book are all connected by visions of cooperativism in a European context that together create a framework for organizational aspirations of a future society. The final chapter, before our conclusion, demonstrates the potential for cooperative development in a community wealth-building context beyond Europe. Maybe this suggests that another form of global cross-pollination of ideas can improve the marketplace locally. In this sense, the work of this volume is to bring to light current examples of a turn towards cooperativism in the 21st century that looks forward to future developments in the way social and economic structures may be re-imagined for a not-too-distant post-crisis, post-growth future. The book, therefore, is driven by the recognized societal demand for some kind of new social and economic structure to emerge in the post-COVID-19 era (Blakeley, 2020), explicitly featuring participatory, collaborative, cooperative opportunities. In the present edition, therefore, we suggest that although the Marxist revolutions have not quite emerged as predicted, changes in terms of finding a sense of meaning, self-awareness and dignity, autonomy, independence and self-governance can be found in the turn towards cooperative ways of organizing work and life.

The book provides an informed, evidence-based speculation of what such a cooperative future might look like. The contributions do not necessarily present the end products of templates for the future, but rather draw courses for actions and outline developments in movement that speak to the importance of organic relational processes and ontological shifts from a society centred on a paradigm of competitive money-making and greed to a different one that emphasizes social value, mutuality and co-operation.

To some readers, this may appear utopic, but philosophically, this is not necessarily new territory. In 1956, Fromm equated 'greediness' and 'ambition' (somehow naturally accepted as normal features of a capitalist perspective on life) with 'insanity' (Fromm, 1956 [2002], p 16). For Fromm, a 'healthy' society would be one that eschewed blind competition. The unhealthiness of work centred on competition and the lack of worker engagement in the fruits of their own production is well-known in the work of Marx. For Marx, the alienation of the workers from themselves was ineluctably linked to being in the service of selling labour as a product for an alien other (specifically, for Marx, the factory owner). In *The German Ideology*, Marx distinguishes between the alienated individual subject to a co-operation that is involuntary and the possibilities of fulfilled and relational cooperativism:

> The social power, i.e., the multiplied productive force, which arises through the cooperation of different individuals as it is determined by the division of labour, appears to these individuals, since their co-operation is not voluntary but has come about naturally, not as their own united power, but as an alien force existing outside them, of the origin and goal of which they are ignorant, which they thus cannot control, which on the contrary passes through a peculiar series of phases and stages independent of the will and the action of man. (Marx, 2011, np)

Structure and organization

The book presents three linked parts, 'Seeds: Identifying the Space for Co-operatives in Addressing Social Challenges', 'Bridges: Co-operative Culture and Education' and 'Growth: The Preston Model, Co-operation and Community Wealth Building'. The first part presents new developments in 21st-century co-operation which speak to the challenges of our times. The second part discusses education and cultural change emerging from the context of the case studies in the first part. This second part acts as a 'bridge' into the third part which reconceptualizes co-operatives as an economic and social network, recently characterized as 'community wealth building'. In this way, the gap between individual case study examples of co-operatives in Part I is re-imagined into a network of co-operatives in Part III by passing through the cultural change implied in Part II.

Part I, Seeds: Identifying the space for co-operatives in addressing social challenges

This section engages with case studies that illustrate disparate experiments in cooperative design and governance in Europe, including digital platform coops, worker coops, cultural coops, and others. While the case studies harbour their own particular elements and circumstances, they are all interconnected by principles of cooperative and democratic governance that explicitly or implicitly push back against the predominant competitive background of a European neoliberal economic paradigm. As such, they contribute to the possibility of a future design for living and working in response to the multiple crises: austerity, social injustice, inequalities, the pandemic, climate change and, in the UK, Brexit – that confront communities in Europe today.

Part II, Bridges: Co-operative culture and education

With the cooperative case studies that challenge forms of governance and ways of perceiving and interpreting life and work, as discussed in Part I, comes a need for changing hearts and minds. This section serves as a bridge between the small case studies of cooperative experience and the larger concepts of co-operation within a community wealth building framework. The part discusses this need and the value of a change in culture, in the broad sense of that word, through education, understood both as pedagogy and also the lived experience of change. Historically, the most successful federation of co-operatives in the world, that of the Mondragón co-operatives in the Basque Country, Spain, began their processes of social and economic change through education. The two chapters in this part discuss the role of education and experience in fostering and sustaining cooperative, social and economic transformation.

Part III, Growth: The Preston Model, co-operation and community wealth building

The combination of the study of development of co-operatives, as in Part I, with the provision or experience of cultural change/education of Part II, takes the reader to Part III, where cooperative principles and values are translated into grander cooperative designs referred to community wealth building, and its chief exponent in the UK, the Preston Model. We also offer an example of how the development of co-operatives within the framework of community wealth building is transferable to other situations and cultures, in the case of our example, a Japanese influenced version of the Preston Model. In this way, the book moves from the small, localized sites within the regions and nations of Europe at the beginning of the book to a potential model for global adoption, at the end.

The chapters

Following the *Introduction* by the Editors in Chapter 1, Chapter 2 (Wallers) brings the reader immediately and radically into the world of changing paradigms that characterizes this volume. Resonating with our discussion of collaboration and co-governance, Waller provides an example of a 'DIY' cinema space that belongs to the 'commons' and is governed cooperatively, but – and this is crucial – not cooperatively in the old, traditional sense of retail or worker-owned cooperativism, but rather a co-operation in a community context which Waller defines as 'new cooperativism'. In many ways the struggle to define the emergence of the cinema in Waller's chapter serves as a definition of our lived present as a time of change and uncertainty, with roots in the solidarity economy of the present and a shape-shifting vision of a possible future.

In the next chapter (Deblangy), the state of cooperativism in France is tellingly illustrated through case studies. Although these examples are based in traditional worker-owned co-operatives, and in that sense differ from the emphasis on the commons of Chapter 2, Deblangy shows how a concern of the commons, and a subject of our times – the ecological crisis – fits smoothly into the preoccupations of worker-owners who are not primarily or only focused on financial profit. If co-operatives are ecologically sound, perhaps they provide templates for a world that survives and sustains the environment.

Chapter 4 discusses the connection between cooperative governance and a sense of meaning at work. Langmead and Webster conclude that work which is meaningful, as opposed to 'decent' – which they define as consisting of external measure of decency mainly in terms of work conditions such as salary, safety, respect, and so on – encapsulates a sense of authenticity in work that provides for society, and, therefore, the environment, as much as in sustaining a living for the individual worker. As such, in line with the previous chapters, there is a sense that co-operatives can provide a paradigmatic challenge to capitalism. At the same time, the authors point out the difficulties in balancing the economic and social missions of these businesses, with specific reference to the Mondragón co-operatives, a theme later picked up in Chapter 12.

Continuing with the theme of 'Seeds', Mannan discusses developments in platform cooperativism, where members who join are in control of providing their labour rather than capital or share investment, and where value is linked to 'reputation' rather than money. The qualities of the by design of platform co-operative provide opportunities for transnational collective equity and democracy through a flat structure guaranteed by the platform's blockchain technology.

The following Chapter 6 discusses how knowledge of history can enable an understanding of a cooperative future. Stewart points to how the harnessing of community spirit, pride and identity developed over generations of work in the steel industry in Scotland created the conditions for the community and cooperative takeover of the local football club as a symbol of this local sense of place and belonging. Motherwell FC supporters became cooperators through a shared sense of working-class identity, strongly linked to the steel industry and a pushback against the apparent inevitability of market forces imposed upon them by politically conservative governments and neoliberal managerial slant. In this way, the disaster of the past became a seed for the future.

This brings the reader to Part II, which suggests the need for a bridge in education and culture to grow these seeds of future change. In the first chapter of this section, Noble shows how cooperative principles and values can be applied to different projects, beyond cooperativism itself. The case study presented in this chapter shows how, without explicitly creating a cooperative project, a cooperative pedagogy facilitated the relationships between the educators, researchers and citizen researchers, and smoothed over possible obstacles to the work that would otherwise arise over power and authority relationships and dynamics.

In Chapter 8, Kuznetsov and Kuznetsova argue for the need to correct the focus of the education provision by universities and business schools in particular to ensure a tighter fit with changing business conditions favouring plurality and new societal demands favouring participatory democracy. They point out that the individualistic, neoliberal approach to business at universities ignores trends towards a greater acceptance of the role of business in society, as demonstrated by the increasing value given to Corporate Social Responsibility. The chapter offers a 'landscape review' to reflect on the state-of-the-art assessment of the gap between competencies and knowledge needed to boost the role of the cooperative sector in a modern economy and the supply of research and training through HE. The chapter identifies related capabilities and skill shortages that need to be addressed and maintains that co-operatives should be more receptive to mainstream business and management education. The analysis lays foundations for international cross-sectoral initiatives that can be delivered by academia in collaboration with the co-operative sector.

Finally, the book opens out into the development of co-operatives and co-operation in terms of an ecosystem. This part asks what a cooperative social system of the future might look like by considering the roles of co-operatives and co-operation in community wealth building projects, with special attention given to the Preston Model as an example of this kind of development in the UK. Webster sets the scene by discussing the history of co-operatives in the UK and Europe. By analysing the decline of the co-operative in the UK, and the rise of the social enterprise for political reasons, Webster leaves the door open for the developments in community wealth building that are discussed in subsequent chapters.

In Chapter 10, Manley and Eseonu describe the potential for identifying cooperative values as a binding agent for ecosystem development in a study of the elusive 'cooperative character' that binds together the creation of a network of cooperative Councils in the UK. This contributes to a consideration of the potential of redefining the parochial nature of localism in community wealth building through the creation of a network of local Councils that are bound by agreement in cooperative principles and values: local and yet spread out across the UK.

Prinos' chapter that follows gives a detailed account of how co-operation binds together the Preston Model of community wealth building. Coming after Manley and Eseonu's chapter, the reader is presented with growing evidence for cooperative principles consisting of the building blocks of new municipal initiatives in community wealth building, within individual local authority policies as well as councils working in mutual support across the country.

Chapter 12 investigates the sustainability and resilience of the cooperative ecosystem in the well-established example of the Mondragón co-operatives. In this chapter, Manley discusses the need for vigilance in keeping the flame of the spirit of co-operation alive in large historical co-operatives. The evidence suggests that despite some cynicism among some academics and some workers in Mondragón, there is much to be hopeful about in others. This suggests that cooperative ecosystems are possible long-term options for society.

Finally, Sakai's chapter exemplifies the potential for cooperative model ecosystems such as Mondragón and Preston to inspire developments abroad as far out as Japan. The chapter is an illustration to the importance of showcasing and exposing cooperative practices. It is aspirational in showing how co-operatives can be active participants in societal transformation and such transformation should not come only from the academic arguments and insights gained through analysis, but also from building public awareness by exposing how the cooperative economy internationally helps to innovate and enrich development models. This chapter constitutes a reflection and forward-looking aspiration in Sorachi, Hokkaido, Japan. Although thousands of kilometres away from Europe, Sakai's chapter demonstrates the reach and universal attraction of cooperative systems originating in Europe.

The editors conclude the book in a chapter that situates the work of colleagues in this edition within the social and economic times that exist today. The concluding chapter discusses the nature of place in an interconnected world, especially in a post-COVID-19 and virtually connected world, which brings up interesting dilemmas of community and place and co-operation. The chapter looks forward to future research that can further link the potential impact of co-operative development and emerging modern-day social movements on addressing social crises, wealth building, local economies and regional regeneration, as well as targeting macro-level emergencies, including climate change and environmental activism, inclusivity, diversity, participatory democracy, social justice, and their opposites in present-day tensions with extremist reactionary positions manifested around the world.

References

Adler, P.S. (2014) 'Capitalism in question', *Journal of Management Inquiry*, 23(2): 206–209.

Adler, P.S. (2019) *The 99 Percent Economy: How Democratic Socialism Can Overcome the Crises of Capitalism*. New York: Oxford University Press.

Alkire, S., Bardhan, P., Basu, K., Bhorat, H., Bourguignon, F., Deshpande, A., Kanbur, R., Lin, Y., Moene, K., Platteau, J.-P., Saavedra, J., Stiglitz, J. and Tarp, F. (2016) 'Stockholm Statement: Towards a consensus on the principles of policymaking for the contemporary world'. Available from www.wider.unu.edu/sites/default/files/News/Documents/Stockh olm%20Statement.pdf [Accessed on 6 August 2022].

Basterretxea, I., Cornforth, C. and Heras-Saizarbitoria, I. (2020) 'Corporate governance as a key aspect in the failure of worker cooperatives', *Economic and Industrial Democracy*, 43(1): 362–387.

Blakeley, G. (2020) *The Corona Crash: How the Pandemic Will Change Capitalism*. London: Verso.

Co-op Economy (2021) 'The Co-op Economy 2021'. Available from www. uk.coop/sites/default/files/2021-06/Economy%202021_1.pdf [Accessed on 5 September 2022].

Costa, M., Delbono, F., Linguiti, F. (2022) 'Cooperative movement and widespread prosperity across Italian regions', *Annals of Public and Cooperative Economics*. Available from https://doi.org/10.1111/apce.12387 [Accessed on 7 September 2022].

Davies, J.S. (2023) 'Urban governance in the age of austerity: Crises of neoliberal hegemony in comparative perspective', *Environment and Planning A: Economy and Space*. https://doi.org/10.1177/0308518X231186151

Develtere, P., Pollet, I. and F. Wanyama (eds) (2008) *Cooperating Out of Poverty. The Renaissance of the African Cooperative Movement*. Geneva: ILO.

Dilger, M.G., Konter, M. and Voigt, K.-I. (2017) 'Introducing a co-operative-specific business model: The poles of profit and community and their impact on organizational models of energy co-operatives', *Journal of Co-operative Organization and Management*, 5(1): 28–38.

Ekberg, E. (2012) 'Confronting three revolutions: Western European consumer co-operatives and their divergent development, 1950–2008', *Business History*, 54(6): 1004–1021.

Ekberg, E. (2017) 'Against the tide: Understanding the commercial success of Nordic consumer co-operatives'. In Hilson, M., Neunsinger, S. and Patmore, G. (eds) *A Global History of Consumer Co-operation since 1850*. Leiden: Brill, pp 698–728.

Emerson, K. Nabatchi, T. and Balogh, S. (2012) 'An integrative framework for collaborative governance', *Journal of Public Administration Research and Theory*, 22(1): 1–29.

Engler, M. and Engler, P. (2022) 'A guide to co-governance. Can movements and politicians work together?'. Available from https://democracyuprising.com/2022/07/05/a-guide-to-co-governance-can-movements-and-politicians-work-together-2/ [Accessed on 13 July 2022].

Errasti, A. Heras, I., Bakaikoa, B. and Elgoibar, P. (2003) 'The internationalization of cooperatives: the case of the Mondragon Cooperative Corporation', *Annals of Public and Cooperative Economies*, 74(4): 553–584.

Fanasch, P. and Frick, B. (2018) 'What makes cooperatives successful? Identifying the determinants of their organizational performance', *Journal of Wine Economics*, 13(3): 282–308.

Flecha, R. and Ngai, P. (2014) 'The challenge for Mondragon: Searching for the cooperative values in times of internationalization', *Organization*, 21(5): 666–682.

Fromm, E. (1956 [2002]) *The Sane Society*. London: Routledge.

Gouveia, R. (2012) 'Consumer co-operatives in Europe: Overview. European community of consumer co-operatives'. Presentation. Available from www.uk.coop/sites/storage/public/downloads/eurocoop_-_nrcc.odp [Accessed on 1 April 2022].

Henriksen, I. (1999) 'Avoiding lock in: Co-operative creameries in Denmark 1882–1903', *European Review of Economic History*, 3(1): 57–78.

Henriksen, I. and O'Rourke, K.H. (2005) 'Incentives, technology and the shift to year long dairying in nineteenth century Denmark', *Economic History Review*, 58(3): 520–524.

Henriksen, I., Lampe, M. and Sharp, P. (2011) 'The role of technology and institutions for growth: Danish creameries in the late nineteenth century', *European Review of Economic History*, 15(3): 475–493.

Henriksen, I., Mclaughlin, E. and Sharp, P. (2015) 'Contracts and cooperation: The relative failure of the Irish dairy industry in the late nineteenth century reconsidered', *European Review of Economic History*, 19(4): 412–431.

Heras-Saizarbitoria, I. (2014) 'The ties that bind? Exploring the basic principles of worker-owned organizations in practice', *Organization*, 21(5): 645–665.

Huckfield, L. (2021) *How Blair Killed the Co-ops: Reclaiming Social Enterprise from its Neoliberal Turn*. Manchester: Manchester University Press.

Hughes, T. and Neale, E.V. (1915) *Foundations: A Study in the Ethics and Economics of the Co-operative Movement, Prepared at the Request of the Co-operative Congress Held at Gloucester in April 1879*, revised by A. Stoddart and W. Clayton, Manchester: The Co-operative Union.

ICA (2020) 'The ICA statement on the cooperative identity'. Available from www.ica.coop/sites/default/files/news-item-attachments/25-anni versary-concept-note-final-draft-554502669.pdf#:~:text=The%20intern ational%20cooperative%20standards%20enshrined%20in%20the%20Statem ent,they%20function%20started%20151%20years%20ago%20around%201 844 [Accessed on 7 July 2022].

Jussila, I., Byrne, N. and Tuominen, H. (2012) 'Affective commitment in cooperative organizations: What makes members want to stay?' *International Business Research*, 5(10): 1–10.

Kalmi, P. (2007) 'The disappearance of cooperatives from economics textbooks', *Cambridge Journal of Economics*, 31(4): 625–647.

Klein, N. (2014) *This Changes Everything. Capitalism Vs the Climate.* London: Simon & Schuster.

Lewin, A.Y., Linden, G. and Teece, D.J. (eds) (2022). *The New Enlightenment. Reshaping Capitalism and the Global Order in the 21st Century.* Cambridge: Cambridge University Press.

MacPherson, I. (1999) *Hands around the Globe: A History of the International Credit Union Movement and the Role and Development of World Council of Credit Unions.* Victoria: Horsdal & Schubart Publishers & WOCCU.

Manley, J. and Aiken, M. (2020) 'A socio-economic system for affect: Dreaming of co-operative relationships and affect in Bermuda, Preston and Mondragón', *Organisational and Social Dynamics*, 20(2): 173–191.

Manley, J. and Whyman, P.B. (2021) *The Preston Model and Community Wealth Building Creating a Socio-Economic Democracy for the Future.* London: Routledge.

Marx, K. (2011) 'Private property and communism'. In S. Sayers (ed) *Marx and Alienation*. Cham: Springer.

Mason, P. (2016) *Postcapitalism: A Guide to Our Future.* London: Penguin.

McLachlan, H. (2020) 'Why "there's no such thing as society" should not be regarded with moral revulsion', *The Conversation*, 24 April 2020. Available from https://theconversation.com/why-theres-no-such-thing-as-soci ety-should-not-be-regarded-with-moral-revulsion-136008 [Accessed on 11 July 2022].

Molina, F. and Walton, J.K. (2011) 'An alternative co-operative tradition: The Basque co-operatives of Mondragón'. In Webster, A., Shaw, L., Walton, J.K., Brown, A. and Stewart, D. (eds) *The Hidden Alternative: Co-operative Values, Past, Present and Future*. Manchester, Manchester University Press, pp 226–250.

Monbiot, G. (2016) *How Did We Get into This Mess?* London: Verso.

Mondragón (2022) 'All our history'. Available from www.mondragon-corp oration.com/en/history/page/3/ [Accessed on 7 July 2022].

Novkovic, S. and Webb, T. (eds) (2014) *Co-operatives in a Post-Growth Era.* London: Zed Books.

Novkovic, S., Miner, K. and McMahon, C. (eds) (2023) *Humanistic Governance in Democratic Organisations: The Cooperative Difference.* Cham: Palgrave Macmillan.

NSP (2016) 'Learning from Emilia Romagna's cooperative economy'. Available from https://thenextsystem.org/learning-from-emilia-romagna [Accessed on 7 July 2022].

OECD (2014) 'The co-operative model in Trentino – Italy'. Available from www.oecd.org/cfe/leed/150202%20The%20cooperative%20model%20 in%20Trentino_FINAL%20wi [Accessed on 4 June 2022].

Parker, M. (ed) (2020) *Life after COVID-19.* Bristol: Bristol University Press.

Parker, M. Cheney, G., Fournier, V. and Land, C. (2014) 'The question of organization: A manifesto for alternatives', *Ephemera*, 14(4): 623–638.

Pellervo (2022). 'Pellervo: Finnish cooperative lobbyists'. Available from https://pellervo.fi/en/english/cooperation-finland/ [Accessed on 7 July 2022].

Pérotin, V. (2012) 'The performance of workers' cooperatives'. In Battilani, P. and Schröter, H.G. (eds) *The Co-operative Business Movement 1950 to the Present.* Cambridge, Cambridge University Press, pp 195–221.

Piketty, T. (2014). *Capital in the 21st Century.* London: Harvard University Press.

Raworth, K. (2017) *Doughnut Economics: Seven Ways to Think Like a 21st-Century Economist.* Vermont: Chelsea Green.

Roelants, B. (2013). *Co-operative Growth for the 21st Century.* Brussels: ICA. [Accessed on 7 July 2022].

Stiglitz, J.E. (2002). *Globalization and Its Discontents.* New York: W.W. Norton & Company.

Tanner, V. (1937) 'The place of co-operation in different economic systems', *Annals of Public and Cooperative Economics*, 13(2): 240–265.

Thompson, M. (2023) 'Whatever happened to municipal radicalism?' *Transactions of the Institute of British Geographers.* https://doi.org/10.1111/tran.12606.

Trebeck, K. and William, J. (2019) *The Economics of Arrival. Ideas for a Grown up Economy.* Bristol: Policy Press.

Varoufakis, Y. (2017). *Adults in the Room, My Battle with Europe's Deep Establishment.* London: Bodley Head.

Webster, A., Shaw L. and Vorberg-Rugh, R. (eds) (2016) *Mainstreaming Co-operation: An Alternative for the Twenty-First Century.* Manchester: Manchester University Press.

Webster, T. and Kuznetsova, O. (2018) 'Harnessing research for a 21st century co-operative movement: Introducing the Co-Operative Early Researchers Network (CERN)', *Journal of Co-operative Studies*, 51(2): 37–42.

Wilkinson, R. and Pickett, K. (2009) *The Spirit Level: Why More Equal Societies Almost Always Do Better.* London: Allen Lane.

Wilkinson, R. and Pickett, K. (2018) *The Inner Level: How More Equal Societies Reduce Stress, Restore Sanity and Improve Everyone's Wellbeing.* London: Penguin.

Wilson, J.F., Webster, A. and Vorberg-Rugh, R. (2013). *Building Co-operation: A Business History of the Co-operative Group, 1863–2013.* Oxford: Oxford University Press.

The World Coop Monitor (nd) Available from https://monitor.coop/en [Accessed on 28 March 2023].

Zamagni, V. (2012) 'A world of variations: Sectors and forms'. In Battilani, P. and Schröter, H.G. (eds) *The Co-operative Business Movement 1950 to the Present.* Cambridge: Cambridge University Press, pp 63–82.

Seeds: Identifying the Space for Co-operatives in Addressing Social Challenges

2

Star & Shadow Cinema: A Grassroots Interface between DIY Culture, New Co-operativism and the Commons

Christo Wallers

Introduction

Star & Shadow Cinema Co-op (S&S) in Newcastle upon Tyne exemplifies a recent pattern of the rediscovery of cinema as a form of dissent against neoliberalism, prefiguring different possibilities for cinema – and as an extension city-making as a spatially located 'social practice' celebrating community, democracy and freedom through the production of urban commons. Adopting an everyday utopian approach to the constituent relations of the cinema screening event – its place, apparatus, organization, audience relations and aesthetics – this mode has been defined as DIY film exhibition (Wallers, 2021). S&S is a 100 per cent volunteer-run cinema and social centre in Newcastle upon Tyne, that evolved out of screening projects between 2001 and 2005 at the Side Cinema and other artist-run spaces. It started as a loose collective of cinema enthusiasts who wanted to organize public film screenings, variously interested in alternative film, artists' moving image, LGBTQ+ cinema and activist documentaries to inform and inspire direct action. They moved to derelict warehouse premises on the edge of one of Newcastle's urban regeneration zone, the Ouseburn, and built a screening space and music venue from scratch, all as volunteers, brushing up on (or teaching themselves) building skills as they went along. Their public programme diversified even more, and as a result the open organizational structure meant that over 1000 volunteers came through the doors and participated actively in sustaining the project. Caught in a typical gentrification cycle in a prime development location, S&S had its lease terminated in 2014, but the story was far from over.

A root urban problem for projects like S&S lies in the asymmetrical power structures that afford big capital the control to dictate the fate of urban space through private ownership. This poses questions for those who envision alternatives, about proactive legal approaches that can protect urban commons on a more long-term basis. In the case of Serbia for example, cinema spaces in Belgrade are but one of many previously state-owned assets that are at risk of top-down privatization, a pattern that commons-activists are doing their best to resist (Čukić and Timotijević, 2020). What models exist in the UK to contest and reverse this form of enclosure and increase democracy in how urban space is managed? Faced with the threat of closure, S&S doubled down and decided to reform as a co-operative community purchasing a building as an 'urban commons' in perpetuity. While cooperativism has traditionally put its weight behind more solidaristic economic systems, recent shifts demonstrate that it need not be viewed solely through an economic lens. Instead its shared qualities with commons and commoning is generating its own body of scholarship, a development termed 'new' or 'open cooperativism' (Vieta, 2010; Conaty and Bollier, 2015; Ridley-Duff, 2021). This chapter, written from the perspective of an activist researcher engaged with the S&S project since its inception, explores some of the theoretical work in the study of commons and new cooperativism in the context of a DIY space for cinema culture, in order to demonstrate and promote the practical synergies made visible by combining these frameworks.

The S&S uses the descriptor 'cinema' but it is significantly more than that. Despite the prevailing consideration of cinema as an entertainment commodity, cinema nevertheless carries connotations of the democratic public sphere, where people can assemble, experience something collectively and reflect on it. Volunteers at S&S have used this potential of free assembly to expand outwards into all manner of activities. In order to better understand the creative uses the S&S enables, looking at the schedule of activities of a regular month demonstrates that, as well as film screenings, volunteer programmers are organizing a whole range of public events and workshops. Once upon a time these might have been offered through public services like libraries, community centres and higher education providers but this provision has been hollowed out as a result of local authority cuts to spending since the 2008 financial crisis. For instance, currently advertised on the S&S website at the time of writing is an open build session, for 'all handy persons and willing bodgers to drop in for a short time or graft all day' on building new storage, installing new hardware and clearing spaces. A free stencil screen printing workshop to make posters and signs for the cinema is on fortnightly on Wednesday evenings, alongside a Fixit Cafe, where people can bring their bits and bobs in need of mending, have a cup of tea and borrow or learn how to use a soldering iron or darning needle. Sometimes this syncs with a community kitchen event, a response to the cost of living crisis that offers a space where local residents and volunteers can come and take part in activities, talk to each other, enjoy a free hot meal and access a free community larder, no questions asked. Beginner DJ classes for women, non-binary and LGBTQ+ communities happen on a Saturday morning, followed by gigs for local and touring bands and alternative club nights in the bar. An art club, an anarchist prisoner letter-writing club and a 'critical thinking and communication' workshop happen on a weekly or monthly basis. All of the meetings of the collective are listed publicly on the website, from film programming to the cafe collective to the coop's general meeting, demonstrating a transparency and inclusivity to the general public. Threaded through this programme are regular screenings, selected by volunteers interested in programming films, ranging from *Twin Peaks: Fire Walk with Me* (1992) to queer classic *The Watermelon Woman* (1997) to the first ever Doctor Who serial *An Unearthly Child* (1963). Significantly, film screenings are designed and conducted to encourage discussion either inside the cinema at the end of the film, or in the bar afterwards, and occasionally include the director present in person or over a video conferencing platform. What this picture hopefully paints is that S&S is whatever volunteers want it to be. It is simply a community-owned space with the resources available for people to build a culture from the ground up.

Do it yourself cinema and using public space

Under the pressures of successive neoliberal governments, the notion of public space has become contested as local authorities place their chips on big property developers to regenerate urban centres through introducing shopping and leisure precincts, luxury flats and student accommodation, often incorporating the alluring idea of cinema into their plans. Rotherham Metropolitan Borough Council have gone this route with their Forge Island scheme which proposes a new leisure quarter for the town centre (Farrell, 2020), as have Burnley Council, who's Pioneer Place development is set to open in 2023, bringing a six-screen cinema, retail units and restaurants to Burnley's town centre (Vaughan, 2020). Alternatively, empty urban buildings have been purchased by property developers and offered as 'meanwhile spaces' to artists and creative workers, allowing developers to minimize the running costs of their assets while they wait for the right moment to knock down and rebuild. The benefit appears mutual, in so far as artist groups get access to space at often below market rates, while developers have their buildings safely occupied and maintained. However the deal is stacked in the developer's favour, who can terminate leases at short notice, leaving the tenants in a precarious situation. DIY Cinema projects are only one of a number of likely cultural groupings to fill these 'meanwhile spaces'. In order to break out of this cycle and to protect democratic, urban cultural space in the long term, S&S reached a consensus that the most reliable option in terms of protecting their autonomy would be to buy their building outright. In summer 2018 they completed the renovation of an enormous old furniture show room, having purchased it from the local authority. Using a prudential loan process, they borrowed and fundraised to redevelop the site and they now have a highly flexible, environmentally sustainable commons resource in east central Newcastle, offering cinema, music space, cafe, bar, library, meeting room and workshop space, volunteer-managed and owned under an open and participatory co-operative governance structure.

The conceptual basis of DIY provides an important and relevant lens for understanding S&S' journey to this point. For these cinema activists, DIY does not merely describe an approach to making things happen rooted in the punk and post-punk countercultures of the 1970s, 1980s and 1990s – be that self-building resources, self-publishing 'zines' (small-run photocopied publications) or putting on alternative bands and film-makers – it means much more. As scholar of punk culture Stephen Duncombe puts it: 'Doing it Yourself is at once a critique of the dominant mode of passive consumer culture and something far more important: the active creation of an alternative culture' (Duncombe, 2008, p 117). To further position the term, Holtzman and colleagues (2007) define DIY as a process working in two ways. First, it foregrounds use value over exchange value, in so far as it is a not-for-profit venture, emphasizing the value of learning through doing things together; second, it reconstructs power dynamics through the creation of relationships or 'counter-institutions' predicated on horizontalism, a process of communication and governance that takes place in a flat hierarchy as opposed to traditional organizations with layers of management who control the permission or determine one's capability to act. DIY as an identifier emerged in the UK alongside punk music, and was picked up in the late 1990s through rave culture and environmental activism (McKay, 1998). The term has expanded since the 2000s to encompass often small-scale responses to counter the alienating narrative of commodification at the level of the individual citizen, made visible in the proliferation of maker collectives, craftivism, open source programming and guerilla or 'tactical' urbanism (Gauntlett, 2011; Campo, 2014; Ratto and Boler, 2014; Crossan et al, 2016; Day, 2017).

DIY Cinema often happens in the interstitial spaces of the city, in squats, or cafes or spaces that have been temporarily adapted to accommodate an audience, rather than in those one might consider as 'proper' cinemas. Often they are ephemeral projects relying on limited funds, borderline legality and a small team of diehard enthusiasts for their survival. They tend towards non-hierarchical organizational models, and encourage a flow between audience and workers which encourages active participation and skill sharing. The types of film culture commonly presented at DIY Cinemas range from activist documentary to underground and avant-garde cinema, home-made films and experimental assemblages of image and sound, alongside a pluralistic celebration of cinema attuned to activists' own interests, enthusiasms or concerns.

Rather than the homogenized environment of the multiplex, the exclusivity of the boutique cinema or the rarefied atmosphere of the art house, DIY film exhibition focuses on creating a critical public space, that is also consciously informal and open, the significance of which is twofold. First, people can collectively interpret the ideologies that circulate not only within films but also the spaces in which they are shown in an unintimidating atmosphere. Second, they can actively share and participate in the *creation* of that culture. Rather than limiting their experience to the consumption of a film, members of the audience may have attended a meeting to have decided on the film, arranged payment for the rights to screen the film, projected the film, run the bar before and after the screening, discussed the form and content of the film at the end, helped tidy the cinema, perhaps even installed the seats, painted the walls or built the raked seating system, or sorted out the electricity bill or the internet connection for the building – the under-acknowledged maintenance required in a shared social space.

DIY, cooperativism and the commons

One more concept bears consideration in the relationship of DIY to the commons: autonomy. A running concern for S&S since it began has been autonomy – from external agenda-setting by the state through its funding restrictions, or the market through the need to prioritize commodification. S&S has navigated a route consciously 'outside' in order to protect this autonomy – outside of the film industry, the funded arts sector and the leisure and entertainment economies, in order to allow for a commons space where different relationships can be cultivated. This route has involved an ambivalent and pragmatic relationship to the state and market, considering this project exists as simultaneously 'anti-', 'despite-' and 'post-' capitalism (Chatterton, 2010). Additionally, while DIY practice is inherently democratic, its 'place' is often veiled in subcultural codes that form boundaries to participation. These may include the taste and habits of a specific group that create a sense of gatekeeping that is hard to penetrate if you are not familiar with the 'house style'. DIY has been critiqued for being 'rooted in idealized inclusion' (Vincent, 2016) and that if you are Black or Brown, or marginalized through disability it can be hard to engage. Because DIY revolves predominantly around voluntarism, there can be an economic barrier to participation for those who lack the financial security to invest their time and energy in unpaid labour. Nevertheless, taking a step back to the 1990s, the surge in DIY culture stemmed from young people feeling ignored and disempowered and channelling their frustration into action. Whether living in trees at road protests, or staying up for days at rural raves and free parties, this culture was inherently 'underground', in that to exercise maximum freedom, the tactical course of action was to maintain as much distance from the mainstream press and media attention. This risked breeding in a form of subcultural elitism only for those in the know, and limited the broader emancipation DIY culture sought to engender. In re-focusing on accessibility, inclusion and plurality over the last decade, DIY cultures and spaces have shifted their cultural status of 'underground' to 'overground', while at the same time holding on to their autonomy from the state and the market. In that sense DIY activists have sought strategies to protect resources as commons open to all, while at the same time ensuring long-term sustainability in a climate of unsupportive economic conditions.

S&S does not follow the conventions of a normal worker or consumer coop, guided as it is by DIY culture. Its adoption of a cooperative governance model reveals a reframing or renewal of co-operative principles that has been noticed by a number of scholars, terming it 'new' or 'open' cooperativism (Vieta, 2010; Conaty and Bollier, 2015; Ridley-Duff, 2021). The pronounced increase in research into commons and 'commoning' has demonstrated a further way of thinking about activist uses of city space which attempt to exceed the limitations imposed through the 'urban ordering' necessary for capitalist reproduction (Stavrides, 2016, p 14). Discourse around the 'commons' has been building significant momentum, precipitated by the work of Elena Ostrom (1990) who first sought to answer the seminal critique regarding the community management of common pool resources (CPR) in the *Tragedy of the Commons* (Hardin, 1968). Ostrom developed an 8-rule system as a list of recommendations to resolve the complex social dynamics of sharing finite resources, which she backed up by international fieldwork to provide evidence in real world practice. The importance for the commons of managing relationships has therefore led to a development in theory beyond the resource in question (commons), to the group who are using it (commoners) and the active mode of participation (commoning), emphasizing the primacy of consensual rules to enable the commons to function and thrive. The categorization of what can qualify as a CPR has also expanded – commons are no longer restricted to the extractive use of finite resources like grazing land or fisheries. On the contrary they can include commons which actually increase through shared use and participation rather than deplete. The online example of the wiki shows how a common resource grows through the additive relationship of its users. For De Angelis and Stavrides a CPR is simply understood as a 'non-commodified means of fulfilling people's needs' (De Angelis and Stavrides, 2010). The separation of shared resources from commodification points towards a different value system to the dominant extractive model, laid bare for example in the efforts of indigenous groups to protect common land rights in the face of logging in Indonesia and the Amazon. In these instances, processes of enclosure backed by big capital are ongoing at catastrophic social and ecological cost.

This dynamic is not only visible in the extraction of natural resources, but has been recognized in the way citizens access, occupy and shape urban space. Stavros Stavrides has addressed this at length, notably in *Common Space: The City as Commons* (2016) in which he paints a picture of the city as an archipelago of enclosures in the urban sea. Private property law marks spaces as varyingly open or closed. Surrounding these enclosures are 'enclave' islands, those spaces controlled through urban ordering. Enclaves include open space, which has the potential to be public or common, but its free use is restricted through the norms and behaviours we may take for granted, but are by no means free of politics and ideology. He offers the examples of gentrified areas, gated communities, public parks or temporarily fenced-off events which bring to the fore forms of control that would otherwise be latent. Urban enclavism for Stavrides is the process of appropriation by capital that renders the urban sea controlled. However, counter to this pressure he places citizen efforts to produce 'expanding commons', in 'threshold spaces'. He outlines three defining qualities of expanding commons – comparability, translatability and egalitarian sharing. The first requires that forms of collaboration are based on multiplicity, and not just coexistence but the comparability and relevance of difference; the second involves the acts of translation that enable a multiplicity of commoners with different languages and backgrounds to cocreate commons; the last – egalitarian sharing – is an essential prerequisite to both limit the potential accumulation of power by one individual or group, and sustain an openness to newcomers, designed through radically democratic governance and decision-making structures. Expanding commoning for Stavrides provides thresholds through which the city can become a space of emancipation or transformation. Threshold spaces are 'hybrid collective works-in-progress' that threaten the dominant order by creating doorways onto other forms of relating; by opening the inside to the outside; and exposing those that cross the threshold to the potentiality of change.

Louis Volont (2019) is one of the few to have previously made the connection between this theorization of commoning and the conceptual framework of DIY urbanism, in his analysis of two Spanish DIY collectives and their efforts to use creative spatial actions to 'generate friction' against profit-led urban development. Todo por la Praxis organizes workshops and collective construction processes to reclaim unused plots and spaces in Madrid in projects like the open-air *Cinema Usera* or the community park *Esta una Plaza*. Recetas Urbanas pre-emptively interrogates the small print of local planning regulations before leading collective actions to push back against the privatization of public space through the judicious positioning of skips, shipping containers and trucks to activate space, around which they build community activities and civic consciousness about how to create a city in common. In Volont's thesis, threshold spatiality forms one part of a tripartite 'field of possibilities' for DIY urbanists to enact political resistance through commoning city space. Acknowledging particularly the dynamics of DIY urbanism's role in gentrification processes, his second point relates to value, asking how the value resulting from commoning can be retained rather than lost to the market when the net result of activities can be seen most visibly and harshly in rising property prices affordable only to the few. The third trait is legitimacy, which in relation to the state or the market can be seen as part of the process of capitalist recuperation, but for Volont it stands for a quality that can be earned through actively doing things differently. Garnering legitimacy with fellow citizens deepens DIY groups' relationship with their publics, and strengthens their hand in negotiating with local government, exemplified in the development of squats into housing associations in the Netherlands, or the 'centri sociali' in Italy.

S&S as a threshold space does its best to 'turn the inside out' as advanced by Stavrides, through communicating to the public its alternative structure. Publicity, signage and social interaction between volunteers and other users of the space all reinforce the conception of S&S as a commons resource. As already noted, in order to exemplify 'expanding commoning', a commons resource needs to promote relationships between commoners that are 'comparable', 'translatable' and 'egalitarian', always welcoming newcomers. Stavrides suggests that comparability happens when 'institutions of this kind encourage differences to meet, to mutually expose themselves and to create grounds of mutual awareness' (2016, p 41). S&S was founded on an open invitation to build a cinema, which has resulted in a considerable diversity of people getting involved. It was initiated with a strong anti–discrimination agenda and it is by no means a homogenous group that frequents and co-manages the space.[1] Earlier forms of DIY activism generally co-ordinated around a single issue or scene, often producing subcultural boundaries. Other less radical cultural venues homogenize their output through marketing departments, branding and hierarchical programming teams. In contrast S&S adopted a much more open approach, embracing plurality and openness rather than a single issue or controlled curatorial line. Any volunteer can program a film, gig or other event, and the regular program demonstrates this multiplicity as evidenced earlier in the chapter. Through sharing space to present public–facing culture, volunteers do more than just coexist, they mutually support one another, learning and skill sharing all the time. In the hand–crafted construction of the space itself they aimed to resist rigid taxonomies of roles based on traditional experts and novices. Dozens of people had a chance to develop confidence in building skills, plaster-boarding spaces or using advanced tools – even a scissor lift. One volunteer who wanted to learn projection made this point about flexibility to newcomers, stating: 'I wouldn't be able to use the facilities like these in any other place. If I wanted to go to the Tyneside [Cinema] and say I would like to project a film here they would laugh at me and close the door.'[2]

The second characteristic of expanding commoning is translation – the 'inherent inventiveness of commoning which always opens new fields and new opportunities for the creation of a common world always in-the-making' (Stavrides, 2016, p 43). This two-way process between newcomers and experienced commoners takes place in numerous spaces as volunteers interact and imagine new common dreams. At S&S this might happen behind the cafe counter, the projection booth or in preparing for an online radio transmission. The perpetual openness to expanding collaboration on film and gig programming, cooking and maintenance encapsulate acts of translation in the context of difference. Last, institutions of expanding commoning need to resist the potential accumulation of power through egalitarian processes of decision-making. In the earliest foundational meetings of S&S in 2005, one of the first agreements was to pursue consensus as a decision-making process. While working groups can self-manage the everyday aspects of stewarding S&S, when it comes to issues that fundamentally affect the organization as a whole, special meetings or assemblies are called and facilitated until consensus is reached. The COVID-19 pandemic had an enormous impact on S&S as opinion about the best course of action polarized. Finding common ground became fraught with difficulty, but the strategy of consensus building protected the commons resource from breaking irreparably apart into factions as could have happened with a majority voting system. The collective reached consensus to close the space before government guidelines were introduced in late March 2020, and took a slow and steady route towards reopening, kept at a measured pace through consensus-based meetings.

The paradigm of commoning is apt for analysing S&S, but what it offers in building a powerful positive vision for sharing resources in the urban context, is somewhat offset by what it lacks in systematic structures for achieving this goal within the eyes of the law, at least in the UK. This is where cooperativism steps in and can offer ethically aligned, practical ways of achieving urban commons. New Cooperativism (NC) represents an evolution of cooperative values beyond the consumer- and worker-oriented cooperative sector. This trend was picked up first by Vieta (2010), who outlined a five-point framework for distinguishing NC. First, this pattern of social innovation is a citizen- and worker-led reaction to neoliberalism. The second characteristic is that this practice does not emerge from within the existing cooperative sector, and therefore is unhindered by set systems in the cooperative movement. In fact, new cooperativism can describe many types of prefigurative action regardless of its governance status as cooperative or not. The third aspect relates to a more egalitarian ethics, disrupting and reconfiguring politics at the most everyday level. Following on from this, NC organizes in more horizontal ways than the traditional hierarchical management model of old cooperativism. Last, rather than focusing on economic benefit to coop members, it focuses on community benefit through social aims.

The position of Star & Shadow Cinema Co-op

How does S&S fit into this rubric? Vieta's first point should by now be self-evident – that this practice is a citizen-led response to the crises of neoliberalism – the 'market knows best' reduction of life to commodification and competitive efficiency with ensuing ecological breakdown, social atomization and inequality. As a DIY act of resistance to neoliberalism, S&S builds an egalitarian community for the exploration of alternative culture outside of the bonds of consumerism, with a light ecological footprint. Vieta goes on to suggest the new form of cooperativism comes from outside rather than within the pre-existing cooperative movement. Unhindered by sedimented ways of working in the cooperative sector at large, these tend to 'prefigure different, less exploitative, and less-alienating forms of economic organization ... as a set of future-oriented possibilities or preliminary sketches that suggest alternative economic, productive, cultural, and social practices in the present and for tomorrow' (Vieta, 2010, p. 4). It is true to say that while the founders of S&S were aware of important small-scale worker co-operatives in Newcastle, such as Amber Films and Tyneside Free Press, the cinema was not born out of the dominant cooperative culture of the times. As has been stated, it was an evolution of DIY activism of the environmental and anti-globalization movements, connected to the proliferation of autonomous social centres that occurred in the early 2000s (see, for example, Pusey, 2010). Third, Vieta notes the NC tendency for developing a politics and ethics at the level of the everyday, rather than focusing on macro change, living the change they want to see in the equitable ways they engage with one another and the earth. At the S&S, cinema – both as films to be seen and a space to be produced – becomes the pretext for a relational critique of the everyday, where the boundaries between consumer and producer are porous and often inverted. The audience member can become the projectionist, and the bar staff. Fourth, in his taxonomy he specifies the significance of collective ownership of the means of production maintained through both horizontal and inclusive labour structures and the egalitarian allocation of surplus. This is readily apparent in the community purchase of the S&S building, and the consensus decision-making process at meetings, but it is visible in the finer detail as well. Volunteers aim for annual participatory budgeting sessions making the financial functioning of the project transparent, and the allocation of surplus democratic. The final point is that NC involves a strong connection to local community development backed up by outward facing social objectives. S&S as a community hub in east central Newcastle, engages in its locality by providing space and facilities but also a meeting place for co-ordinating actions or sharing information, and opportunities to find social connection and a sense of agency and empowerment in how urban space is allocated and managed. The crossovers between DIY, commoning and new cooperativism are by now clear to see. Yet it is worth reasserting that in Vieta's model, NC describes a tendency in social innovation that is not necessarily formally tied to cooperativism as a governance system. How can this disconnection from traditional coop forms be accounted for?

The recognition of change stems from critiques that old cooperativism has moved too close to the capitalist logic of the market, weakening its radical roots; and that it has lost touch with the original co-operative principles of open membership and democratic control (Ridley-Duff, 2021). In his research on NC, Ridley-Duff harvested critiques from three groupings – the P2P Foundation in the Netherlands, which researches and promotes peer-to-peer production predominantly online; the Transition Network developing community resilience in the face of climate change; and FairShares, a group of researchers and cooperators seeking fair recognition and allocation of wealth to all stakeholders in social enterprises. In his research he noted a consistent proposition across all of these sources in favour of commons resources for mutual benefit (p 7). This pattern has already motivated exploration of the convergence between cooperativism and the commons. Pat Conaty and David Bollier, in their commons strategy report *Toward an Open Co-operativism* (2015), seek to provide an argument for the blending of innovative commoning (particularly peer-to-peer production) with the experience and wisdom of the cooperative movement. Their model proposes cooperative entrepreneurs co-producing commons through a variety of technical structures and strategies, from commons-based reciprocity licenses to expanding multi-stakeholder co-operatives; increasing community land trusts, cooperative housing and mutual currencies; forging synergies between open network platforms and familiar cooperative structures; and encouraging collaborative partnerships between citizens and local governments to co-develop commons and protect common wealth. The system of open cooperativism, while embracing and utilizing commoning strategies, clearly is weighted towards the solidaristic economy of the cooperative movement, contrasting with Stavrides' commons theory which prioritizes political standpoints in relation to common pool resources. The journey for S&S exemplifies the tension between these two positions, one political and the other economic that reflects a similar tension between 'new' and 'open' cooperativism.

Star & Shadow Cinema Co-op and co-operation

S&S has undeniably embraced cooperative principles, evident from the poster of the seven cooperative rules up on the wall when you first enter the space. The cinema was initially an unincorporated group, when running activities under the name New Side Cinema Collective, before hastily constituting as a Community Interest Company (CIC) in 2006 in order to take on the lease of a building. It was only when the possibility of community purchasing a building came up that latent interest in cooperative structures developed into an urgent need to have a governance model that could own an asset like a building, while staying true to S&S' DIY ethic. The CIC model lacked a stated value system, or any sense of solidarity with a wider movement. S&S opted for a multi-stakeholder community benefit society (CBS) based on the 2014 Somerset Rules. This governance model harmonizes with DIY practice and commoning in a number of ways. As a CBS, it prioritizes benefit to the community rather than to cooperative members first and foremost. This keeps the organization grounded in its social purpose. Written in relatively plain language rather than legalese, it closely follows the international cooperative principles by writing in a strong focus on democracy, autonomy, independence and sustainable development, empowering members and stakeholders at the most local level possible. It includes an asset lock which after dissolution protects any assets from exploitation by coop members. It opens up ownership and democracy to diverse groups of stakeholders rather than focusing power exclusively in the membership and it builds in social accounting as a safeguard to ensure the social mission is maintained.

S&S is not a pure commons resource in that it is designed around two models of participation, one closely aligned with commoning, the other angled towards the reality of functioning in a market system. The primary model has historically been described by S&S activists as 'with not for'. Based on mutual reciprocity, this conception centred on collectively building and co-managing a space and resource in common, thus enabling the sharing of culture on participants' own terms, outside of the logics of both the market and the state funded arts sector. By contributing voluntary time to the maintenance of the resource, participants can share open access to the physical, technical, administrative and financial assets aggregated in the project, just like other examples of common pool resources. Any accumulated value generated by activity, be that social, material or capital, remains within the organization and is distributed by democratic means through working groups. In the case of profit, this gets reinvested according to the social aims of the coop through an expanded program of events, improved resources or other activities decided through participatory budgeting. The value of the knowledge created or generated is distributed to existing and potential members through updates to digital platforms like the wiki or the shared cloud drive meaning new knowledge is not siloed, but transparent and accessible. The social value is embodied by those that participate in an enriched sense of agency and ownership of their city. Activity is guided by mutual benefit, 'with' one another rather than 'for' a customer or service user. On the other hand, the second model of participation implies a more conventional supplier-consumer relationship of visitors to events or 'external' users of the space. Audiences for films and gigs for example, or those that want to hire a space for a meeting but do not have the time or inclination to volunteer, fall into this category. They are charged well below market rates for access to the resource. These two levels of participation are reflected in the membership categories of the S&S Cooperative as Class 1, referred to as community membership, which includes volunteer-workers; and Class 2 defined as non-community members who are supporters and friends of S&S. The two classes are subdivided further in acknowledgement of their different stakeholder status, for example autonomous and associate collectives make up part of the Class 2 membership. Canny Library, a radical library project, and Film Bee, an artist-run film lab constitute some of these associate stakeholders. In exceptional circumstances, the proportional voting rights of different classes of membership ensure that while decision-making is democratic, the interests of the core membership (or commoners) are prioritized. However, in all but the rarest case, any member of an open meeting can engage in the consensus process, a feature enshrined in the Local Rules as the dominant decision-making process. It has also enabled S&S to subsume the powers of directors (referred to as stewards) to the general meeting, which is the sovereign body of the organization. Membership of the co-operative is open to anyone, as long as they behave in accordance with the safer spaces agreement agreed upon democratically at a general meeting. This means that S&S' horizontal structure is 'baked into' its governing document. This legal structure has enabled the S&S to purchase a building owned in common by members of the co-operative.

Conclusion

The legal frameworks for community ownership of land and assets have undergone significant progressive changes since the early 2000s through legislation like the Community Right to Buy and the Localism Act 2011. Alongside pubs, community shops and sports fields, cinemas have galvanized activists to protect important community resources at risk of loss. The Wellington Orbit, a small volunteer-run cinema in Shropshire has recently put out a community share issue to raise funds to buy the leasehold of their building. As of June 2022, Oxford's Ultimate Picture Palace secured the community share capital to buy their building. Theatre Gwaun became the owners of their cinema in Fishguard through a Community Asset Transfer from Pembrokeshire County Council. The Independent Cinema Office has rolled out workshops on community purchase of cinemas using the government's mechanism of the Community Ownership Fund as part of the Levelling Up agenda. These are positive stories of communities taking charge of assets that form the fabric of shared civic life. Yet the narrative has been framed by notions of community rescue and preservation, rather than proactive challenge to a neoliberal order. A DIY project like Star & Shadow Cinema demonstrates that alternatives exist. In effect, they have created a cooperatively managed commons, synthesizing the theoretical positions outlined earlier. S&S volunteers now self-identify as DIY activists, as cooperators and as commoners, presenting a convergence of recent thinking about the solidarity economy. New cooperativism and urban commoning provide the basis for a paradigm shift in thinking about democratic access to community resources, taking steps beyond preservation into the active construction of alternative social relationships. This chapter has explored how these mutually supportive concepts can interact in the creation of long-term-sustainable and democratically controlled urban cultural spaces. Following renewals in the cooperative movement can be seen to have opened up a different set of tools for DIY urbanism and the production of the city as commons. Cooperativism is replete with rules-based systems that tally with Volont's threefold field of possibilities. It can provide governance models that protect threshold spaces, dedicated to expanding commoning; it can ensure that value produced and accumulated stays within the group that generated that value; it can provide developing and ongoing legitimacy with important stakeholders without fundamentally compromising the core ethical system, particularly through multi-stakeholder involvement in the ownership and management of the commons resource. Furthermore it can enshrine ideals in a governing document that place political concerns in comparable importance to economic ones. To that end it can protect urban commons long term, enabling commoners to reimagine and enact new possibilities beyond the current capitalist order. This proactive approach needs to be expressed more forcefully in order to publicly shift the argument in favour of solidaristic civic activism more broadly.

Notes

[1]   S&S has struggled in reaching people of colour based in Newcastle upon Tyne to feel included. S&S has become a safe(r) space for LGBTQA+, people with disabilities and those with mental health issues.

² Arto Polus (Star & Shadow volunteer) interviewed by Christo Wallers, Newcastle, July 2018.

References

Campo, D. (2014) 'Iconic eyesores: Exploring do-it-yourself preservation and civic improvement at abandoned train stations in Buffalo and Detroit', *Journal of Urbanism: International Research on Placemaking and Urban Sustainability*, 7(4): 351–380.

Conaty, P. and Bollier, D. (2015) 'Toward an open co-operativism', *Commons Transition*, 10 February. Available from https://commonstransition.org/toward-an-open-co-operativism2/ [Accessed on 18 May 2021].

Crossan, J., Cumbers, A., McMaster, R. and Shaw, D. (2016) 'Contesting neoliberal urbanism in Glasgow's community gardens: The practice of DIY citizenship', *Antipode*, 48(4): 937–955.

Čukić, I. and Timotijević, J. (eds) (2020) *Spaces of Commoning: Urban Commons in the Ex-Yu Region*. Belgrade, Serbia: Ministry of Space/Institute for Urban Politics.

Day, A. (ed) (2017) *DIY Utopia: Cultural Imagination and the Remaking of the Possible*. Lanham, MD: Lexington Books.

Duncombe, S. (2008) *Notes from Underground: Zines and the Politics of Alternative Culture* (2nd edn). Bloomington: Microcosm.

Farrell, S. (2020) 'Approval recommended for major mixed-use development'. Insider Media. Available from www.insidermedia.com/news/yorkshire/approval-recommended-for-major-mixed-use-development (Accessed on 1 August 2022).

Gauntlett, D. (2011) *Making Is Connecting*. Cambridge: Polity Press.

Hardin, G. (1968) 'The tragedy of the commons', *Science*, 162(3859): 1243–1248.

Holtzman, B., Hughes, C. and Van Meter, Kevin (2007) 'Do it yourself … and the movement beyond capitalism'. In Biddle, E. Graeber, D. and Shukaitis, S. (eds) *Constituent Imagination: Militant Investigations//Collective Theorization*. Oakland, CA: AK Press, pp 44–61.

McKay, G. (ed) (1998) *DIY Culture: Party and Protest in Nineties Britain*. New York: Verso.

Ostrom, E. (1990) *Governing the Commons: The Evolution of Institutions for Collective Action*. Cambridge: Cambridge University Press (The political economy of institutions and decisions).

Pusey, A. (2010) 'Social centres and the new cooperativism of the common', *Affinities: A Journal of Radical Theory, Culture and Action*, 4(1): 176–198.

Ratto, M. and Boler, M. (eds) (2014) *DIY Citizenship: Critical Making and Social Media*. Cambridge, MA: MIT Press.

Ridley-Duff, R. (2021) 'New co-operativism as social innovation: Progress or regress?', *Journal of Co-operative Studies*, 53(3): 5–24.

Stavrides, S. (2016) *Common Space: The City as Commons*. London: Zed Books.

Vaughan, C. (2020) 'Burnley approves cinema and leisure scheme: Place North West'. Available from www.placenorthwest.co.uk/planning-burnley-approves-cinema-and-leisure-scheme/ [Accessed on 1 August 2022].

Vieta, M. (2010) 'Editorial: The new cooperativism', *Affinities: A Journal of Radical Theory, Culture, and Action*, 4(1): 1–11.

Volont, L. (2019) 'DIY urbanism and the lens of the commons: Observations from Spain', *City & Community*, 18(1): 257–279.

Wallers, C. (2021) 'From caves to commons: DIY cinema in the UK'. Available from https://centaur.reading.ac.uk/104245/ [Accessed on 7 September 2022].

3

Beyond Green-Washing: Sustainable Development and Environmental Accountability through Co-operators' Eyes (A French Perspective)

François Deblangy

Introduction

This chapter explores the processing of environmental issues by democratically run organizations from the perspective of their members, be they active or retired, founding or new. It is specifically based upon a qualitative analysis of three French workers' co-operatives from different backgrounds, operating in different sectors and of different sizes. A survey was carried out comprising of 16 individual, face-to-face interviews with members of all co-operatives playing various roles and fulfilling various functions within them. Questionnaires submitted to the interviewees were split into two parts: part 1 was made up of around 15 open questions – some of which were adapted to fit the peculiar history and socio-economic profile of the coop – to better understand the raison d'être of the organization and its members' understanding of their missions; part 2 was a series of a dozen scaled-response questions to assess the co-operators' political attitudes and personal stance regarding industrial democracy, ecology and the market economy. Each interview lasted two hours on average but time was unfortunately lacking to consider completing this work with field, let alone participatory, research.

This chapter also draws heavily upon an in-depth knowledge of workers' co-operation and industrial democracy built up by the author over the last four years of academic research and a fairly regular record of the co-operatives' activities during the same time span. The study suggests that, while a democratic structure alone might not be a determining or sufficient factor to promote and apply ambitious green reforms within a company, direct participation in collective decision-making enhances and strengthens members' political consciousness and broadens their areas of concern through a process of collective empowerment and sharing of this political power. This political 'awakening' is likely to be even more acutely experienced in the presence of direct adversity. It will also most probably be efficiently maintained and nurtured by an unremitting horizontal questioning, both internally (of the daily working organization) and externally (relating to the social and political environment) oriented.

The impact of democratic decision-making in producers' co-operatives has already been discussed in an extensive literature, especially in the late 20th century. Most of this focused on the quite narrow economic question of productivity, though (Stephen, 1982; Defourney et al, 1985; Grunberg, 1986; Estrin et al, 1987). Furthermore, authors were sometimes inclined to refer to the fairly polysemous term of 'participation' which encompasses very diverse schemes ranging from mere profit-sharing to total workers' self-management. Other pioneering works attempted to research more deeply into the social transformations implied by an active participation in the running of their organization by worker-members and its entanglements with wider social and political movements such as feminism but remained rather isolated contributions (Wajcman, 1983). More recent studies tried to highlight the link between employee participation and their companies' involvement in favour of environmental sustainability but their scope was limited to top-down strategies designed by conventional corporations themselves through the prism of human resources management (Benn et al, 2015; Farooq et al, 2019). Thus previous contributions do not appear to satisfactorily address the relation between workplace democracy and growing awareness of the environmental impact of productive activities nor the politicizing and awareness-raising potential of self-management in workers' collectives.

Yet the current ecological crisis raises a vast range of issues that mainly young citizens across the world have started to tackle by organizing themselves politically on the streets, through alternative media, but also through the ballot box. Tomorrow, the workplace may well give them a whole new field of battle. Indeed, one can hardly dissociate the climate emergency and current social as well as political turmoil in many countries, intertwined as they are by concerns about taxation, income inequality and political representation. Recent social upheavals in France with the 'yellow vests' movement give us a tell-tale illustration of those interconnections. That is why this chapter will be dealing with the translation of ecological consciousness and its development in working environments managed by the workers themselves or their direct representatives. Workers' co-operatives were chosen first because they generally embody the purest form of workplace democracy and second because they are sufficiently developed in France to allow further longitudinal or cross-sectorial observations in the future.

Workers' co-operation in France: background

France has a very long and rich cooperative history. Great Britain is often considered the birthplace of the wider co-operative movement – sometimes referred to as the 'cooperative commonwealth' – and the pioneering role of Robert Owen, his contribution to social reform and utopian socialism cannot be overstated (Pollard and Salt, 1971). However, British co-operation has historically been dominated by consumers' cooperative societies and even represented by them alone for most of the previous two centuries. Decades after Beatrice Webb's first critical account of 'producers' democracies' (Webb, 1891), labour historian George D.H. Cole still came to the same conclusion that 'industrial Co-operation among producers exists in Great Britain only as an adjunct to the Consumers' Movement, on which it entirely depends' (Cole, 1944, p 395). Things happened quite differently on the other side of the Channel. The first worker-run productive cooperative society appeared in Paris as early as 1834 following the model of workers' associations (*Associations Ouvrières*) designed by Philippe Buchez and later promoted in his monthly newspaper *L'Atelier* (The Workshop). Buchez's social experiments and the 1848 February Revolution were a major inspiration to the first circle of British Christian Socialists who founded the Society for Promoting Working Men's Associations in 1850 and supported the establishment of the first viable producers' co-operatives in the last quarter of the century (Jones, 1894; Backstrom, 1960).

The restoration of the French Empire in 1852 swept away most of the urban working class' associations and social aspirations. In 1871, the short-lived Paris Commune promptly issued a decree declaring the seizure of workshops and factories left behind by their owners which were to be managed by workers formerly employed in them. Once again, workers' associations were nipped in the bud by the ensuing bloody military repression. But cooperative and mutual societies, including workers' coops, then became valuable in the eyes of most governments of the Third Republic in which moderate democratic socialists played a leading role (Toucas-Truyen, 2005). Laws were even passed in the 1880s and 1890s to allow them priority in securing public contracts and they began to thrive on a lasting basis, especially after the establishment of their first central organization – the Consultative Board of Productive Workers' Cooperative Associations – in 1884. In the beginning of the 20th century, France became a stronghold of workers' co-operation thanks to sympathetic legislation and a growing radical trade union movement.

Workers' co-operatives among the biggest in Europe and arguably the world at that time were founded such as Albi Workers' Glassworks (*Verrerie Ouvrière d'Albi*, 1895) and the Workers' Association in Precision Instruments (*Association des Ouvriers en Instruments de Précision*, 1896). The 1920s and 1930s were still a boom period for the French cooperative movement, both productive and retail. In 1937, the central organization of the workers' cooperative movement was reorganized pretty much along the same lines as the trade union movement with sectorial and geographical branches and renamed General Confederation of Productive Workers' Cooperative Societies (CGSCOP). Eighty-five years later, the CGSCOP is still the central promotional and advisory body of the movement today.

The French post-war government and its left-wing members – mainly communists – also played a determining role in the advancement of productive co-operation and industrial democracy globally. The government order of 22 February 1945 created the French Works Councils (*Comités d'Entreprises*) which stated 'the need to associate workers to the government of the economy and the management of their companies'. In 1947, a general legal framework was given to cooperative societies and activities, although strictly limited to their commercial and economic function. French workers' coops were growing especially in a handful of key sectors such as the building and printing industries. By this time, only around 40 workers' coops were still operating in Great Britain, most of them affiliated to the declining Co-operative Productive Federation (CPF). Both countries experienced massive working-class protests and industrial unrest from the end of the 1960s but these came to quite different ends. While factory occupations began to erupt across France from the very beginning of May 1968, they quickly receded after the Grenelle agreements which granted employees a 35 per cent increase in minimum wage and the creation of company-level trade union branches. The British wave of sit-ins was rather less intense but lasted into the beginning of the 1970s. It also took its root in other structural changes, namely a nationwide industrial rationalization causing heavy job cuts during a high tide of British trade unionism. Some industrial action was still going on in France after 1970 and, interestingly, some highly publicized large-scale sit-ins transformed into spontaneous work-ins and then became formalized as workers' co-operatives with the implication of government officials on strikingly similar times. Indeed both the 'Benn coops' and the French clock-making factory LIP were set up within a few months in 1973–74[1] (Coates et al, 1976; Piaget, 2021).

The historical robustness and resilience of workers' co-operation in France has attracted interest among British practitioners and writers (Oakeshott, 1978, pp 121–144; Thornley, 1981, pp 131–150). In July 1978, the law no. 78–763 specifically defined productive workers' cooperative societies as being 'formed by workers of all occupations and qualifications associated to carry out their jobs collectively in a company they directly manage or through authorised representatives chosen by and among them'. Today, there are 2,300 workers' co-operatives operating in France employing over 50,000 people[2] in a great diversity of sectors, all affiliated to the CGSCOP and linked-up together in regional federations. Many of them are at the cutting-edge of sustainability and green practices in their own fields (Kerfourn, 2018; Nivet, 2018a, 2018b) and, as workers' coops, of workplace democracy and participative management. Therefore, the central question here is whether or not we can observe some kind of casual relationship between these two characteristics. Are cooperators in their dual role of workers and members more sensitized to the environmental impact of their productive activity? Does political representation within a company raise workers' awareness about wider issues so that they are led to take greater care of their direct environment than private capital-owners would? Or are democratically organized structures simply more likely to attract those individuals with already ingrained ecological sensibility? Findings tend to show, first, that these hypotheses do not rule out one another and, second, that workers' propensity to seize upon these questions depends on the decision-making process and power sharing scheme as well as the 'political history' of the co-operative. Before taking a closer look at their members' experience and attitudes, let us first introduce the workers' coops studied here.

The sample analysed

The sample introduced here was carefully arranged to reflect the diversity of the French workers' cooperative movement. All co-operatives differ greatly from one another by their size – ranging from just a few members to over 50 – their age – from 2 to over 40 years old – and their origins – from an unprompted political assertion to a long-lasting factory occupation.

Co-operative A

Alternatives Économiques is a medium-sized organization which produces and publishes a monthly economic magazine: 80 per cent of its capital is owned by the 40 worker-members and around 20 per cent by a readers' association. It was founded in 1980 and first run as a nonprofit organization by its sole founder, an economics teacher who wanted to prove Margaret Thatcher wrong when she famously stated there was 'no alternative' (see Interview 1.g). The magazine became a workers' co-operative as soon as it had hired enough staff in 1984 and started to gain popularity among the teaching community thanks to the accessibility of its contents for a non-academic readership and the unorthodoxy of its analysis. The co-operative is committed to promote an educational approach to economics but also social sciences and, more recently, ecology. The editorial policy can be situated on the centre-Left of the political spectrum and the magazine has fairly strong historical and ideological ties with social democratic movements in France. However, members also stress the unique profile of their organization as one of the few genuinely independent newspaper in the French press (Interview 1.f).

The company is operating on two different sites with journalists and executives – mainly highly qualified jobs – working in Paris and after-sales, shipping or subscription services – lower-skilled jobs – located in the birthplace of the magazine near Dijon in eastern France.[3] Wages account for the major part of the operating costs which cannot be easily reduced and co-operative A went through hard years around 2010 when journals and newspapers had to quickly develop a digital strategy in order to follow new reading habits and survive. Today, the co-operative has achieved a sound financial situation thanks to growing online subscriptions but also loyal paper version readers. In addition to running a paper and online magazine, co-operative A is also dedicated to the promotion of alternative thinking in academic and business circles. It therefore contributes to and organizes various conferences and colloquia in France and stands out as a flagship member of the social economy in France.

Co-operative B

Les Passants is a small cooperative bakery created only recently and run as a workers' coop from the beginning in 2019. It was founded by two friends and now employs five bakers – all of whom were interviewed – in Poitiers, western France. All members are relatively young graduates who changed career and had to go through some initial training before joining the co-operative. Workers can decide how much time they want to spend on the job according to what is needed for the bakery to run efficiently. They mainly produce sourdough bread baked in the oldest wood-fired oven in the city and made from local and organic products. Founding members of the co-operative consider their main objective a social one, though, and insist on their aim to offer 'a high-quality bread at an affordable price' (Interview 2.a, 2.b). Co-operative B directly sells its products to the general public through its shop and on the weekly market but its biggest customers are local community-supported farming organizations (CSFO).[4] Le Chaudron d'Or, for example, offers a wide range of local organic products from around 15 producers including dairy, seasonable fruits and vegetables or meat and eggs directly on the city campus every week. Customers must become members of the organization and get a basket of the weekly production for a fixed contribution.

Co-operative C

SCOP-TI can be considered as a 'phoenix' workers' co-operative born out of the conversion of a conventional private firm which the owner – a huge multinational corporation – wanted to close down. However, this production site was repeatedly proven to be viable by the trade union members, and supported by the social and political underlying aspirations of some of their leading figures, undoubtedly making it fit into the category of 'alternative conversions' (Cornforth et al, 1988, p 9). This industrial co-operative is the final outcome of a four-year long tooth-and-nail fight led by around 80 workers – helped by many political sympathizers – to protest against the closure of their infusion- and tea-producing factory near Marseille, in southern France. The story began in 2010 when the parent company announced its plan to close the plant, a dozen years after closing a first one near Le Havre. Workers organized and drew up an alternative plan to keep the machines operating on the site which set out a case and plan for them to run the factory themselves. Trade unionists gave the struggle a highly symbolic and political complexion demanding a 're-appropriation of the industrial equipment' (Interview 3.a). They describe this struggle as a five-dimension one, comprising of 'a political, economic, industrial, judicial and media battle' (Interview 3.a). Indeed, during the successive chapters of this industrial saga, the workers welcomed the French president to-be François Hollande during his electoral campaign and several ministers during his mandate.

After 1,336 days of conflict, the remaining workers were finally able to resume work and created their own co-operative to be run democratically by the people employed. Cooperative status was adopted primarily because 'it allowed the most horizontal management structure within the capitalist economy' (Interview 3.d). Machines were transferred to the city of Marseille for the symbolic sum of one euro but the new worker-members were denied the transfer of the ownership of the nationally famous brand under which they had been producing and production contracts. Thus, the co-operative had to start building a new commercial brand from scratch and still lives on mainly as a subcontractor of private labels. During their occupations of the factory, workers also founded a nonprofit organization to spread the news and promote their cause all over the country and also abroad, creating links with other working-class movements in Greece, for example (Interview 3.b). Founding members of co-operative C also identified a real need to re-educate workers to work cooperatively and foster democratic practices on a daily basis.

Findings and discussion

Green policy within workers' coops

All worker-members interviewed stated that environmentalism was a major concern in the daily running of their co-operative and were able to provide at least a short list of measures taken within them to either reduce the environmental impact of their activity and/or advertise for green alternatives. This part examines the methods adopted by each co-operative to actively contribute to the preservation of the environment in their respective sector and on their scale.

When co-operative A was founded some 40 years ago, the environment was not a regular issue on its agenda as its founder himself admitted. Although the very first issue of the magazine was already printed on recycled paper, the contents exclusively focused on economic matters. From a personal perspective, he was an early anti-nuclear militant already interested in green power issues. Besides, the mid-1970s saw the birth of a new school of thought in France which became known as political ecology embodied by philosophers and political thinkers such as André Gorz and René Dumont (Dumont, 1973; Gorz, 1975). Thinkers of political ecology called for dramatic changes in our social and economic systems to restore a healthy relationship between human beings and nature, especially after the excesses of war and consumerism. Most of the members who gradually joined the co-operative were influenced by their writings and a significant part of them soon became involved in green politics. An early member recalls that 'the self-management movement supported by the French Democratic Confederation of Labour (CFDT)[5] and political ecology were at the core of the magazine's identity during the 1980s'. Yet, it was not until the retirement of the founder and his replacement by a new president of the co-operative in 2000 that journalists started to tackle environmental issues in their articles. From then on, they gradually became one of the key development areas of the editorial policy. The co-operative now employs two specialists on the question and ecology was introduced as one the four main sections of the journal when a whole new layout was designed.

The most impactful way for a press company to contribute to the ecological cause is probably through sensitization of its readership and propaganda and co-operative A has obviously been doing this for over 20 years. But on a more microeconomic scale, members also adapted its internal functioning to reduce its environmental footprint. Power at co-operative A is provided by a pioneering French green energy company also run as a co-operative named Enercoop. Magazines are still printed on recycled paper although it is widely considered less attractive to readers. Another regular committed position by the co-operative is to intentionally display major questions such as climate change and degrowth on their front-page even when other political headlines tend to sell more (Interview 1.e).

Ecology was at the very heart of the initial project of Co-operative B. The bakery was founded only three years ago by rather young and politically active members. All raw materials used for the different products are organically – whether under French and European labels or not[6] – and locally grown. Products are sold in their shop in the city centre and on the weekly market just a few hundred metres away. Bakers presently drive their car there but are exploring innovative carbon-free transportation modes for the future (Interviews 2.a, b, e). Car deliveries to farms outside the city are also indispensable but the co-operative sometimes turns down too distant customers when they can afford it. The production process produces little pollution but still undergoes regular improvements. The oven used to bake the bread dates back to the early 20th century and is still the only heating device. It is powered by wood, a renewable energy though its combustion emits carbon dioxide. Before being baked, dough has to be laid to rise for several hours at a given and steady temperature. Bakers usually use electric fermentation chambers to ease this process which are similar to huge refrigerators but workers at co-operative B managed to do without it during a whole period of the year by using the basement of their premises and slightly modifying quantities in their ingredients.

While all members are convinced of the need to take greater care of the environment and reduce as much as possible the impact of their productive activity on it, ecology is considered by some members to be more of a fact than a philosophy in the workplace (Interview 2.b). On a larger scale, the co-operative also supports an eco-friendly citizen movement against intensive farming by providing bread at cost price (Interviews 2.a, e).

As an industrial production site, co-operative C has by far the heaviest environmental impact. The factory was initially built to provide for a mass market on a European scale with a production capacity of up to 6,000 tonnes a year. Radical shifting to eco-friendly supply and production was a consistent aim of the cooperative project. During the elaboration phase of the alternative project to factory closure, different commissions were created to think about its various aspects, one of which was dedicated to ecology. Before the conversion of the company into a co-operative, herbs such as lime tree leaves were imported from Eastern Europe through Hamburg, then shipped back to Poland for packaging and brought back west again to be sold in France. Now lime tree leaves are bought from local producers in Southern France whom the co-operative helped develop the organic culture of an ancient variety of lime trees. Furthermore, thyme used for another tea flavour is grown 12 miles away from the factory. By the end of the 20th century, the pre-coop company had given up on natural flavouring to move on to artificial flavouring, which allowed heavy cuts in jobs by replacing 15 cooks by two operators. A former cook in the private company felt he was 'not a cook anymore but a mere workman in front of a cement mixer' (Interview 3.b).

When the co-operative changed packaging, products were still packed in old boxes for weeks to use them up and avoid wasting materials (Interview 3.a). Right from the beginning of production, cooperators launched a new wholly organic product range under a specific brand. Of course, the peculiar situation of this phoenix workers' co-operative puts a strain on its environmental ambitions. Because of its size and high fixed costs, they need to sell considerable volumes so as not to run at a loss and therefore have to deal with large retailing store chains, which is often considered a deal-breaker by specialized organic food stores. Since the production site and buildings are very large and the region is very sunny, some worker-members have been considering installing solar panels on the roof but the company is not in a position to afford such investments yet. The average age is high among the 57 workers now employed and most of them belong to a generation who were not confronted with environmental crisis as children or teenagers, yet they generally feel highly concerned by the issue. Some of them explained they felt really appalled by the green-washing strategies of their private, multinational competitors who resort to low-cost country sourcing to bypass social and environmental regulations.

Such critical political views on our modern capitalist societies are widely shared by interviewees of all co-operatives in the sample, as will be seen in the next section.

Worker-members' attitudes towards ecology

Scaled-response questions were asked in all interviews to try and assess cooperators' attitudes and opinions about industrial democracy, political ecology and potential global solutions to environmental issues. Answers given could vary from 1 (totally disagree) to 10 (totally agree). Averages were calculated for each co-operative and each question and compared. The first conclusion is that results are quite – and sometimes strikingly – similar to one another. Standard deviations[7] between the means were also calculated and are usually very low, ranging from 0.27 to 1.13. These figures suggest interviewees' thoughts, no matter what co-operative they work in, sharply coincide (Figure 3.1). Co-operative C, whose members have gone through a long and exhausting industrial dispute against the former owners of their factory, gave the highest number of extreme occurrences – either 1 or 10 – revealing decided opinions. On the other hand, co-operative A, the oldest and best-established, gave more moderate answers, though clearly converging.

All cooperators interviewed agree that ecology is a major national and international issue, 80 per cent of them – and all worker-members of co-operative B – choosing the highest answer for a global average of 9.53. When asked whether the state or citizens should play a leading role in the setting-up of schemes for the preservation of the environment,

Figure 3.1: Average answer given to response-scaled questions by co-operative

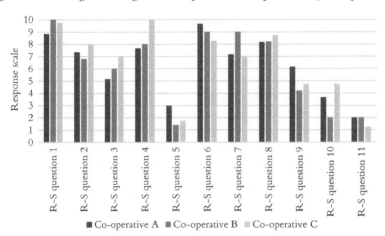

interviewees also agreed on the company level that state intervention would best suit the situation. Worker-members of co-operatives B and C gave near-average results to both options and co-operative C gave the highest average answer which reflects a deeply rooted belief in self-determination and 'grassroots' initiative. This can possibly be explained by the process of collective emancipation triggered during the sit-in and work-in which led to the foundation of the co-operative and presumably by some kind of distrust towards state officials and recent governments' neoliberal legislation in a highly unionized co-operative. Interestingly, results obtained from members of co-operative A show the widest gap between the two options to the advantage of state action which is consistent with its dominating reformist ethos.

As far as industrial democracy and workers' participation are concerned, worker-members in all co-operatives generally agree that giving more powers to workers within their companies would enable a better understanding of the environmental impact of their productive activity and its taking into account in the overall strategy. Once again, members of co-operative C remarkably stressed their support of this hypothesis with a maximal average of ten. The conversion of members from the status of employees to that of cooperators and the ensuing disruption in the company's ethos have most probably strengthened this utter conviction. As one of the founding members puts it: 'Most workers in the co-operative now feel concerned about the environment because we frequently discuss the environmental impact of our decisions' (Interview 3.d). One of his co-members elaborated on the crucial need to share information to foster this participation: 'We explain everything to co-operators with complete transparency and it gives meaning to all of this. Cooperators have a right to get to know the product they manufacture and to get to grips with it' (Interview 3.b).

All worker-members strongly rejected 'green capitalism' as a trustworthy way out of the present environmental crisis with Co-operatives B and C giving average answers very close to the bottom end. Members of co-operative B were the youngest in the sample and held clear-cut anti-capitalist views. One founding member of co-operative B wished we talked more about 'class struggle ... capitalist exploitation and working conditions' during electoral campaigns. Members of co-operative A also expressed suspicion about capitalism but were overall less adamant in their denunciation. In contrast to the lukewarm feedback given so far, they were the most convinced that the protection of the environment needs to be part of a wider political struggle (R–S question 6). This position perfectly matches the editorial policy of co-operative A as well as its political identity and its ideological roots. As described earlier, political ecology strongly influenced founding and early members, part of whom have been involved in the French green party for a long time. These results are quite consistent with those obtained for R–S questions 2 and 3 dealing with the respective roles of the state and citizen movements in the protection of the environment. Although members of co-operative C stressed more the need for state intervention, answers from members of co-operative A show a wider gap between the two questions and, therefore, a deeper faith in 'macro-political' solutions compared to 'micro-political' ones (Junqing, 2008). The managing director of co-operative A believes that: 'A company alone has only very limited scope of action. The issue cannot be solved within the co-operative. ... Environmental considerations only come in fifth or sixth position in the press federation, when it doesn't cost any penny. Ecology must be tackled on a state-level and requires regulations' (Interview 1.g).[8]

R–S questions 8 to 10 were aimed at ascertaining cooperators' expectations regarding the flow of democratic participation and decision-making process within the co-operative. Answers allow to assess their position in relation to top-down or bottom-up cooperative management. Interviewees were asked whether the main function of board members was to forward and implement propositions made by rank-and-file members (R–S question 8) or to initiate them and impel their co-members to carry them out (R–S question 9). Three worker-members put both suggestions on equal footing and all others agreed that the leading role of the general assembly in initiating decision-making processes should be more important than the managing board's. Members of co-operatives B and C valued bottom-up flow of participation almost twice as much as its opposite. These results reflect stronger idealistic stances and totally horizontal management structures in co-operatives where all jobs are opened to rotation and managing positions either diffuse, are reluctantly assumed (Interviews c) or simply non-existent (Interviews a). Co-operative

A is run in a more formal way which is characteristic of medium-sized workers' co-operatives in France.

Finally, members had to express their views on collective decision-making by comparing majority rule and consensus. Answers below the average – 5 – mean workers interviewed consider majority rule less important than a consensus and vice versa. The sample overall favoured consensus over majority rule. This is particularly true for members of co-operative B whose small size and very informal management structure allow to reach effective consensus: 'We hardly ever vote "coldly" on anything' (Interview 2. d). The two other co-operatives are sometimes constrained to resort to majority rule because of the scale of the business they manage and the coexistence of different departments, which explains less decided choices. This reluctance to govern by simple majority rule in democratic organizations where votes keep coming one after the other can be globally observed. As a member of an American agricultural co-operative puts it 'a large minority hurts the cooperative' (Anderson and Henehan, 1994, p 42). In practice, all workers' co-operatives studied here are run in a rather flexible way which combines different – sometimes hybrid – decision-making processes alternatively used to reach agreements smoothly and effectively. The final section of this chapter will focus on the democratic machinery of each co-operative and its specific role in facilitating worker-members' participation in discussions and decisions affecting its environmental policy and strategy.

The implications of workers' co-operation for ecological awareness at work

Co-operative A is run on pretty much the same lines as most workers' co-operatives in France. The general assembly of all members elect a board of directors comprising of 12 members, 8 of whom must be employees of the co-operative. The members of the board elect the president of the co-operative and name the managing director on proposal from the president. A management committee is responsible for the daily running of the co-operative which includes the president, the managing director and heads of the different departments. Co-operative A offers a perfect example of an organization run by an elected board in which operational decision-making authority resides with the managers under collective mechanisms for holding them accountable to the non-management workers. Democratic government is essentially representative[9] but the organizational model is nearly sociocratic,[10] that is semi-autonomous working groups can decide on a wide range of issues as long as they consult impacted members, and experts if necessary. The managing director described its management style as directly influenced by the advice process whose objective is to promote members' initiatives and delegate powers among qualified members. Feedback, reviews or suggestions to the whole membership is also encouraged: 'Everything can be discussed at any time' (Interview 1.g). Besides, the highest positions of president and managing director are voted every year to strengthen the system of checks and balances.

As described earlier, political ecology within the co-operative has grown to be become a most important characteristic of its identity. A large section of members, especially founding and executive ones, have long been advocates of environmentalism. Some of them have been involved in green militancy and politics. Therefore, it is hard to demonstrate that workplace democracy has ever played a decisive role in the policy of the co-operative in this sphere. As a magazine of unorthodox economics and social sciences, their main contribution consists in informing readers and advertising for green alternatives, which they do by writing on potentially polarizing topics such as degrowth. However, internal levers controlling or impacting editorial policy are in the independent hands of specific department heads such as the editorial board or Human Resources for the recruitment of journalists. Although all members can exercise control over the co-operative's strategy and policy during annual meetings of the general assembly, it has proven to be challenging to genuinely involve non-editorial staff working on the second site. It seems that the biggest room for improvement both in members' participation and environmental awareness is to be found there.

Yet, it would be wrong to assume that just because environmental awareness is already ingrained in members' minds, co-operation has no further role to play. First of all, working for the only worker-owned and worker-run magazine in a highly concentrated press sector gives worker-members 'the feeling to work for a common cause' (Interview 1.c). Such engaging feelings undoubtedly nurture the co-operative's democratic life and foster members' participation in collective consultations which enriches its political agenda. The actual meaning of co-operation was obviously observed through interviewees' repeated assertions that such environmental – and generally speaking political – consciousness might as well develop in conventional or hierarchical companies but would simply either be muted or remain unheard. This strongly indicates that even among a highly sensitized membership, collective participation is needed as a 'democratic anticoagulant'.

Indeed, other studies show that voting is not always the be-all and end-all of industrial democracy. Voicing members' opinions is also a powerful tool – and sometimes ranked as the most effective way – to exert democratic control (Anderson and Henehan, 1994, pp 35 and 61). This is partially the case in co-operative A but even more so in co-operative B. This is why R–S question 11 addressed the co-operative's permeability to surrounding political, social and economic debates. Members overall strongly opposed the view that divisive issues should be kept out of the co-operative (Figure 3.1). This shared conception of the intellectual life of a co-operative is in sharp contrast to what has been experienced by former employees of conventional companies.

Co-operative B gives another telling example of how opened debates and discussions within co-operatives can help members informally participate in cooperative policy making. The co-operative is typically run as what is commonly called a collective. This management structure is frequently adopted in smaller organizations where every worker performs a similar job and participates in most decisions, even relatively minor operational ones. Major strategic decisions are generally taken during monthly meetings of the whole membership, where they are always approved by consensus of all workers. There is no formal division or delegation of authority and all workers are paid at the same hourly rate. Strategic decisions such the use of local and organic products were self-evident to all members and did not require any vote or discussion. Other operational decisions affecting the working environment and conditions of all members such as the use of an electric fermentation chamber were discussed during the meeting of the general assembly after being raised by a member during a shift. Members often collectively decide to make one of them responsible for carrying out a specific task such as investigating on a label and dealing with the administrative procedure (Interview 2.c). The nominated delegate then reports to the general assembly before taking a final decision. Despite its small size, members of co-operative B agree that 'different decisions require *different degrees or modes of participation*' (Thomas and Cornforth, 1989, p 6).

Most of the time, worker-members of co-operative B work in shifts of two persons and this is where ideas are shared and suggestions made. All members usually meet on Thursday morning on shift change and members can use this opportunity to raise an issue and add it to the agenda of the next monthly meeting of the general assembly. As in co-operative A, all cooperators feel extremely concerned about environmental issues and co-operation acts more as a daily treatment for democratic and political vitality.

Co-operative C, a medium-sized factory, is too big to be run exactly as a collective much to all founding members' regret. During their long-standing fight to maintain their activity and secure their jobs, workers were actively seeking a system to manage their own factory in the most horizontal and democratic manner. The workers' co-operative (*Société Coopérative Ouvrière de Production*) status proved to best meet their requirements but they still wish they could run their co-operative without even naming a president or a managing director. The general assembly of workers elect a board of directors comprising of 11 members elected for four years, all of whom are dismissible and chosen from the workers. This board appoints a steering committee (*comité de pilotage*) of three members or more including the president and the managing director who are responsible for managing the daily operations. Other seats are opened to different suitably skilled members of the co-operative to form an enlarged steering committee according to the specific decisions to be made. All decisions are submitted to the board of directors and applied as long as they are not contested. If so, decisions are suspended and sent back for discussion with worker-members. The scheme built by co-operative C is best described as a 'consent' management style with a fairly accountable elected board.

'Phoenix' co-operatives are arguably the less prone to meaningfully transform members' paradigm and trigger politicization among them as collective decision-making is not sought as a democratic experiment per se but rather a half-hearted choice to save jobs when no industrialist or outside investors are willing to take their factory over (Wajcman, 1983; Eccles, 1981). Co-operative C can be considered to stand out as an exception to this law. As Thomas and Cornforth wrote:

> It is often assumed that the amount of member participation increases as one moves from management to members' decision making. However, it is not obvious that members' influence over decision will increase likewise. ... There must be a genuine commitment to power sharing and mutual influence by potentially powerful groups, such as management. (1989, p 10)

This 'genuine commitment to power sharing' is precisely at the very heart of the cooperative project trade union representatives have been fighting for. Observers of workers' co-operations have often witnessed situations where managers are given the lion's share of prerogatives, and voting rights on the persons to assume these positions constitute the only expression of democracy from members behaving as 'passive citizens' (Francoual, 2012, p 69). Although the president notes that 'some workers still come to work just as they did before the co-operative was founded' (Interview 3.a), widely shared social commitments act as a compass for the management of the co-operative. And these commitments are not confined to social or economic claims. For example, workers formerly employed in the 'kitchen' eagerly supported the return to natural flavouring. Worker-members also quickly linked their fight to national or global issues, such as the promotion of a local and eco-friendly agricultural supply chain.

The eventful and highly publicized story of co-operative C shows that the existence of a radical trade union opposition to managerial authority can play a leading role in welding together workers around an alternative way of producing. Deliberations were organized to help all impacted workers on different jobs understand the need to switch to different processes. For example, individual plastic packaging were replaced by recyclable paper and plastic packaging limited to boxes and the product range of loose-leaf tea was developed. Members can directly participate in democratic management on many occasions using a ballot box. This is how pay scales limiting differentials to 1:1.3 were adopted with 80 per cent support among the membership.

Although a large part of these drastic changes were first instilled by the most militant founding members, they were freely espoused and taken up by trusting worker-members. The only real deterrent to far-reaching social and environmental policies remains the co-operative's uncomfortable commercial position. Co-operative C has now become a textbook case of what changes co-operation can bring about in workers' self-confidence, political and ecological attitudes and aspirations.

Conclusions

The case studies presented here offer conclusive evidence that workers' co-operatives, as laboratories of workplace democracy in France, are strong vehicles of political expression outside traditional consultative rituals such as electoral campaigns. They not only allow but also foster workers' participation in manifold decisions affecting their daily lives, thereby offering them a rare opportunity to voice their opinion and defend their interests. However, democratic participation alone cannot be considered sufficient to avoid environmental ignorance and recklessness. New start and especially 'alternative' co-operatives such as co-operatives A and B seem to better take into account their environmental impact primarily because they are set up by convinced members with strong political views and experience in militancy. But converted or 'phoenix' co-operatives such as co-operative C are living proof that democratization of industry by and for the producers can lead to a better understanding of the environmental impact of their activity. There is no apparent reason why industrial democracy should only apply to purely economic and social questions and accounts collected suggest environmental issues are thoroughly considered by workers in co-operative organizations. Most probably, the importance and scope of the current ecological crisis is widely acknowledged and understood by workers and democratic participation in the workplace essentially enables them to voice their opinion and influence policy. Collective decision-making best serves the common interest of members who are overall less obsessed by profit maximization at any cost than managers appointed mainly to this end.

Outside the world of workers' co-operatives, labour representative organizations (LRO) have started to get to grips with green issues in the framework of industrial relations. Nevertheless, recent legislation in France has had a 'scissors effect' on them by increasing the diversity and complexity of their missions while reducing their means. In 2018, a first decree amalgamated shop stewards (*délégués du personnel*), works councils (*Comités d'Entreprise*) and hygiene, safety and working conditions committees (*Comité Hygiène, Sécurité et Conditions de Travail*) into a single representative body named social and economic committee (*Comité Social et Économique*).

In many cases, this concentration led to cuts in representative staff as well as companies' financial contribution.[11] On the other hand, the recent law no. 2021–1104 of August 2021 (also called 'Climate and Resilience law') modified several rules of the French labour code stating the missions of the new social and economic committee. These committees are now allowed to question a company's environmental policy and access a database gathering information about the environmental impact of its activity during legally held consultations. They can also be assisted by chartered accountants in their inquiries regarding the environmental strategy.[12] While these legal reforms could seem to open new opportunities for workers' representatives, they are unlikely to bear fruit without any appropriate and binding schemes to expand workplace democracy beyond one-sided consultation.

Such a lukewarm attempt to tackle the major issue of environmental protection by giving under-geared LROs a mere right of inspection over company policy emphasizes how ahead of their time co-operatives can be. There is a strong case for trade unionists and working-class movements to question not only the sharing of wealth but also its production process and its ends, that is how we are to work and what for. Only when workers feel their voice is being heard will they be willing to use it. This is a rule all co-operatives studied here understood and complied with successfully either by including all members in the decision-making process or by rotating managing positions. Awareness of global issues such as ecology is also a mental disposition which needs to be fostered through inward and outward connections with different actors from the wider social environment – intellectual and academic collaboration, business relationships with neighbouring cooperative or community projects or support in similar social and industrial struggles. All these exchanges help cooperators and workers consider the big picture and grasp the wider implications and meaning of their local struggle for global change.

Notes

[1] The period from the mid-1970s to the late 1980s saw an upsurge in the number of British workers' co-ops which were created by the hundreds with great help from the Industrial Common Ownership Movement and Labour local authorities. In France, the growth was older, less dramatic and much steadier.

[2] Liste des sociétés coopératives ouvrières de production pour l'année 2021, *Journal Officiel de la République Française*, n°0128, 04 June 2021; this figure reaches 2,590 according to the CGSCOP to which we can add around 1,200 multi-stakeholder co-operatives (www.les-scop.coop/chiffres-cles).

[3] Unfortunately, no co-operator employed on this site could be interviewed which is likely to slightly distort obtained results.

[4] These are known as AMAP in France which stands for organizations for the preservation of farming agriculture (Associations pour le Maintien d'une Agriculture Paysanne). Most of French CSFO were founded over the last 20 years and developed into a rather well-established and influential network.

[5] The French Democratic Confederation of Labour (*Confédération Française Démocratique du Travail*) is one the biggest French trade-union which promoted industrial democracy and self-management during the 1970s and was actively involved in the fight of LIP workers mentioned earlier in the chapter.

[6] Members are somewhat critical of 'mainstream' organic label which they regard as insufficiently demanding and socially blinded.

[7] Standard deviations measure how dispersed the results in a data series are in relation to the mean. A low standard deviation means data are clustered around the mean and a high standard deviation indicates data are more spread out. In this chapter, standard deviations are used to quantify like-mindedness among the different samples of co-operators and express how much members' views differ or coincide with each other.

[8] A member of co-operative B took a similar stand taking low-cost airlines as another example.

[9] French co-operative law gives the general assembly of members the right to either delegate or retain powers assigned to it, thereby leaving it the possibility to fashion its own functioning somewhere between a purely direct and indirect democracy where most powers are given to appointed managers (Francoual, 2012, p 60).

[10] For a short introduction to sociocracy, you can visit www.sociocracyforall.org/sociocracy/.

[11] Béchaux, S. (2020), 'Des nouveaux comités d'entreprise au rabais', *Alternatives Économiques*, issue 398.

[12] LOI n° 2021-1104 du 22 août 2021 portant lutte contre le dérèglement climatique et renforcement de la résilience face à ses effets, *Journal Officiel de la République Française*, n°0196, 24 August 2021 (Art. 40–44).

References

Anderson, B.L. and Henehan, B.M. (1994) 'Decision making in membership organizations: A study of fourteen US cooperatives', *Research Bulletin*, 94(5): 1–103.

Antoni, A. (1970) *La Coopération Ouvrière de Production*. Paris: Confédération Générales des Sociétés Coopératives Ouvrières de Production.

Backstrom, P.N. (1960) 'John Malcolm Forbes Ludlow, a little known contributor to the cause of the British working man in the 19th century', Boston University (PhD thesis), Available online from: open.bu.edu/handle/2144/22323 [Accessed on 3 March 2023].

Benn, S., Teo, Stephen, T.T. and Martin A. (2015) 'Employee participation and engagement in working for the environment', *Personnel Review*, 44(4): 492–510.

Coates, K., Eccles, A.J., Benn, T., Fletcher, R., Fleet, K., Jones, D.C. and Mackie, A. (eds) (1976) *The New Worker Co-operatives*. Nottingham: Spokesman Books.

Cole, G.D.H. (1944) *A Century of Co-operation*. Manchester: The Co-operative Union.

Cornforth, C., Thomas, A., Lewis, J. and Spear, R. (1988) *Developing Successful Worker Co-operatives*. London: SAGE Publications.

Deblangy, F. (2022) 'From workshop democracy to democratic workshop: A historical sketch of production cooperation in Great Britain', *RECMA*, 363(1): 132–147.

Defourney, J., Estrin, S. and Jones, D.C. (1985) 'The effects of workers' participation on enterprise performance: Empirical evidence from French cooperatives, *International Journal of Industrial Organisation*, 3: 197–217.

Dumont, R. (1973), *L'utopie ou la mort*. Paris: Le Seuil.

Eccles, A.J. (1981) *Under New Management. The Story of Britain's Largest Worker Co-operative – its Successes and Failures*. London: Pan Books.

Ellerman, D. (1990) *The Democratic Worker-Owned Firm: A New Model for the East and the West*. London: Routledge.

Estrin, S., Jones, D.C. and Svejnar, J. (1987) 'The productivity effects of worker participation: Producer cooperatives in western economies', *Journal of Comparative Economics*, 11: 40–61.

Farooq, O., Farooq, M. and Reynaud, E. (2019) 'Does employees' participation in decision making increase the level of corporate social and environmental sustainability? An investigation in South Asia', *Sustainability*, 11(2): 511–524.

Francoual, P. (2012) 'Le travailleur dans la société coopérative ouvrière de production', Toulouse University (Master's thesis in labour law).

Gorz, A. (1975), *Écologie et politique*. Paris: Éditions Galilée.

Grunberg, L. (1986) 'Safety, productivity and the social relations in production: An empirical study of worker cooperatives', *International Journal of Sociology and Social Policy*, 6(4): 87–102.

Jones, B. (1894) *Co-operative Production*. Oxford: Clarendon Press.

Junqing, Y. (2008) 'On micro-political philosophy', *Diogenes*, 221(1): 58–72.

Kerfourn, F. (2018) 'Cas 1. Elemas, une SCOP leader français de la terre cuite en quête d'un développement équilibré et durables'. In Confédération générale des Scop, *Les Scop*. Caen: EMS Éditions, pp 17–33.

Nivet, J.-B. (2018a) 'Cas 2. SCIC Coopa coopératives multisociétariale, pour développer un service innovant de mobilité'. In Confédération générale des Scop, *Les Scop*. Caen: EMS Éditions, pp 34–74.

Nivet, J.-B. (2018b) 'Cas 6. Natureshop, un management participatif pour un développement coopératif'. In Confédération générale des Scop, *Les Scop*. Caen: EMS Éditions, pp 171–205.

Oakeshott, R. (1978) *The Case for Workers' Co-ops*. London: Routledge & Kegan Paul.

Piaget, C. (2021) *On fabrique, on vend, on se paie*. Paris: Éditions Syllepse.

Pollard, S. and Salt, J. (eds) (1971) *Robert Owen: Prophet of The Poor. Essays in Honour of the Two-hundredth Anniversary of his Birth*. London: Macmillan Press.

Stephen, F. (1982) *The Performance of Labor-Managed Firms*. London: MacMillan Press.

Thomas, A. and Cornforth, C. (1989) 'A model for democratic decision-making: The Case of worker co-operatives', *Economic Analysis and Workers' Management*, 1(23): 1–15.

Thornley, J. (1981) *Workers' Co-operatives. Jobs and Dreams*. London: Heinemann Educational Books.

Toucas-Truyen, P. (2005) *Les Coopérateurs: Deux Siècles de Pratiques Coopératives*. Paris: Les Éditions de l'Atelier/Éditions Ouvrières.

Wajcman, J. (1983) *Women in Control: Dilemmas of a Workers' Co-operative*. Milton Keynes: Open University Press.

Webb, B. (1891) *The Co-operative Movement in Great-Britain*. London: Swan Sonnenschein & Co.

Winslow, M. (2005) 'Is democracy good for the environment?', *Journal of Environmental Planning and Management*, 48(5): 771–783.

4

Exploring the Role of Worker Co-operatives in the Co-creation of Meaningful Work

Kiri Langmead and Anthony Webster

Introduction

The experiences of people at work have attracted increasing interest in recent years (Taylor et al, 2017). This has been driven by numerous factors, including the impact of new technologies on jobs, the decline of trade unionism (especially in the UK), the growing casualization of work, the aftermath of the financial crash of 2008 and, most recently, the effects of the COVID-19 pandemic. All this has generated growing concern about the quality of work and its impact on the wellbeing of workers (Oswald et al, 2015). Worker co-operatives have played an important role in responding to these factors, offering secure and good quality work even in times of crisis (Roelants et al, 2012; Birchall, 2013; Berry and Bell, 2018). This has been attributed to their dual socio-economic purpose and solidarity with their community, and structural characteristics including democratic decision-making and worker ownership (Cheney et al, 2014; Peredo and McLean, 2020; Billiet et al, 2021). More broadly, there has long been strong advocacy of the ethical dimension of cooperative commercial enterprise, notably emphasizing member democracy (Rothschild, 2009), concern for the wider community and the environment (Novkovic, 2008; Mellor, 2012; Phelan, McGee and Godon, 2012), and a commitment to high standards of working conditions (Restakis, 2010; Ruccio, 2011; Carlone, 2013).

Taking two UK worker co-operatives, this chapter will explore the extent to which the experiences of worker-members differ from those working in 'mainstream' commercial organizations. More specifically it will explore how worker ownership and democratic member control can enable workers to put social and environmental values into practice, and through this, cocreate work that is meaningful. Drawing on secondary literature on worker cooperatives, the chapter will draw some tentative conclusions about common experiences across Europe, and the extent to which they reflect the UK examples analysed. The chapter draws upon the increasingly complex debate about what constitutes 'meaningful' work, and the extent to which cooperative experiences meet these definitions.

Worker co-operatives and work as a field of study

There are extensive literatures on 'decent' and 'meaningful' work, and on worker co-operatives. This section will lay out some of the key arguments and findings in these fields and will provide a wider context for the in-depth studies later in the chapter. The quality of work experience has attracted growing interest (Taylor et al, 2017). In 1999 the ILO defined the key components of 'decent' work (ILO, 1999; 2008). These include a fair income, productive work, protection of workers' rights at work, wider social protections for them and their families, work–life balance, worker representation and appropriate systems for compensation; as well as equal opportunities for personal development and freedom to express views at work (Baruch, 2006; Judge et al, 2010; Valizade et al, 2016).

Alongside 'decent' work, 'meaningful work' has emerged as a more nuanced and complex evaluation of the ways in which work can enhance human experience and life. Calls for meaningful work respond to a recognition that, while work increasingly demands employees' time, effort and emotional investment, it is frequently experienced as meaningless (Cederstrom and Fleming, 2012; Michaelson et al, 2014). These experiences constitute feelings of incoherence, unease and estrangement from the self (Costas and Fleming, 2009), the fragmentation of identity, 'a weakening [of] social cohesion in the workplace and beyond' (Kociatkiewicz et al, 2021, p 4), and a loss of 'hope of pleasure in the work itself' (Morris, 1886, p 21). Literature has linked such experiences to the valorization, discipline and rationalization inherent to the capitalist labour process (Chatterton and Pusey, 2020; Peredo and McLean, 2020). Yeoman (2014a, p 3) contends that disempowerment and the devaluation of the worker severely undermines the possibility of achieving meaningful work.

In contrast to 'decent work' that focuses mainly upon the external conditions confronting workers, 'meaningful work' focuses more on how people find significance and meaning in their work and through it a sense of purpose in their lives. Terkel's (1974) work was probably the first academic attempt to unpick how some people are able to find emotional, moral and intellectual value in their work which enriches and gives purpose to their lives, as well of a sense of personal moral fulfilment. Subsequent literature has framed meaningful work as a hybrid concept, that combines a sense of moral worth and purpose, with the meeting of emotional needs such as autonomy, unity with others, developing confidence and competence, and a sense of personal commitment and investment (Wolf, 2010; Duffy et al, 2016; Michaelson, 2021). Others have argued that meaningfulness cannot be understood as a static emotional or moral outcome. Rather, meaningfulness is viewed as an ongoing process that sees meaning negotiated in different temporal, social and cultural contexts (Mitra and Buzzanell, 2017). Through this lens, meaningfulness arises not only through the enactment of values and the fulfilment of purpose, but through the process of negotiating contradictions between those values and present reality (Lips-Wiersma and Morris, 2009). It arises also through deliberative engagement with others, where values are reinforced, challenged and reinterpreted. Thus, 'becoming co-authorities in the creation and maintenance of values' is a source of meaningfulness in itself (Yeoman, 2014b, p 243). From this perspective, the creation of meaningful work necessitates the restructuring of work to enable workers to define meaningfulness through co-operation and democratic participation. As Ashforth and Reingen (2014) and Kociatkiewicz et al (2021) show, worker co-operatives open such opportunities.

The potential of worker co-operatives, in which worker-members own and control the businesses for which they work, is reflected in what CICOPA (2005, p 2) defined as the first basic characteristic of worker co-operatives: to generate wealth 'in order to improve the quality of life of the worker-members, dignify human work, allow workers' democratic self-management and promote community and local development'. Thus, unlike consumer co-operatives or wider stakeholder co-operatives, the link between membership, work and the quality of work experienced in worker co-operatives is arguably more immediate and unmediated. There are extensive literatures on worker co-operatives across Europe, though as will be seen, a focus upon experiences of work has been quite recent.

Much of the work on European workers' co-operatives has focused upon those in Spain, France and Italy, where these organizations are most numerous. In 2012–2014, there were 25,000 worker coops in France, 2,500 in Spain, and 17,000 in Italy but a much more modest 500–600 worker co-operatives in the UK (Pérotin, 2016, p 240). This more modest number is reflected in the relatively few studies focused on UK worker co-operatives. Drawing on data from three UK worker co-operatives, Wren (2020) identified several features which typify worker-members' experiences. These include the development of a 'whole life perspective', where workers see their work as a central and integrated part of their life. In line with Langmead's (2018) research, this feature encompassed opportunities for members to freely express themselves, as well as a commitment to prioritizing paying a living wage, offering secure employment and structuring work around workers wellbeing rather than profit. Second, Wren identified 'consistently shared values', that is commonly held beliefs, work practice and attitudes which need to be actively cultivated through careful induction, training and reinforcement through day-to-day work. Third, self-ownership, understood by Wren as an active form of participation in decision-making, again facilitated by training and inculcation into the democratic practices of the co-operative. When discussing this feature, Wren highlights the challenges associated with developing meaningful democratic participation. These challenges are explored in-depth in Powell's (2021) research with established and scaled worker co-operatives, and Langmead's (2018) research with small-scale worker co-operatives. In both cases, developing and sustaining collectivist-democratic organizing is understood as an ongoing struggle beset with tensions and contradictions, including between cooperative values and the need to survive in an intensely competitive (and some would argue exploitative) capitalist marketplace. Sustaining democracy within workers co-operatives therefore requires the 'ongoing attention of members' (Powell, 2021, p 151). While challenging, this 'work of democracy' is understood as central to the creation of meaningful work (Ashforth and Reingen, 2014; Yeoman, 2014a).

Spain – and specifically the Mondragon consortium of co-operatives – has attracted significant academic interest. Mondragon was founded to 'provide work and employment to local people at a time of great societal economic need' (Heales et al, 2017, p 7). As such, it has 'decent', secure work, and the 'satisfaction of people's needs' at its core (Ridley-Duff, 2010; Webb and Cheney, 2014). Crucial to achieving this goal is a commitment to Mondragon's cooperative principles, including to democratic governance, pay solidarity and worker control over the production, appropriation and distribution of surplus (Gibson-Graham, 2003; Ridley-Duff, 2010). In their research with worker-members of Mondragon, Heras-Saizarbitoria (2014, p 656) found that the 'principle of secure membership and employment' remains a central tie that binds workers to the co-operative. This tie was reflected in the much lower rate of unemployment in the Mondragón region in 2012, standing at just 5 per cent compared to 25 per cent in Spain (Webb and Cherney, 2014, p 81). This trend, enabled by worker-owners actively deciding to retain employment levels often at the expense of renumeration, has also been observed in co-operatives in the Emilia-Romagna region of Italy (Zamagni, 2019).

Notwithstanding these benefits, there is some debate about the extent to which workers in the Mondragon co-operatives are satisfied with their working lives and how well principles of self-management and democratic member control are observed (Heras-Saizarbitoria, 2014). Two factors have especially influenced this debate. First the question of 'degeneration', or the alleged tendency of co-operatives to lose commitment to cooperative principles as younger members, without the personal experience of cooperative formation, come to control the co-operative (Cherney, 1999). To counter this tendency, as outlined in Manley's chapter in this volume, Mondragon organizations sought to 'regenerate' themselves by programmes to instil cooperative principles and values among new members. There is much debate about the effectiveness of these efforts. The second factor is the impact of internationalization of some of the Mondragon consortium's activities on adherence to cooperative principles. Research here finds that, notwithstanding efforts to extend cooperative principles (and even cooperative governance), foreign subsidiaries have been treated as bodies subordinate to the aims of the parent Mondragon co-operative, in ways uncomfortably similar to capitalist multinationals (Flecha and Ngai, 2014; Bretos et al, 2018; 2019). The common denominator for these factors is the corrosive impact that capitalist culture and competition can have upon worker cooperative models over time and space.

Other analyses of European worker co-operatives provide some contrasting assessments of worker experience. A unique personal assessment of how workers in a French sheet metalworker co-operative are able to use informal means to challenge managerialist authority, and thereby stall trends towards degeneration, offers a striking picture of how worker-members at a grass roots level can push back against overbearing managerial power (Jaumier, 2017). Basterretxea and Storey's comparative study of John Lewis Partnership in the UK and the Eroski retailer of Mondragon contends that poorly managed worker co-operatives are both poor in performance and in worker experience; and that effective management sensitive to the needs of workers democracy is essential for these aspects to be successful (Basterretxea and Storey, 2018). A study of the Italian cooperative sector similarly contends that the growth of effective management in both national umbrella organizations and individual co-operatives since the end of the Second World War was instrumental in preventing degeneration, maintaining adherence to cooperative principles, and averting demutualization (Battilani and Zamagni, 2012). A key theme running through this literature is the tension and balance between effective managerial authority and worker democracy.

In contrast, literature from Poland and Greece builds a picture of radical worker co-operatives that reject managerial authority in favour of collectivist-democracy. For the Greek co-operatives described by Kokkinidis (2014) and Howarth and Roussos (2023), a commitment to horizontality and direct participation in decision-making was underpinned by a desire to foster care and mutual aid relationships (Howarth and Roussos, 2023) and to providing space for members to realize their 'self-creating, self-altering and self-instituting capacities' (Kokkinidis, 2014, p 848). Kociatkiewicz et al's (2021) research with two Polish worker co-operatives connects a sense of agency and efficacy enabled by collectivist-democracy to the creation of disalienation at work that encourages the 'assumption of responsibility' (p 20) and the 'authentic expression of the self' (p 21). In all of these examples, we begin to see how worker co-operatives create spaces for meaningful work, not only by performing work with a social purpose, but through processes of democratic organizing that meet workers' emotional needs of autonomy and unity with others.

More recently, much work has focused upon co-operative responses to changes in the global labour market caused by new technologies and labour casualization. Following the economic downturn of the 1990s, and in response to fast rising unemployment, there was a dramatic rise in worker co-operatives in Finland among those professions and vocations in which self-employment is often the norm. Puusa and Hokkila (2020) show that many of the key reasons for the rapid growth of these co-operatives arise from the positive experiences of working for them; notably the senses of empowerment, freedom, autonomy and communality with other members. Sandoval (2016) reinforces this view in respect of the cultural sector, identifying the worker cooperative model as one which addresses many of the dissatisfactions arising from precarity and powerlessness experienced by workers in the sector. Similarly responding to experiences of increased precarity, platform co-operatives are being developed as an alternative to the corporate digital economy (Scholz, 2016). In contrast to investor-owned platforms, platform co-operatives are owned and run by their users, who also receive a share of the profits (Schneider, 2020). By putting control back in the hands of gig workers, platform co-operatives aim to make platform-based work less 'capital-centric' and, in tandem, less alienating for workers (Chatterton and Pusey, 2020, p 40).

Worker co-operatives

Before exploring the extent to which worker co-operatives open opportunities for the creation of meaningful work, this section will outline the key features of worker co-operatives and introduce the two case study organizations.

Worker co-operatives are: 'trading enterprises, owned and run by the people who work in them, who have an equal say in what the business does, and an equitable share in the wealth created from the products and services they provide' (Banton et al, 2012, p 1).

This definition highlights the two key features of worker co-operatives. First, workers retain ownership of their labour, and any surplus arising from their labour. This is important, not only in providing workers with 'an equitable share in the wealth created' but also gives them the power to reframe surplus, not as source of future individual equity, but as a means of achieving collectively determined social ends (Cornforth, 2004; Cornwell, 2012). Second, worker co-operatives extend autonomy and participation in decision-making to all worker-members, who collectively determine the goals of the organization, and the means through which these goals are achieved. To explore how these features support the creation of meaningful work we draw on data collected by one of the authors from two worker co-operatives: Beanies Wholefoods and Regather Trading Cooperative.

Beanies is a Company Limited by Guarantee, run as a worker co-operative. According to its articles (1986), its objects are: 'To act cooperatively and collectively as purveyors and promoters of whole and organically grown foods and such other related products and to create general awareness of such benefits as may be derived from the consumption and utilisation of such products.'

They fulfil their objects by running a small shop selling wholefoods, and fruit and vegetables; operating a city-wide organic fruit and vegetable delivery service in Sheffield; and promoting local, vegetarian and organic food through participation in national events such as Organic September and Cooperative Fortnight. At the time of the study Beanies had seven full-time members, one part-time bookkeeper and between six and eight part-time staff who work on the shop floor. Neither the part-time staff, nor the bookkeepers were members of the co-operative.

Regather registered under the Industrial and Provident Societies Act in 2010 as a cooperative consortium; a cooperative constituting members who are self-employed. Between 2010 and 2014 members increasingly expressed a desire to be employees of Regather. This resulted in a shift in organizational type from a cooperative consortium to a worker co-operative. This was formalized in their governing documents in 2016.

Regather's mission is to: 'give people the choice and opportunity to live, work and play cooperatively and create a mutual local economy'. This mission is fulfilled through member and community-led projects that form the core of Regather's commercial trading activity. Over the last ten years these have included: the creation of an events space to support emerging local talent and provide opportunities for people to 'find friends and develop relationships'; a community kitchen set up to provide affordable space for local food start-ups; an organic vegetable box scheme developed to increase access to locally sourced and affordable organic produce; and most recently, Regather Farm, established to support the development of a more sustainable local food system. During the research, Regather had seven worker-members who ran and sustained the projects and participating in decision-making. Worker-members were supported by volunteers who participated in activities such as vegetable box packing, and helping with events.

Data from both co-operatives was collected through focus groups and participant-observation. The latter included volunteering and attending meetings for a 15-month period between November 2014 and February 2016. Following an in-depth discussion about anonymity, and an opportunity to review research findings, participants requested that the researcher include their names and the name of their co-operatives in publications (Langmead, 2017, p 100). This reflected their desire to share their experience with others, 'warts and all' (Chris, Beanies). As Rachel (Regather) explained: 'Anonymising us would go against our vision of allowing people to learn from our mistakes'.

Experiences of meaningless work

At the start of the research, members were asked to share written narratives outlining their journey to cooperative working. Within these narratives members described past experiences of work in hierarchical organizations. Their descriptions expressed a sense of meaninglessness and disempowerment that motivated their decision to join a worker co-operative. For example, Tim explained how working for the Environment Agency left him feeling 'quite removed from the work and the ramifications of [his] daily tasks'. This disconnection from the purpose and meaning of work was also articulated by Jake who expressed his discomfort at working for the Health and Safety Executive, at a time when they were 'doing more [and more] commercial work ... mostly for oil companies and their suppliers'. Describing the oil companies as 'evil' because of the damage their industry does to the environment, Jake began to experience a sense of unease and estrangement from the self that are characteristic of work that lacks meaning.

Like Tim and Jake, Nicole's reflection on work in a corporate music venue captures a reflexive moment in which she lost hope of achieving a true and coherent sense of self through her work:

> '[After 4 years it] became clear to me [that the corporate music venue] had very little interest in Sheffield as a city nor in its people or local economy, and that my role offered me little or no opportunity to influence this. I felt more and more of my energy was being spent simply helping to make some already wealthy people become even wealthier.'

Clearly, the focus on generating profit for the owners and shareholders of the music venue directed and limited Nicole's work activities (Langmead et al, 2020; Battilana et al, 2022). While she repeatedly tried to instigate projects that would enable her to support and reconnect with the local community, she found herself pushing against a closed door, constrained by both the economic and organizational structures that she was working in (Yeoman, 2014b; Mitra and Buzzanell, 2017). The disappointment and despondency running through her words reveals a loss of hope that the job would ever hold any meaning or pleasure (Morris, 1886).

Across these narratives, we see Holloway's (2010, p 9) claim that: 'Ever more people simply do not fit in to the system, or, if we do manage to squeeze ourselves on to capital's ever-tightening Procrustean bed, we do so at the cost of leaving fragments of ourselves behind, to haunt. That is the basis of our cracks and of the growing importance of a dialectic of misfitting.'

Participants in the research aligned with Holloway in refusing to understand experiences of dialectic misfitting as an inevitable and necessary consequence of work. Rather, as the next section shows, they viewed their misfittings as openings for new forms of work that enabled them to reclaim the lost fragments of the self.

Reclaiming meaning

This section explores how the structure and practices of worker co-operatives opened opportunities for members to cocreate meaningful work. It focuses specifically on how meaning was created through cooperative acts of reclaiming social and environmental values that had been excluded from work in hierarchical, profit motivated organizations. This was demonstrated by Lisa who explained how work at Regather provided her with an opportunity to re-embed her environmental values within her work: "Working at Regather appeals to me because I feel that I am involved with something that has the potential to make improvements to my local environment. I feel like I have tried working in a sector where rules are coming from above and I would like to try to make more difference locally."

Lisa highlights the limits posed by top-down management, implying in her last sentence that this approach does not allow space for people to make real improvements to their local environment. In doing so she acknowledged, like Langmead et al (2020), that when acting as an agent of the owner (in the case of a capitalist enterprise) or the state (in the case of the civil service), management is 'constitutively irresponsible' (Langmead et al, 2020, p 16) and actively seeks take responsibility away from worker by controlling their efforts towards the 'achievement of externally determined goals' (Langmead et al, 2020, p 8). Other members similarly described how a desire to reconnect with their values drove them to make 'positive decision[s] to reject the system' (Gareth) and embrace the opportunity that co-operatives provided for collective self-determination. In this rejection they recognized that creating meaningful work that allowed them to enact their values meant considering, not only what the organization does but how it does it (Parker et al, 2014). More specifically, they recognized the need for a fundamental shift towards organizational models that are founded on principles of worker ownership and control, and that foster mutuality, co-operation and self-determination (Yeoman, 2014a; Battilana et al, 2022).

The importance of worker ownership came across strongly in a discussion on the co-operatives' ten-year vision. Within this discussion, Rachel described her aim to establish Regather as:

'a centre for social action in the area. Like empowering people to take more action on things that they are passionate about and to have our own funds to be able to support that that are independently generated from our own trading activities … So, to be generating profits that are set aside to support other local people to make their projects possible.'

In Rachel's passionately stated aim we see meaning emerging, not only from a sense of moral purpose associated with supporting and empowering the local community, but also through a feeling of unity with that community. This sense of unity was shared by Tim who expressed his appreciation for working 'close to home' and having his 'values and life centred around [Regather]'. In Rachel's final sentence she describes a desire to set aside profits in order to meet her aim, and foster Regather's connection to their local community. The fact that workers who perform necessary and surplus labour also own the surplus they produce means that it is up to them, and not a manager or shareholder, to decide how that surplus is used (Ruccio, 2011, p 336). Thus, in contrast to its positioning as a source of future individual equity, collective ownership enabled members to reimagine surpluses of time, money and skills as social and environmental potentiality and a means to achieve meaningful work (Cornwell, 2012; Langmead, 2018).

Regather's organic vegetable box scheme and, more recently, the development of Regather Farm further demonstrates how co-operation and self-determination enables environmental and social values to be put into practice. Regather's mission is to 'create a mutual economy' and, as with all of their projects the vegetable box and farm were developed to meet this mission. Both projects emerged from a local need for a sustainable food system, and from member's values, skills and past experiences of community agriculture. Through these food projects members were able to derive meaning from the interconnection between past and present events, building on the knowledge gained from past agricultural projects and utilizing relationships they had developed with like-minded people outside of Regather (Mitra and Buzzanell, 2017, p 598). Thus, in addition to the meaning arising from 'mak[ing] more difference locally', meaning emerged through the process of working cooperatively to determine and enact shared values by putting skills and knowledge into practice (Michaelson et al, 2014).

Further emphasizing the importance of the co-operatives' structure, the exchange, shows how collective decision-making created opportunities for members to articulate their values in a way that informed action, thus contributing to the creation of meaningful work (Lips-Wiersma and Morris,

2009). Discussing their choice of energy supplier, members questioned the economic logic of adopting the cheapest supplier by introducing environmental concerns that are commonly confined to the domestic sphere.

Mark: I will just put in ethical energy suppliers into google and see what comes up.

Dave: At the end of the day we have to keep the business afloat.

Rocky: Some of the ethical ones have not so obvious tangible benefits as well. Like I use Good Energy at home ...

Mark: Yes, that's it, we use Good Energy.

Rocky: A lot of people who work here use these ethical things but then through the business, that is *your* business collectively, [you are] using these horrible corporates that build nuclear power stations and destroy the planet.

The initial absence of consideration for the environment is evidence of what Jake described as 'the odd paradox' that sees people enacting certain values at home, while simultaneously working for a company that is collectively acting in ways that are 'quite destructive'. However, in contrast to the experiences of disempowerment outlined in the previous section, worker ownership enabled members to resist such destructive actions and act instead with regard and responsibility towards the environment (Langmead et al, 2020). Thus, the quote conveys four key sources of meaning. First, the meaning arising from being united with others through the expression of shared values. Second, the meaning associated with having the freedom to act autonomously, not in an individualistic sense of acting in one's own interests, but in a collective sense of acting with regard to, and responsibility for, human and non–human others (Notes from Nowhere, 2003, p 110). A third source of meaningfulness arises from the active negotiation of the 'ideal' of using a more environmentally sustainable energy supplier, and the 'reality' of ensuring ongoing financial viability (Lip–Wiersma and Morris, 2009). This negotiation is founded in the dual social–economic characteristic of worker co-operatives. The paradoxical nature of this characteristic is widely acknowledged (Cornforth, 2004; Somerville, 2007; Zamagni and Zamagni, 2010; Audebrand, 2017). Also acknowledged are the ways in which the democratic structure of co-operatives, and specifically practices of participatory democracy, continually keeps this social–economic duality at play 'through oscillating decisions and actions that enable each [position] to be upheld over the long term' (Ashforth and Reingen, 2014, p 484). This 'oscillation' sat in stark contrast to Nicole's, and Jakes' experience of work in hierarchical organizations where economic concerns were prioritized above social and environmental values; a prioritization over which they had no control. However, Lip-Wiersma and Morris (2009, p 507) argue that it is not just the power to pursue and enact an inspirational ideal that is a source of meaningfulness. The very act of making reality visible *alongside* ideals is meaningful in itself. The authors describe how focusing only on the ideal results in feelings of inauthenticity, and contend that work becomes more meaningful 'when one can be aware of ... the fact that the problems facing humanity can be overwhelming' (Lip-Wiersma and Morris, 2009, p 506). This again highlights the importance of deliberation to the creation of meaningful work.

The final source of meaningful work arose through the acknowledgement, and deliberation over, multiple sources of meaning (Lip-Wiersma and Morris, 2009). Underlying Dave's comment that 'we have to keep the business afloat' is not a drive to maximize profit, but a desire to pay members a decent wage and to have a thriving co-operative to pass on to the next generation of workers – a desire shared by members of Italian co-operative, SACMI (Webb and Cheney, 2014, p 76). This value of care for current and future members made work meaningful, both in itself and through the ways in which it was carefully balanced against the desire to have green energy 'at all costs'.

It is not, of course, easy to balance to the multiple, and at time conflicting, needs of members, the co-operative, society and the environment. In both co-operatives, the researcher observed members making personal sacrifices that defied their own ethic of care (Sandoval, 2016; Soetens and Huybrechts, 2023). Fran described earning just 'enough money to survive'; Gemma reflected on the pay cut that she had accepted when taking the job at Beanies; and Nicole recounted the additional, unpaid hours that she was working for Regather. Reflecting on the issue of pay, Dave described how the 'strong ethics of coop members in putting others first' contributed to the acceptance of these sacrifices. Members' willingness to 'continue with this life' (Fran) was heightened by benefits that their co-operatives afforded, including the opportunity to 'see work as a part of my life' (Fran), to develop a sense of personal coherence, to be 'part of the decision-making process' (Gemma), and to take ownership over their work. This is not to say, however, that personal sacrifice was accepted without challenge. Over the course of the research members engaged in a number of lengthy and contentious discussions about pay, annual leave and working hours. It was in these discussions that attention turned to the self and its relation to human and non-human others, and through them that members created 'time ... to discern what [is] the morally right thing to do' (Lip-Wiersma and Morris, 2009, p 505). As Lip-Wiersma and Morris (2009) argue, such deliberations are themselves a key part of what makes work meaningful.

Conclusion

This chapter set out to explore the extent to which worker co-operatives support the creation of meaningful work. The context was the shadow of the 2008 financial crisis and, more recently, the COVID-19 pandemic. Both of these global events have brought to the fore experiences that illustrated the exploitative nature of work in the capitalist economy, and raised concerns over the quality and meaning of work. While organizations have sought to address these concerns by, for example, paying attention to job design and providing opportunities for employee participation (Michaelson et al, 2014), the impact of these interventions will be limited so long as control over the process and surplus of production remains with the owners, rather than the workers, of an organization (Yeoman, 2014a).

Research carried out in Greece (Kokkinidis, 2014), a country hit particularly severely by post-2008 austerity, shows that worker co-operatives offer an alternative, collective approach to addressing these concerns. This is supported by research with Polish (Kociatkiewicz et al, 2021) worker co-operatives, which found that worker ownership and participatory democracy enabled members to assume responsibility for, and collectively determine, work activities in a way that prioritized social and environmental values over economic concerns. In addition to providing members with a sense of moral purpose, this gave meaning to their work by enabling the 'authentic expression of the self' (Kociatkiewicz et al, 2021, p 21), and by supporting a sense of unity with other cooperative members and wider society. However, as experienced in Mondragon, data from the two case studies reveals that balancing co-operatives' dual socio-economic aim, and thus sustaining a sense of moral purpose and authenticity, is not easy. Participatory democracy has been shown to play an important role here (Langmead, 2017; Battilana et al, 2022). It does so by creating a space for social and environmental aims, and economic realities to be made visible and openly deliberated. In addition to providing a source of resistance against degeneration, this process contributes to the creation of meaningful work by giving members the time to reflect on and negotiate the paradoxes they face (Lip-Wiersma and Morris, 2009; Audebrand, 2017).

Finally, we argue that worker ownership and democratic control provides opportunities for workers to negotiate two paradoxes inherent to meaningful work: the paradox that seeking meaning to satisfy one's needs can drive workers to harmful excesses; and the paradox that 'meaningfulness arises in the context of self-fulfilment and self-actualization, yet it is dependent on the "other" for its realization' (Bailey et al, 2019, p 490). Worker co-operatives confront these paradoxes in two ways. First processes of deliberation, enabled by participatory democracy, create opportunities for members to negotiate tensions between satisfying a need for meaningfulness and preventing the harmful individual consequences of pursuing meaningfulness, such as overwork or the acceptance of poor working conditions (Bailey et al, 2019, p 489). The ongoing prioritization of decent work was similarly observed in Mondragon (Ridley-Duff, 2010; Webb and Cheney, 2014) and Emilia-Romagna (Zamagni, 2019). Second, cooperative structures of worker ownership embed within them an interdependence on, and deep recognition of, others' needs (Webb and Cherney, 2014; Langmead, 2018). This in turn addresses the paradox between meaningfulness arising from self-fulfilment and meaningfulness arising through our dependence on others by enabling members to understand the self as it exists in relation to others (Bailey et al, 2019, p 490). Thus, worker co-operatives support the creation of meaningful work, not only by enabling members to put cooperative, social and environmental values into practice, but by positioning workers as 'co-authorities' (Yeoman, 2014b) in the creation of meaning and enabling meaning to be negotiated on an ongoing basis (Mitra and Buzzanell, 2017).

References

Ashforth, B.E. and Reingen, P.H. (2014) 'Functions of dysfunction: Managing the dynamics of an organizational duality in a natural food cooperative', *Administrative Science Quarterly*, 59(3): 474–516.

Audebrand, L.K. (2017) 'Expanding the scope of paradox scholarship on social enterprise: The case for (re) introducing worker cooperatives', *M@n@gement*, 20(4): 368–393.

Bailey, C., Lips-Wiersma, M., Madden, A., Yeoman, R., Thompson, M. and Chalofsky, N. (2019) 'The five paradoxes of meaningful work', *Journal of Management Studies*, 56(3): 481–499.

Banton, A., Cannell, B., Crook, R., Hope, L., Russell, E., Werner, B. and Whellens, S. (2012) *The Worker Co-operative Code*. Manchester: Co-operatives UK.

Baruch, Y. (2006) 'Career development in organizations and beyond: Balancing traditional and contemporary viewpoints', *Human Resource Management Review*, 16(2): 125–138.

Basterretxea, I. and Storey, J. (2018) 'Do employee-owned firms produce more positive employee behavioural outcomes? If not why not? A British-Spanish comparative analysis', *British Journal of Industrial Relations*, 56(2): 292–319.

Battilani, P. and Zamagni, V. (2012) 'The managerial transformation of Italian co-operative enterprises 1946–2010', *Business History*, 54(6): 964–985.

Battilana, J., Yen, J., Ferreras, I. and Ramarajan, L. (2022) 'Democratizing work: Redistributing power in organizations for a democratic and sustainable future', *Organization Theory*, 3(1): 1–21.

Berry, D. and Bell, M.P. (2018) 'Worker cooperatives: Alternative governance for caring and precarious work', *Equality, Diversity and Inclusion*, 37(4): 376–391.

Billiet, A., Dufays, F., Friedel, S. and Staessens, M. (2021) 'The resilience of the cooperative model: How do cooperatives deal with the COVID19 crisis?', *Strategic Change*, 30(2): 99–108.

Birchall, J. (2013) 'The potential of co-operatives during the current recession: Theorizing comparative advantage', *Journal of Entrepreneurial and Organizational Diversity*, 2(1): 1–22.

Bretos, I., Errasti, A. and Marcuello C. (2018) 'Ownership, governance, and the diffusion of HRM practices in multinational worker cooperatives: Case-study evidence from the Mondragon group', *Human Resources Management Journal*, 28(1): 76–91.

Bretos, I., Errasti, A. and Marcuello C. (2019) 'Multinational expansion of worker co-operatives and their employment practices: Markets, institutions and politics in Mondragón', *ILR Review*, 72(3): 580–605.

Carlone, D. (2013) 'Infecting capitalism with the common: The class process, communication, and surplus', *Ephemera*, 13(3): 527–544.

Cederstrom, C. and Fleming, P. (2012) *Dead Man Working*. Winchester: Zero Books.

Chatterton, P. (2010) 'So What Does It Mean to be Anti-capitalist? Conversations with Activists from Urban Social Centres'. *Urban Studies*. 47(6): 1205–24.

Chatterton, P. and Pusey, A. (2020) 'Beyond capitalist enclosure, commodification and alienation: Postcapitalist praxis as commons, social production and useful doing', *Progress in Human Geography*, 44(1): 27–48.

Cheney, G. (1999) *Values at Work: Organizational Communication Meets Market Pressure at Mondragón*. Ithaca, NY: Cornell University Press.

Cheney, G., Santa Cruz, I., Peredo, A.M. and Nazareno, E. (2014) 'Worker cooperatives as an organizational alternative: Challenges, achievements and promise in business governance and ownership', *Organization*, 21(5): 591–603.

CICOPA. (2005) *World Declaration on Worker Cooperatives*. Brussels: CICOPA.

Cornforth, C. (2004) 'The governance of co-operatives and mutual associations: A paradox perspective', *Annals of Public and Cooperative Economics*, 75(1): 11–32.

Cornwell, J. (2012) 'Worker co-operatives and spaces of possibility: An investigation of subject space as collective copies', *Antipode*, 44(3): 725–744.

Costas, J. and Fleming, P. (2009) 'Beyond dis-identification: A discursive approach to self-alienation in contemporary organizations', *Human Relations*, 62(3): 353–378.

Duffy, R.D., Blustein, D.L., Diemer, M.A. and Autin, K.L. (2016) 'The psychology of working theory', *Journal of Counselling Psychology*, 63(2): 127–148.

Flecha, A. and Ngai, P. (2014) 'The challenge for Mondragon: Searching for the cooperative values in times of Internationalization', *Organization*, 21(5): 666–682.

Gibson-Graham, J.K. (2003) 'Enabling ethical economies: Cooperativism and class', *Critical Sociology*, 29(2): 123–161.

Heales, C., Hodgson, M. and Rich, H. (2017) *Humanity at Work: Mondragon, A Social Innovation Ecosystem Case Study*. London: The Young Foundation.

Heras-Saizarbitoria, I. (2014) 'The ties that bind? Exploring the basic principles of worker-owned organizations in practice', *Organization*, 21(5): 645–665.

Holloway, J. (2010) *Crack Capitalism*. UK: Pluto Press.

Howarth, D. and Roussos, K. (2023) 'Radical democracy, the commons and everyday struggles during the Greek crisis', *British Journal of Politics and International Relations*, 25(2), 311–327.

Jaumier, S. (2017) 'Preventing chiefs from being chiefs: An ethnography of a co-operative sheet-metal factory', *Organization*, 24(2): 218–239.

Judge, T.A., Piccolo, R.F., Podsakoff, N.P., Shaw, J.C. and Rick, B.L. (2010) 'The relationship between pay and job satisfaction: A meta-analysis of the literature', *Journal of Vocational Behavior*, 77(2): 157–167.

ILO. (1999) *Decent work. Report of the Director-General, International Labour Conference, 87th Meeting*. Geneva: International Labour Office.

ILO. (2008) *Decent work: Some strategic challenges ahead. Report of the Director-General, 97th Session of International Labour Conference*. Geneva: International Labour Office.

Kociatkiewicz, J., Kostera, M. and Parker, M. (2021) 'The possibility of disalienated work: Being at home in alternative organizations', *Human Relations*, 74(7): 933–957.

Kokkinidis, G. (2014) 'Spaces of possibilities: Workers' self-management in Greece', *Organization*, 22(6): 847–871.

Langmead, K. (2017) 'Challenging the degeneration thesis: The role of democracy in worker cooperatives?' *Journal of Entrepreneurial and Organizational Diversity*, 5(1): 79–98.

Langmead, K. (2018) *Exploring the Performance of Democracy and Economic Diversity in Worker Cooperatives*. Sheffield: Sheffield Hallam University.

Langmead, K., Land, C. and King, D. (2020) 'Can management ever be responsible? Alternative organizing and the three irresponsibilities of management'. In O. Laasch, R. Suddaby, R.E. Freeman, and D. Jamali, D. (eds) *Research Handbook of Responsible Management*, Cheltenham: Edward Elgar Publishing, pp 40–55.

Lips-Wiersma, M. and Morris, L. (2009) 'Discriminating between "meaningful work" and the "management of meaning"', *Journal of Business Ethics*, 88(3): 491–511.

Mellor, M. (2012) 'Co-operative principles for a green economy', *Capitalism Nature Socialism*, 23(2): 108–110.

Michaelson, C. (2021) 'A normative meaning of meaningful work', *Journal of Business Ethics*, 170(3): 413–428.

Michaelson, C., Pratt, M.G., Grant, A.M. and Dunn, C.P. (2014) 'Meaningful work: Connecting business ethics and organization studies', *Journal of Business Ethics*, 121(1): 77–90.

Mitra, R. and Buzzanell, P.M. (2017) Communicative tensions of meaningful work: The case of sustainability practitioners. *Human Relations*, 70(5): 594–616.

Morris, W. (1886) *Useful Work Versus Useless Toil*, No. 48, Socialist League Office.

Notes from Nowhere (2003) *We Are Everywhere: The Irresistible Rise of Global Anti-Capitalism*. London: Verso.

Novkovic, S. (2008) 'Defining the co-operative difference', *The Journal of Socio-Economics*, 37(6): 2168–2177.

Oswald, A.J., Proto, E. and Sgroi, D. (2015) 'Happiness and productivity', *Journal of Labor Economics*, 33(4): 789–822.

Parker, M., Cheney, G., Fournier, V. and Land, C. (2014) *The Routledge Companion to Alternative Organization*. Abingdon: Routledge.

Peredo, A.M. and McLean, M. (2020) 'Decommodification in action: Common property as countermovement', *Organization*, 27(6): 817–839.

Pérotin, V. (2016) 'What do we really know about workers' co-operatives?' In Webster, A., Shaw, L. and Vorberg-Rugh, R. (eds) *Mainstreaming Co-operation: An Alternative for the Twenty-First Century?* Manchester: Manchester University Press, pp 239–260.

Phelan, L., McGee, J. and Godon, R. (2012) 'Cooperative governance: One pathway to a stable-state economy', *Environmental Politics*, 21(3): 412–431.

Powell, O.H. (2021) *Creaking, Slipping and the Goldilocks Zone: Cultivating Relevance in Established and Scaled Worker Cooperatives*. Bangor: Bangor University.

Puusa, A. and Hokkila, K. (2020) 'Co-operatives of independent workers in Finland: A unique forum for self employment'. In Roelants, B., Eum, H., Eşim, S., Novkovic, S. and Katajamäki, W. (eds) *Co-operatives and the World of Work*. Abingdon: Routledge, pp 188–204.

Restakis, J. (2010) *Humanizing the Economy: Co-operatives in the Age of Capital*. Gabriola Island: New Society Publishers.

Roelants, B., Dovgan, D., Eum, H. and Terrasi, E. (2012) *The Resilience of the Cooperative Mode*. Brussels: CECOP-CICOPA.

Ridley-Duff, R. (2010) 'Communitarian governance in social enterprises: Case evidence from the Mondragon Cooperative Corporation and School Trends Ltd', *Social Enterprise Journal*, 6(2): 125–145.

Rothschild, J. (2009) 'Workers' cooperatives and social enterprise: A forgotten route to social equality and democracy', *American Behavioral Scientist*, 52(7): 1023–1041.

Ruccio, D.F. (2011) 'Cooperatives, surplus, and the social', *Rethinking Marxism*, 23(3): 344–340.

Sandoval, M. (2016) 'Fighting precarity with co-operation? Worker co-operatives in the cultural sector', *New Formations*, 88(4): 51–68.

Schneider, N. (2020) 'An internet of ownership: Democratic design for the online economy'. In Roelants, B. Eum, H. Eşim, S. Novkovic, S. and Katajamäki, W. (eds) *Co-operatives and the World of Work*. Abingdon: Routledge, pp 234–246.

Scholz, T. (2016) *Platform Cooperativism: Challenging the Corporate Sharing Economy*. New York: Rosa Luxemburg Foundation.

Soetens, A. and Huybrechts, B. (2023) Resisting the Tide: The Roles of Ideology in Sustaining Alternative Organizing at a Self-managed Cooperative. *Journal of Management Inquiry*, 32(2): 134–51.

Somerville, P. (2007) 'Co-operative identity', *Journal of Co-operative Studies*, 40(1): 5–17.

Terkel, S. (1974) *Working: People Talk About What They Do All Day and How They Feel About What They Do*. New York: Pantheon/Random House.

Taylor, M., Marsh, G., Nicol, D. and Broadbent, P. (2017) *Good Work: The Taylor Review of Modern Working Practices*. London: Department for Business, Energy & Industrial Strategy.

Valizade, D., Ogbonnaya, C., Tregaskis, O. and Forde, C. (2016) 'A mutual gains perspective on workplace partnership: Employee outcomes and the mediating role of the employment relations climate', *Human Resource Management Journal*, 26(3): 351–368.

Webb, T. and Cheney, G. (2014) 'Worker-owned-and-governed co-operatives and the wider co-operative movement: challenges and opportunities within and beyond the global economic crisis'. In Parker, M., Cheney, G., Fournier, V. and Land, C. (2014) *The Routledge Companion to Alternative Organization*. Abingdon: Routledge, pp 88–112.

Wolf, S. (2010) *Meaning in Life and Why It Matters*. Princeton: Princeton University Press.

Wren, D. (2020) 'The culture of UK employee-owned worker cooperatives', *Employee Relations*, 42(3): 761–776.

Yeoman, R. (2014a) *Meaningful Work and Workplace Democracy: A Philosophy of Work and a Politics of Meaningfulness*. London: Palgrave Macmillan.

Yeoman, R. (2014b) 'Conceptualising meaningful work as a fundamental human need', *Journal of Business Ethics*, 125(2): 235–251.

Zamagni, S. and Zamagni, V. (2010) *Cooperative Enterprise: Facing the Challenge of Globalization*. Cheltenham: Edward Elgar Publishing.

Zamagni, V. (2019) *Why We Need Cooperatives to Make the business World More People-centered*. Geneva: UNTFSSE International Conference in Geneva.

5

The Promise and Perils of Corporate Governance-by-Design in Blockchain-Based Collectives: The Case of dOrg

Morshed Mannan

Introduction

This chapter analyses the emergence of new collectivist organizations in response to the growth of the platform economy, with a particular focus on a blockchain-based software developers' collective, dOrg. This digital collective seeks to respond to a 21st-century challenge: providing decent conditions and agency to workers in a world experiencing globalization, digitalization and rising inequality. As with other contributions to this volume, this chapter shows what alternative business structures, such as co-operatives and collectives, can offer to discussions on the future of work, while also highlighting how organizations like dOrg innovate long-standing cooperative governance structures. Through a case study of this transnational collective, I describe how its governance structure innovates upon, and departs from, Rothschild and Whitt's (1989, pp 62–63) two ideal types of organization – the bureaucratic organization and the collectivist-democratic organization. I then go on to demonstrate how dOrg addresses agency problems by way of what I call *corporate governance-by-design* (Mannan, 2018, p 191). In the last part of the chapter, I explain how this concept varies from traditional corporate governance and evaluate the extent to which the measures introduced to achieve corporate governance-by-design, such as reputation-weighted voting, address the governance challenges faced by such organizations. I conclude by reflecting on the lessons that organizations like dOrg can offer co-operatives in the 21st century.

It is necessary to clarify the usage of certain terms. In this chapter, a platform refers to a business model used by firms to bring together various groups and intermediate transactions of tangible and intangible resources between them (Montalban et al, 2019, p 807). There is a wide variety of businesses that use the platform business model (that is, platform firms) in existence, but this chapter focuses particularly on *labour platforms*. These are platforms where users on one side of a platform provide labour for users on other side(s) of the platform. Through the suite of technologies used by labour platform firms – from their proprietary matching algorithms to their users' smartphone sensors – the platform collects, processes and uses data to encourage and facilitate these interactions (Mannan, 2022). These firms are *asset-light* in the sense that they do not own physical assets or produce goods or provide services themselves but rely on the labourers to use their own assets to supply goods and services to other users by transacting on the platform's marketplace. As the firms' revenue is typically predicated on the number of transactions made on their platform, for-profit platform companies seek to maximize transactions by nudging and manipulating the choices of labourers and consumers (Pignot, 2021, p 3).

There are many types of labour platforms in existence, which can be divided according to the qualifications needed to complete work and the geographic proximity of workers to their end-consumer. This chapter is concerned with remote, high-qualification labour. I focus on highly-skilled freelancers, many of whom are highly mobile, and work at a distance from their clients, each other and the jurisdiction where their organization is registered (Hannonen, 2020). As other scholars have noted recently, freelancing entails 'looking for freedom while facing the consequences of highly individualised forms of work' (Mondon-Navazo et al, 2022, p 738), where the allure of potential autonomy in setting the terms and conditions of one's working life is often dashed by attempts of clients to control and restrain this autonomy. This arrangement entails several risks and responsibilities for the worker, including client non-payment, the cost of health and personal liability insurance, the maintenance of work equipment, and the payment of tax and social security contributions. For some freelancers, organizing or joining a co-operative offers a way of sharing these burdens and countering this tendency towards individualization with a more solidaristic approach (Murgia and de Heusch, 2020). This chapter presents and analyses a case concerning an organization that strives for such a solidaristic approach, while also addressing the coordination problems that hamper the governance of large and/or transnational co-operatives.

dOrg, while sharing some resemblances with freelancers and self-management co-operatives, is the world's first blockchain-based limited liability company and is organized as a collective. It has several features and objectives that are distinct from the aforementioned co-operatives, most notably, due to the organization operating fully online, having a transnational membership and implementing part of its governance system on a *blockchain* (Reijers et al, 2021). In the interests of space, I will not delve into a descriptive definition of blockchain-based networks, which is available elsewhere (De Filippi and Wright, 2018), but will highlight its distinctive characteristics relative to other networks, which are: '(a) decentralization, (b) transnationality, (c) tamper-resistance, (d) pseudonymity, (e) lack of coercion, (f) trustlessness [i.e., trust in third-parties or other participants is not required for the network to function], and (g) operational autonomy' (De Filippi et al, 2022). While these features make blockchain-based networks difficult to regulate, people can build applications and tools that harness these features to achieve new forms of decentralized governance. Difficulties in scaling trust and overcoming cultural differences have been used to explain why co-operatives have struggled to grow beyond a certain size or operate across borders (Spear, 2004; Errasti et al, 2017). The example of dOrg illustrates how building *confidence* – a concept that is related to, but distinct from, trust (discussed later) – can aid in scaling solidaristic efforts. dOrg seeks to build confidence through a combination of 'on-chain' and 'off-chain' governance (Reijers et al, 2021), or more plainly, through the rules for interactions and decision-making that are embedded in a blockchain protocol and other non-blockchain tools (for example, ranging from online forums and polling mechanisms to drafting members' covenants). In doing so, dOrg strives for corporate governance-by-design.

By presenting a case study of a novel type of organization that prefigures a new way of organizing work and governing workplaces across borders, this chapter adds to the 'library of alternative case studies' suggested by Parker and Parker (2017, p 1382). While having strong limitations in terms of generalizability (Farquhar, 2012), conducting a case study offers lessons for other, similarly oriented organizations to learn from if they wish to scale transnationally. Indeed, dOrg from the outset wished to make itself an example for other groups with similar objectives, with it publishing a statement at the time it became the first legally registered decentralized autonomous organization (DAO): '[w]e want to make what we just did accessible to anyone in the world ... [u]ltimately the process of configuring and deploying a legally registered DAO will be as easy as creating a social media account' (Gravel & Shea PC, 2019).

The case study was constructed through online discussions and workshops with a co-founder of dOrg (pseudonym: 'AB') between 2020 and 2022, an analysis of their governance documentation available online and in their public Discord server (a voice and text messaging platform) and a series of semi-structured interviews with AB and another member of dOrg (pseudonym: CD) for remaining clarifications. The scope of this chapter is limited to describing the operation and governance of dOrg to build an argument that the collective seeks to achieve corporate governance-by-design.

The corporate governance of co-operatives is a subject that has received renewed attention in the governance literature due to the business failures of both financial and non-financial co-operatives in recent years (Yamori et al, 2017; Basterretxea et al, 2022). While this is in part due to exogenous socio-economic trends, such as increased global competition (Errasti et al, 2017, p 182), endogenous factors such as the size and geographic scope of the co-operative, along with the specialized knowledge and decision-making skills of members, are also relevant. Indeed, a recent article focuses primarily on seven endogenous 'paradoxes' that pose a dilemma for cooperative governance: (1) cohesion between members with varying interests, (2) maintaining the motivation of board members without extrinsic incentives, (3) striking a balance between board members collaborating with professional management and monitoring them, (4) sustaining member participation, (5) striking a balance between choosing expert board members and representative board members, (6) determining how to measure the success of the co-operative, and (7) mainstreaming the co-operative without losing its distinct democratic identity (Michaud and Audebrand, 2022). As Spear (2004) has demonstrated, some of these tensions are accentuated when the co-operative reaches a certain size and geographic scope – encouraging active member participation being one example. This chapter contributes to this discourse as it shows how one novel collective addresses these dilemmas, potentially providing lessons for more traditional collective organizations operating in the contemporary digital economy as well. In addition, this chapter also contributes to the small, but growing, body of literature concerned with how blockchain technology can be used to improve corporate governance more broadly and even enable new forms of distributed governance altogether (Reyes et al, 2017; Kaal, 2020a, 2020b). This literature relies on hypotheses on how applications of blockchain technology may revolutionize corporate governance but only refers to working industry examples in passing. Reyes (2021, pp 442, 463) is an exception and while dOrg is mentioned in her article for how the organization automates operational and management processes, the article does not extensively discuss the organization's features or governance practices.

The case of dOrg

The formation of dOrg can trace its origins in late 2018 when a group of software developers met at hackathons (that is, events in which people come together to write or improve software programs) and wanted to find a way of collaborating. The project they informally worked on initially was a tool to launch DAOs. A DAO is a 'blockchain-based system that enables people to coordinate and govern themselves mediated by a set of self-executing rules deployed on a public blockchain, and whose governance is decentralised (i.e., independent from central control)' (Hassan and De Filippi, 2021). Decentralization is a slippery term and has several connotations and meanings, depending on context. In one view, for an organization to be considered a DAO the rules of governance must at least be *technically*, if not also *operationally*, decentralized (COALA, 2021). This means that a smart contract that can be unilaterally altered by a single party, with no other input, would not qualify as a DAO. However, a governance system reliant on '(crypto-)token voting' –where the proportion of tokens held by someone determines their voting power –would still qualify as being decentralized, even if it opens the possibility of a single entity having a majority voting power within the governance system (COALA, 2021). As tokens can be acquired in many ways, from monetary payments (as with shares) to labour contributions, several governance systems can be experimented with in this space, from plutocracy to different variations of democracy (Himmelreich, 2021). For others, a DAO must have both technical and operational decentralization, with the latter included through some form of multi-stakeholder governance.

The founders of dOrg sought to implement such an experimental governance system themselves by creating a DAO and then registering as a Blockchain-Based Limited Liability Company (BBLC) in Vermont, with the legal entity conferring the benefits of legal personhood and limited liability to the DAO. The ownership interests (that is, units) in the LLC were tied to tokens in the DAO known as REP. Their choice of using an LLC was motivated by their desire for a 'lightweight' structure that would also be able to readily accommodate foreign members. At the same time, there is a connection to the cooperative movement as dOrg can elect to be taxed as a co-operative according to its Operating Agreement. In contrast to typical remote freelance work – where a steady revenue stream is not guaranteed, there is an absence of a community to learn from, and there is subservience to a corporate platform (Wood and Lehdonvirta, 2021) – dOrg offers a workplace in which there is a high degree of operational autonomy *and* opportunities for collective decision-making. As the example of dOrg shows, blockchain-based organizations can instantiate democracy within a firm – in the broad sense of having a collective decision-making system that gives each member equal, fair opportunities to influence dOrg's decisions (Himmelreich, 2021, p 2) – but does so in a manner that is distinct from a capitalist company and a collectivist worker co-operative.

How dOrg works

Unlike many DAOs operating in the (decentralized) finance sector (El Faqir et al, 2020), dOrg did not sell a token to the public through a so-called Initial

Coin Offering (ICO), before or at its launch. Members of dOrg receive REP tokens based on the value they produce, which is determined by the US dollars they earn from working on internal or client projects. One REP is earned by a member for every US dollar that is earned, as well as for certain activities that support the internal operations of dOrg (for example, organizing in-person meetings and work referrals). The amount of REP a member holds determines their voting power. The advantage of REP in blockchain-based systems is that they can be stored transparently, while also being resistant to Sybil attacks and other forms of gaming/abuse. At the time of writing in June 2022, there was a total token supply of 4,420,883 tokens held by 97 token holders. While the token holders are pseudonymous to the outside world – as they are identified by their Ethereum addresses – most of the token holders only have a fraction of one per cent of the issued tokens, with the five most significant token holders, having 8.03 per cent, 6.49 per cent, 5.89 per cent, 5.18 per cent and 4.6 per cent of the total tokens. This token is different from payment or utility tokens (Shirole et al, 2020), as well as withdrawable share capital in a co-operative (Co-operatives UK, 2020) since it is *non-transferable* and as such cannot be sold on secondary markets or withdrawn from the collective.

REP alludes to the idea of reputation as a 'digital representation of an entity's standing or status in a specific domain' (De Filippi et al, 2021). In the context of dOrg, formal status and voting power are gained through income earned through dOrg but a more substantive understanding of members' abilities and expertise is gained through means other than metrics, such as off-chain personal interactions. Having an effective reputation system that ensures parties act honestly and in good faith can help attract and retain consumers of non-financial services offered by blockchain-based organizations (Mannan, 2018, p 201; Kaal, 2020b).

Joining, and working through, dOrg

Initially, any interested person could 'propose' to join dOrg. In this process, they would have to demonstrate their skills (for example, making a software application). dOrg would vote on whether their skills were sufficient before countersigning the proposal. If the application was successful, the new dOrg member would get 100 REP and 100 US dollars. In the view of one of the interviewees, AB, this was too lax a system for admission. The awkwardness of voting against potential new members meant that most applications for membership were accepted. Moreover, only a few existing members were voting. This meant that oversight of the admission system was not sufficiently rigorous. For AB, this 'hurt our image that we are an elite software development agency'.

dOrg's early efforts at client acquisition illustrate some of the problems of this initial admission system. Salespersons who brought projects for the organization got 10 per cent of the project value as a commission (10 per cent also went to the dOrg treasury). This is an important incentive for members to bring clients to dOrg and work with other members, instead of working independently. At the same time, the existence of this incentive presented challenges for the collective. First, it creates the possibility of more work being brought to the collective than it is prepared to complete. Second, and relatedly, it can generate tensions between old and new members of dOrg, a horizontal agency problem that is often discussed in the worker cooperative literature (Pencavel, 2013; Armour et al, 2017b).

Indeed, this is what happened in dOrg with more client projects being referred to the collective by members involved in business development than they could handle. As a consequence, some members went on a hiring spree, with there being 14 new activation proposals (member applications) in a month instead of the usual two to three. Older members were concerned about this as it had the potential of diluting the quality of the services provided by dOrg. They were able to prevent new members from joining by using their joint higher REP to vote against them, to maintain the 'integrity' of the collective. There was also a moratorium for a short period in appointing new members. The members that had been involved in business development then went on to work in other capacities. With this experience in mind, dOrg is currently in the process of appointing a specialized sales team.

At present, people fill out a form to join and are effectively placed on a waiting list. A talent coordinator then matches what dOrg needs in terms of skill sets and client requests with the pipeline of candidates. If the candidate passes the subsequent interviews and their profile is seen to be acceptable, the talent coordinator member who vetted the candidate proposes that an offer be made to the candidate by dOrg. No payments are now made to the member to join. In effect, the lesson from the early experience with member admissions led to a reversal of the procedure by which members may join the organization: instead of members proposing to join, the organization makes an offer for new members to join. Unlike most worker co-operatives, where a purchase of cooperative share capital is common (Vieta et al, 2016), dOrg does not require any capital contributions to be made to join; only contributions of labour.

For AB, this new admission system is suitable for dOrg for the time being as they do not wish to be an organization with 10,000 members. While they are still figuring out what the ideal size for dOrg will be, in his view it will not be more than 150–200 people, working on about two dozen high-quality projects at any one time.

New client projects are obtained by dOrg through a contact form or a personal connection/referral (dOrg, 2022e). Anyone can signal their interest in reaching out to a potential client that has used the contact form, and members are encouraged to collaborate in the process of closing the deal. If the interested members deem the project to be promising, a statement of work is completed and a proposal is submitted for the broader organization to vote on, before the commencement of work. When a new project is started, the members self-organize to complete the work and arrange for the internal coordination and quality assurance of the project.

Payments can be made through a combination of tokens pegged to the US dollar and REP (US$ 50 + 50 REP/hour or US$ 25 + 25 REP/hour) or only in REP (150 REP/hour). To incentivize working for the internal needs of dOrg, members can work up to 22 hours a month without submitting a proposal or a funded initiative (dOrg, 2022a), effectively providing members with access to a minimum income. In the 42 months since its foundation, dOrg has generated over 5 million USD in on-chain revenue.

Governing dOrg

dOrg has implemented a type of collective governance, where there is neither a board of directors nor professional management. Instead, numerous governance decisions are made directly by the members themselves through the use of blockchain-based systems and other online tools. According to the Operating Agreement of the Blockchain-Based Limited Liability Company (BBLLC), this includes the admission and expulsion of members, the transfer of member units, upgrades or modifications to the dOrg DAO and related software, and changes to the Operating Agreement itself. In short, the digital tools used by the BBLLC are an integral component of the Operating Agreement, in addition to the written text itself. While there has been a degree of automation of the higher levels of management in dOrg (Reyes, 2021), humans remain in the loop. One such human is the Administrative Member of dOrg, responsible for interacting with the state and third-party service providers for the benefit of the collective. They have the power to act as the agent of the collective, file documents and are elected by the membership. The Operating Agreement seeks to exculpate the Administrative Member of any fiduciary duties and indemnifies them for acts for, or on behalf, of the collective. At the time of writing, the Operating Agreement is in the process of amendment and there is a proposal to remove this role. Instead, the DAO will be able to delegate specific administrative responsibilities to individual members through governance proposals.

In dOrg, earning reputation is not only meant to signal the quality of the work, level of commitment or bonus entitlements of members but, more importantly, represents their proportional share of voting power and ownership within the collective (dOrg, 2022b). These votes are not merely polls of the interests or sentiments of members, as their outcome is legally binding. This is because the reputation-based voting power is tied to the one unit of the Blockchain-Based Limited Liability Company that each member receives upon joining dOrg. At present, dOrg uses Snapshot, a popular voting tool that records user votes in a decentralized storage system known as the Interplanetary File System. This allows dOrg to avoid the 'gas fees' (that is, a type of transaction fee) inherent in using a public permissionless blockchain-based system (Faqir-Rhazoui et al, 2021, p 5558), while still benefitting from the transparency that is a distinguishing feature of such platforms from more centralized tools (Hussey, 2021). At the same time as the decisions resulting from these votes need to be executed on-chain, tokenholders elect signers of a multi-signature wallet to perform this function. Voting for proposals, on issues ranging from the operational (for example, pay-out of earnings, legal fees) to the maintenance of the organization's treasury (that is, a pool of funds that are invested in the collective itself) to the strategic (for example, proposing the admission of new members), are based on REP-based voting, where 'one token equals one vote'. According to Kaal (2020b, p 26), reputation systems lead to a 'positive-sum game', creating non-fungible value for dOrg members and dOrg itself. However, a foreseeable problem with such a system is that it enables the emergence of a form of technocracy or epistocracy (Moraro, 2018). Such technocratic governance risks replicating the vertical principal-agent problems and accountability concerns that bedevil certain centralized platforms, where some founders and shareholders hold outsized voting power (Armour et al, 2017b; Mannan and Schneider, 2021). To pre-empt this problem, reputation in dOrg is *inflationary*, where the weight of a member's reputation declines over time relative to active members if they become inactive. The level of activity of a member is gauged every three months to assess whether they have earned dollars – and hence REP – in the preceding period.

To avoid a flood of governance proposals, and to allow for proper deliberation, a proposer must first open a forum topic to discuss a potential proposal; it is only when a decision needs to be made that a proposal is posted. Proposals are voted on by the membership and then if passed, the proposal is executed by seven elected multi-signature wallet signers, typically comprising top REP holders, professionals (for example, an accountant) and active members.

As with traditional co-operatives and collectives, maintaining participation is a concern for dOrg. So far, this is addressed by providing active reputation holders with a bonus from the organization's treasury – in addition to sociocultural and ideological incentives. An interesting example of how 'off-chain' social norms intersect with 'on-chain' governance processes is provided by the enforcement of dOrg's members' covenant. Upon joining the collective, members are expected to uphold the principles of the covenant in all the spaces associated with dOrg and contribute to an 'open, welcoming, diverse, inclusive, and healthy community'. Failure to do so can lead to expulsion from the collective. The standards that the members are expected to uphold are:

- Demonstrating empathy and kindness toward other people
- Assuming good intentions
- Being respectful of differing opinions, viewpoints, and experiences
- Giving and gracefully accepting constructive feedback
- Taking ownership of our commitments and communicating changes with multiple weeks' notice
- Accepting responsibility and apologizing to those affected by our mistakes, and learning from the experience
- Encouraging transparency and collaboration while preserving privacy where reasonably expected
- Focusing on what is best not just for us as individuals, but for the overall community. (dOrg, 2022c)

A range of behaviours may be deemed unacceptable under these standards, including sexual harassment and hate speech. When problematic behaviour is raised, the members are encouraged to first reconcile and then enter into mediation, failing which an enforcement proposal is submitted for the members to review and decide upon. The members can then decide on the practical and reputational consequences that will ensue for the infringing party (dOrg, 2022d). The burning of the member's REP is particularly significant as it has both financial and control implications for the member. If all REP is burnt it practically leads to a member's expulsion. It is also possible for members to voluntarily and formally withdraw from dOrg or become inactive for a while. In both the case of voluntary and involuntary withdrawal, the unit record of the BBLLC will be automatically updated to reflect this.

Aside from internal matters, software issues can create governance concerns for dOrg. A bug in dOrg DAO's smart contract(s) could compromise the operation of the organization and the splitting of the underlying Ethereum blockchain protocol into two parallel, competing chains can lead to the duplication of REP and questions over the rights attached to the REP. The Operating Agreement of dOrg countenances these difficulties by providing that the funds of dOrg are to be ringfenced in a multi-signature wallet – jointly controlled by an Administrative Member and another member – for the time needed to patch the bug. Before a contentious fork, members will have the opportunity to vote on which chain to follow, thereby definitively the chain on which dOrg DAO will continue to exist. However, as blockchain technology is more of a tool for dOrg than a fundamental technical infrastructure, the degree of risk of such exogenous shocks to dOrg is less substantial than with other DAOs.

Applying Rothschild and Whitt's two ideal types of organization to dOrg

An earlier article that discussed dOrg considered it to be a 'distributed business entity' (Reyes, 2021). Her comparison was primarily with hierarchical corporations and hypothetical algorithmic entities. Given the nature of dOrg's governance, it would be fruitful to compare the organization with both collectivist-democratic organizations (for example, collectively-run bookstores) and traditional bureaucratic organizations (for example, modern multinational corporations). Rothschild and Whitt (1989, pp 62–63) compared these two ideal types across 8 dimensions. First, while *authority* in a bureaucratic organization resides in individuals owing to their expertise or incumbency, in collectivist-democratic organizations authority resides in the collective as a whole and is only ever delegated temporarily. Although an elected group of seven members of dOrg have certain signing authority, dOrg bears a stronger resemblance to the latter as several key governance decisions require the vote of the membership, administrative roles are delegated temporarily, and the REP holders are (potentially) subject to change.

Second, bureaucratic organizations formalize fixed, universal *rules*, while collectivist-democratic organizations have minimal rules and instead rely on ad hoc decisions and a shared notion of substantive ethics. The standards specified in the members' covenant of dOrg do indicate that there is a coalescence of ethical values within the collective, the dOrg Handbook, Operating Agreement and its digital tools demonstrate that several rules have been formalized and *permanently stored* on a distributed ledger. Thus, in this dimension, dOrg has a closer resemblance to a bureaucracy. Third, *social control* in bureaucratic organizations is primarily carried out through direct supervision or the use of standardized sanctions but is based on personal, moralistic appeals in collectivist-democratic organizations. Here, dOrg treads a line between either pole, as it follows a gradually escalating approach in handling disputes, starting from personalized appeals (for example, initial personal conversations when a covenant dispute arises) to imposing standardized sanctions (for example, on-chain removal procedures). Fourth, bureaucratic organizations conceive *social relations* as being impersonal and instrumental, while collectivist-democratic organizations are more holistic and appeal to ideas of community. Given the importance that dOrg gives to a Swarm approach, it is clear that the organization leans more towards the latter.

Fifth, *recruitment and advancement* in bureaucratic organizations are premised on 'specialised training and formal certification' and offer the prospect of a career. In contrast, in collectivist-democratic organizations, recruitment is based on friendship and informally assessed skills and as there is no hierarchy, there isn't a traditional notion of a career ladder either. dOrg initially bore a strong resemblance to collectivist-democratic organizations in this regard, but as it tightened its member admission requirements, it gravitated towards the middle of these two ideal types. In the past, anyone could apply to be a member and now there is a careful vetting of the applicant's skills and experience and an offer of membership is only made if there is a pressing need. Sixth, *incentives* in bureaucratic organizations are mainly financial, while in collectivist-democratic organizations they are ideological or solidaristic. In this regard, dOrg has features like the latter, as the social and community aspect is as important as the economic objectives of the collective, if not more so. Seventh, in terms of *social stratification*, in bureaucratic organizations rewards are differentially distributed based on office and a degree of inequality is accepted, though in collectivist-democratic organizations the approach to rewards is more egalitarian and differences are strictly limited. dOrg permits there to be differences in earnings and reputation power, although the basis of stratification is not wealth but the extent of recent labour contributions. As such, in this dimension, dOrg resembles the former type, even if the degree of social stratification is comparably less than in other DAOs (Ilyushina and MacDonald, 2022). Finally, bureaucratic organizations have maximum *differentiation*, in terms of both division of labour and job specialization; collectivist-democratic organizations do not and generally demystify specialized expertise. Although dOrg projects have lead roles with certain experience and knowledge, these positions are notionally accessible by anyone and are democratically appointed. Indeed, anyone can submit a governance proposal and any member could be authorized to perform specific administrative tasks. Therefore, concerning differentiation, dOrg has a minimal division of labour and generalizes the holding of rules and functions.

This analysis reveals that, in a strict sense, dOrg is not purely a collectivist-democratic organization or a bureaucratic organization but has elements of both. dOrg can be considered as a new ideal type – a 'distributed business entity' – which incorporated the authority system, division of labour, incentives, and social relations of collectivist-democratic organizations while adopting the rules and social stratification of bureaucratic organizations. In terms of social control and recruitment processes, dOrg falls somewhere in between. This is summarized in Table 5.1. While there may also be several co-operatives that fall within this spectrum between two ideal types, an important reason why dOrg does so is because of its technical innovations when it comes to, for example, voting and member removal.

Corporate governance-by-design

As a hybrid organization, with a transnational, pseudonymous group of members and clients, it is unsurprising that dOrg is confronted with some

Table 5.1: Distributed business entities as a hybrid of collectivist-democratic and bureaucratic organizations

	Bureaucratic organization	Distributed business entity	Collectivist-democratic organization
Authority	Individual	*Collective*	*Collective*
Rules	*Maximal, formal, fixed rules*	*Formal, fixed rules*	Minimal, informal, often unwritten rules
Social control	Direct supervision and standardized sanctions	Escalation from personal appeals to on-chain enforcement	Personalistic or moral appeals
Social relations	Impersonal and instrumental	*Communitarian*	*Communitarian*
Recruitment and advancement	Specialized training and formal certification; Prospects for career	Rigorous vetting of skills but no formal certification	Friendship and informal assessment; No career progression
Incentives	Financial	*Social and ideological*	*Social and ideological*
Social stratification	*Differential rewards and inequality permissible*	*Differential rewards and inequality permissible*	Egalitarian differential in rewards and limited inequality
Differentiation	Maximal division of labour and maximal specialization	*Minimal division of labour and emphasis on generalization*	*Minimal division of labour and emphasis on generalization*

Note: The areas in italic highlight similarities with either ideal type.
Source: Adapted from Rothschild and Whitt (1989, pp 63–63)

agency costs. Armour and colleagues (2017a) identify three agency problems from which agency costs arise, namely the vertical agency problem between principals and agents, the horizontal agency problem between majority-minority principals and the firm-stakeholder agency problem. In the context of traditional corporations, the first problem manifests when hired management (that is, agents) pursue their interests instead of the wealth-maximizing interests of shareholders (that is, principals). The second agency problem arises when majority shareholders (that is, agents) exploit their voting power to benefit themselves instead of the shareholders as a class, thus potentially jeopardizing the interests of minority shareholders (that is, principals). The third problem arises when a firm as a whole (that is, agent) opportunistically uses its position to benefit itself to the detriment of stakeholders, such as workers or consumers (that is, principals). These agency problems may be exacerbated if the principals are heterogeneous and dispersed, as they face costs in terms of collecting *information* and *co-ordinating* among themselves (Spear, 2004, p 44). In short, deficiencies in trust lead to these problems. Agency problems also occur in collectives and co-operatives, although in a different manner. The interests of cooperative members are not limited to wealth maximization and include a wider array of social and utility concerns, which present distinct challenges for cooperative board members seeking to encapsulate their interests. The fact that co-operatives commonly have 'one member, one vote' systems means that there isn't a member with the same powers of control as a majority shareholder, however there can still be horizontal agency problems due to heterogeneous preferences among members due to factors such as length of service in the co-operative.

While agency theory is a contested basis for understanding governance problems (Spear, 2004, p 50), in both corporations and co-operatives, it continues to be an influential theoretical framework, including in research of blockchain-based organizations (Kaal, 2020b; Michaud and Audebrand, 2022). Through this lens, the purpose of good corporate governance is to address these costs (Pargendler, 2016, p 367). There are various legal strategies – both regulatory and governance-based – that can be used to reduce costs arising from any principal-agent relationship. *Rules* and *standards* are two regulatory strategies that are prescribed by a jurisdiction, with the former used to permit or prohibit corporate behaviour ex-ante and the latter used to discretionarily evaluate corporate conduct ex-post (Armour et al, 2017a). Two other regulatory strategies are setting conditions on *entry* (for example, disqualification of certain individuals from holding managerial roles) and *exit* (for example, appraisal rights of dissenting shareholders) for interactions with the firm. This allows principals to screen new agents and enables principals to escape from poor management by an agent if necessary. *Selection* and *removal* of key decision-makers, such as board directors, are central to corporate governance and both mandatory provisions of corporate law and voluntary provisions of corporate governance codes address these two processes, particularly in the case of public companies (Armour et al, 2017a). This empowers principals to appoint agents that serve their interests or remove those that do not.

These strategies were developed with publicly-traded corporations in mind. As discussed in the previous section, dOrg is a different type of organization with distinct agency costs. The strategies needed to mitigate these costs also differ accordingly. dOrg is subject to far fewer mandatory rules concerning its internal governance than an archetypical publicly-traded corporation. This is due to its choice of legal entity. LLCs, including BBLLCs, are very flexible structures, allowing founder members to privately order the initial governance system (Kaal, 2020b, p 11). In other words, there are fewer exogenous rules and standards as to the governance system that dOrg mandatorily has to comply with. For example, one of the few standards applicable to member-managed LLCs, are the duties of loyalty and care that members owe the LLC and to each other – which may be limited, but generally cannot be eliminated (Johnson and Tanner, 2018, pp 34–35). Second, and relatedly, dOrg does not have a board and has a limited delegation of discretionary roles. There is a minimal division of the functions of monitoring, management, and work, with several members performing all three. Thus, a different set of entry terms are needed. Unlike publicly-traded corporations, or even many DAOs (Kaal, 2020b, p 13), dOrg does not have transferable equity or tokens. As a consequence, members exiting the organization or a potential hostile takeover cannot be used as threats to discipline the management of the collective.

As with companies in general, the selection and removal of role-holders are important considerations for dOrg and are determined through the nomination and voting of individuals. However, even the role with the most extensive managerial duties on behalf of dOrg, the Administrative Member, has strict limits on their discretion and representative power as the members as a whole have a fundamental role in directing the operations and affairs of the entity. Thus, the selection and removal of role-holders have less of an impact in this context. In contrast to publicly-traded companies, the initiation of decisions has a crucial role in the governance of dOrg and the scope of these decisions range from day-to-day minutiae (for example, appointing an intern) to strategic decisions (for example, deleting a member's REP).

Given the inefficacy or inapplicability of several legal strategies to dOrg, how does the entity remedy the agency costs that invariably arise? I argue that it does so through corporate governance-by-design. This neologism draws inspiration from regulation-by-design and privacy-by-design. Regulation-by-design broadly refers to design-based interventions (for example, the design of railway carriages) to change human behaviour to achieve certain policy objectives (for example, reduced noise on trains) (Yeung, 2008). Privacy-by-design refers to the idea that data protection should be addressed proactively by automatically protecting data by default in IT systems and ensuring that these safeguards are always in place. These embedded protection mechanisms should be 'visible and transparent' to users and predisposed to respecting user privacy (Pagallo, 2021, p 114). As with these design-based interventions, corporate governance-by-design seeks to pre-empt agency costs through the ex-ante use of mechanisms provided in their techno-legal governance assemblage, that is, their Operating Agreement alongside the DAO's smart contract(s) and other digital tools linked to therein. Let's first consider the vertical agency problem. The good corporate governance practices of public companies would suggest that the opportunism of an agent can be mitigated through selection or removal strategies, while research on the governance of large co-operatives suggests the strengthening of a member-elected board to monitor professional management (Basterretxea et al, 2022, p 366). dOrg, instead, avoids delegation for the most part and drastically reduces the discretionary powers of agents ex-ante (that is, in its Operating Agreement), while strengthening the capacity for any member to asynchronously present governance-related proposals through the dOrg online forum and Snapshot. As decisions are voted upon by a relative majority within the collective, the opportunities for individual opportunism are limited.

Turning to the horizontal agency problem, in the context of public companies, the legal strategies followed to protect the principal (that is, the minority shareholder) from the opportunism of the agent (that is, the majority shareholder) range from the appointment of independent directors to the conferral of exit rights. In large co-operatives, the heterogeneous preferences of various member groups can create horizontal agency problems between, for example, old members and new members, thereby slowing down decision-making and allowing miscommunication between management and members (Basterretxea et al, 2022, p 372). dOrg addresses this problem in a variety of ways. Costs arise in this context owing to the differential ownership of REP, with a few members having significantly higher REP than others. However, this is formally and dynamically addressed through the continuous inflation of REP, a feature that had been included from the outset. The reputation scores of all members can be viewed on-chain through a gamified, accessible interface and this REP can diminish if valuable recent work is not done, which means that a member with a large relative REP now may not always retain it. As this on-chain record is tamper-resistant and the REP updates are automated, members can have a high degree of confidence in its accuracy. Relatedly, as there is an emphasis on getting things done, proposals to decide on an issue are voted upon within a short set period. To counteract the possibility of large REP holders exploiting this, a quorum of five members is needed for a vote – irrespective of how much REP each of the members hold.

With both vertical and horizontal agency problems, information asymmetries prevent principals from holding agents to account. Various forms of disclosures are a common approach towards mitigating these asymmetries, in both companies and co-operatives. In dOrg, the online forums, proposal platforms and secure recording of votes on-chain allow for the continuous, ambient collection and publication of operational and governance data, which is transparently available to the membership. While being dispersed across various online spaces, this data serves the purpose of disclosures and enables continuous monitoring by members.

These are all design-based governance interventions in the sense that they *shape* the conditions surrounding a member in a desirable direction (for example, enabling members to participate in collective decision-making), *soften* the impact of some behaviour that might cause harm (for example, REP inflation to limit long-term control by inactive members) and outright *prevent* others (for example, preventing Administrative Members from entering into third-party contracts unilaterally) (Yeung, 2008, p 87). By pre-empting the emergence of certain notable agency costs, dOrg strives to achieve continuous compliance with certain long-established corporate governance principles.

Yet, there are certain shortcomings of corporate governance-by-design. As decisions are collectively-made, and top REP holders have significant influence, the stakes for other members diminish and there may be a sense of reduced personal autonomy and moral responsibility over decisions. This can be seen in the public Snapshot interface of dOrg, where participation in most individual proposals is very low. It appears that a focus on a procedural conception of democracy has eroded intrinsic motivations to participate (Himmelreich, 2021, p 3). While the Operating Agreement allows for all members to vote upon changes to be made to the blockchain protocol software used, as well as other technological modifications, the apathy that can seep in may make it difficult for rank-and-file members to break out of comfortable habits and demand change of the technology or existing governance processes. It is implicit in corporate governance-by-design that the role of external actors will be minimal, yet it may be difficult to resolve all internal disputes through forum discussions, mediation and voting processes. As the history of corporate law teaches us, neutral third-party enforcement can help resolve competing policy objectives – an issue that is pertinent for an entity that embraces both commercial and communitarian logics.

Conclusion

In this chapter, I have constructed and presented a case study of a novel, transnational group of Web3 software developers, dOrg. In addition to fleshing out the features of dOrg that make it distinct from both bureaucratic and collectivist-democratic organizations, I have honed in on its particular approach to corporate governance through the ex-ante use of techno-legal mechanisms. While this approach to corporate governance, which I have called corporate governance-by-design, can steer behaviour in favourable directions and cushion or prevent certain harmful actions, thereby diminishing agency costs, it may also have unintended effects. One such effect may be a disinclination to regularly participate in governance processes.

In several respects, dOrg is an outlier, not only for building a solvent business while using experimental technologies and a new legal entity form, but also for recognizing early on the need for human involvement in distributed governance. Several DAOs aspire for a greater degree of automation (Reyes, 2021), which may lead to even greater uses of corporate governance-by-design and further unintended consequences.

The experience of dOrg can offer salutary lessons for new co-operatives in the 21st century as well. On the one hand, it shows that the availability and use of governance tools are not in themselves sufficient for addressing the problem of active governance participation, which has long been a concern for co-operatives (Michaud and Audebrand, 2022). On the other hand, dOrg may prefigure a new way of organizing cooperative work and cooperative governance. While not being a substitute for a stable job or statutory employment rights (The Blockchain Socialist, 2022), dOrg provides access to work opportunities and a voice in governance that is otherwise absent in the domain of remote digital work. This can help achieve one of the objectives of the platform cooperativism movement, which is to improve the working terms and conditions of platform labour. dOrg does not have a 'one member, one vote' model of governance – a hallmark of cooperative governance – and yet it does not have a voting system tied to contributions of financial capital either. While dOrg's model of voting power tied to recent, valuable labour contributions may not supplant the long-standing practice of one member, one vote at cooperative general assemblies, the model and tools used could be implemented in other domains of a co-operative's operations (for example, management of day-to-day work processes) to address the forms of agency problems typical in worker co-operatives (for example, horizontal agency problem between senior and junior members). Beyond the specific case of dOrg, DAOs and co-operatives have much to offer each other in terms of lessons in governing large, complex structures in a collaborative manner, with the former charting new paths in technological innovation and the latter offering a rich historical tradition, principles and best practices to learn from (Thompson et al, 2022; Mannan, 2018). The emergence of 'DAO co-operatives' like SongADAO co-operative (a daily music production co-operative) and the Employment Commons LCA (an employment co-operative that helps workers of DAOs with payroll, tax compliance, and access to certain benefits) indicate that this mutually beneficial cross-pollination has begun to take place (Radebaugh and Muchnik, 2021).

Acknowledgements

This research received funding from the European Research Council (ERC) under the European Union's Horizon 2020 Research and Innovation Programme (Grant Agreement No. 865856). The author wishes to thank Sofía Cossar, Primavera de Filippi, Jamilya Kamalova, Vashti Maharaj, Tara Merk and two members of dOrg for their comments on an earlier version of this chapter. Usual disclaimers apply.

References

Armour, J., Hansmann, H. and Kraakman, R. (2017a) 'Agency problems and legal strategies'. In Kraakman, R., Armour, J., Davies, P., Enriques, L., Hansmann, H., Hertig, G., Hopt, K., Kanda, H., Pargendler, M., Ringe, W.-G. and Rock, E. (eds) *The Anatomy of Corporate Law* (3rd edn). Oxford: Oxford University Press, 29–48.

Armour, J., Hansmann, H., Kraakman, R. and Pargendler, M. (2017b) 'What is corporate law?'. In *The Anatomy of Corporate Law* (3rd edn). Oxford: Oxford University Press, pp 1–28.

Basterretxea, I., Cornforth, C. and Heras-Saizarbitoria, I. (2022) 'Corporate governance as a key aspect in the failure of worker cooperatives', *Economic and Industrial Democracy*, 43(1): 362–387.

COALA (2021) Model Law for Decentralized Autonomous Organizations (DAOs). Available from https://coala.global/wp-content/uploads/2022/03/DAO-Model-Law.pdf [Accessed on 10 June 2023].

Co-operatives UK (2020) *Community Shares Handbook*. Manchester: Cooperatives UK.

De Filippi, P., Shimony, O. and Tenorio-Fornés, A. (2021) 'Reputation', *Internet Policy Review*, 10(2): 1–9.

De Filippi, P., Mannan, M. and Reijers, W. (2022) 'The alegality of blockchain technology', *Policy and Society*, 41(3): 358–372.

De Filippi, P. and Wright, A. (2018) *Blockchain and the Law: The Rule of Code*. Cambridge, MA: Harvard University Press.

dOrg (2022a) *Funded initiatives, dOrg Handbook*. Available from https://docs.dorg.tech/workflows/doing-internal-work/funded-initiatives [Accessed on 15 March 2023].

dOrg (2022b) *Governance, dOrg Handbook*. Available from https://docs.dorg.tech/governance [Accessed on 15 March 2023].

dOrg (2022c) *Member Covenant, dOrg Handbook*. Available from https://docs.dorg.tech/covenant [Accessed on 15 March 2023].

dOrg (2022d) *Removal, dOrg Handbook*. Available from https://docs.dorg.tech/lifecycle/removal#proposing-removal [Accessed on 15 March 2023].

dOrg (2022e) *Sourcing a New Client Projects, dOrg Handbook*. Available from https://docs.dorg.tech/workflows/sourcing [Accessed on 15 March 2023].

El Faqir, Y., Arroyo, J. and Hassan, S. (2020) 'An overview of decentralized autonomous organizations on the blockchain'. In *Proceedings of the 16th International Symposium on Open Collaboration*. New York: Association for Computing Machinery (OpenSym 2020), pp 1–8.

Errasti, A., Bretos, I. and Nunez, A. (2017) 'The viability of cooperatives: The fall of the Mondragon Cooperative Fagor', *Review of Radical Political Economics*, 49(2): 181–197.

Faqir-Rhazoui, Y., Arroyo, J. and Hassan, S. (2021) 'A Scalable Voting System: Validation of Holographic Consensus in DAOstack', *Hawaii International Conference on System Sciences 2021 (HICSS-54)*.

Farquhar, J. (2012) *Case Study Research for Business*. London: SAGE Publications.

Gravel & Shea PC (2019) 'dOrg launches first limited liability DAO', *Gravel & Shea: Attorneys at Law*. Available from www.gravelshea.com/2019/06/dorg-launches-first-limited-liability-dao/ [Accessed on 15 March 2023].

Hannonen, O. (2020) 'In search of a digital nomad: Defining the phenomenon', *Information Technology & Tourism*, 22(3): 335–353.

Hassan, S. and De Filippi, P. (2021) 'Decentralized autonomous organizations', *Internet Policy Review*, 10(2).

Himmelreich, J. (2021) 'Should we automate democracy?' In Véliz, C. (ed) *The Oxford Handbook of Digital Ethics*. Oxford: Oxford University Press, pp 1–36.

Hussey, D.M. (2021) 'What is snapshot? The decentralized voting system', *Decrypt*, 4 June. Available from https://decrypt.co/resources/what-is-snapshot-the-decentralized-voting-system [Accessed on 15 March 2023].

Ilyushina, N. and MacDonald, T. (2022) 'Decentralised autonomous organisations: A New research agenda for labour economics', *The Journal of the British Blockchain Association*, 5(1): 50–53.

Johnson, J.D. and Tanner, S.W. (2018) 'Modification of fiduciary duties in limited liability companies', *In-House Defense Quarterly*, Summer: 32–37.

Kaal, W.A. (2020a) 'Blockchain solutions for agency problems in corporate governance'. In Balachandran, K.R. (ed) *Economic Information to Facilitate Decision Making*. Singapore: World Scientific Publishers, pp 313–329.

Kaal, W.A. (2020b) 'Blockchain-based corporate governance', *Stanford Journal of Blockchain Law & Policy*, 4(1): 1–28.

Mannan, M. (2018) 'Fostering worker cooperatives with blockchain technology: Lessons from the Colony Project', *Erasmus Law Review*, 11(3): 190–203.

Mannan, M. (2022) 'Theorizing the emergence of platform cooperativism: Drawing lessons from role-set theory', *Ondernemingsrecht Tijdschrift*, 2: 64–71.

Mannan, M. and Schneider, N. (2021) 'Exit to community: Strategies for multi-stakeholder ownership in the platform economy', *Georgetown Law Technology Review*, 5(1): 1–71.

Michaud, M. and Audebrand, L.K. (2022) 'One governance theory to rule them all? The case for a paradoxical approach to co-operative governance', *Journal of Co-operative Organization and Management*, 10(1): 100151.

Mondon-Navazo, M., Murgia, A., Borghi, P. and Mezihorak, P. (2022) 'In search of alternatives for individualised workers: A comparative study of freelance organisations', *Organization*, 29(4): 736–756.

Montalban, M., Frigant, V. and Jullien, B. (2019) 'Platform economy as a new form of capitalism: A Régulationist research programme', *Cambridge Journal of Economics*, 43(4): 805–824.

Moraro, P. (2018) 'Against epistocracy', *Social Theory and Practice*, 44(2): 199–216.

Murgia, A. and de Heusch, S. (2020) 'It started with the arts and now it concerns all sectors: The case of smart, a cooperative of "salaried autonomous workers"'. In Taylor, S. and Luckman, S. (eds) *Pathways into Creative Working Lives*. Cham: Springer International Publishing (Creative Working Lives), pp 211–230.

Pagallo, U. (2021) 'On the principle of privacy by design and its limits: Technology, ethics and the rule of law'. In Chiodo, S. and Schiaffonati, V. (eds) *Italian Philosophy of Technology: Socio-Cultural, Legal, Scientific and Aesthetic Perspectives on Technology*. Cham: Springer International Publishing, pp 111–127.

Pargendler, M. (2016) 'The corporate governance obsession', *Journal of Corporation Law*, 42(2): 359–402.

Parker, S. and Parker, M. (2017) 'Antagonism, accommodation and agonism in critical management studies: Alternative organizations as allies', *Human Relations*, 70(11): 1366–1387.

Pencavel, J. (2013) 'Worker cooperatives and democratic governance'. In Grandori, A. (ed) *Handbook of Economic Organization*. Cheltenham: Edward Elgar Publishing, pp 462–480.

Pignot, E. (2021) 'Who is pulling the strings in the platform economy? Accounting for the dark and unexpected sides of algorithmic control', *Organization*. https://doi.org/10.1177/1350508420974523

Radebaugh, J. and Muchnik, Y. (2021). 'Exclusive report: Solving the riddle of the DAO with Colorado's cooperative laws', *The Defiant*, 16 December. Available from https://thedefiant.io/solving-the-riddle-of-the-dao-with-colorados-cooperative-laws [Accessed on 15 March 2023].

Reijers, W. Wuisman, I., Mannan, M., De Filippi, P., Wray, C., Rae-Looi, V., Veléz, A. and Orgad, L. (2021) 'Now the code runs itself: On-chain and off-chain governance of blockchain technologies', *Topoi*, 40(4): 821–831.

Reyes, C. (2021) 'Autonomous business reality', *Nevada Law Journal*, 21(2): 437–490.

Reyes, C., Packin, N. and Edwards, B. (2017) 'Distributed governance', *William & Mary Law Review*, 59(1): 1–32.

Rothschild, J. and Whitt, J.A. (1989) *The Cooperative Workplace: Potentials and Dilemmas of Organisational Democracy and Participation*. Cambridge: Cambridge University Press.

Shirole, M., Darisi, M. and Bhirud, S. (2020) 'Cryptocurrency token: An overview'. In Patel, D Nandi, S., Mishra, B.K Shah, D., Modi, C.N., Shah, K. and Bansode, R.S. (eds) *IC-BCT 2019 Proceedings of the International Conference on Blockchain Technology*. Singapore: Springer, pp 133–140.

Spear, R. (2004) 'Governance in democratic member-based organisations', *Annals of Public and Cooperative Economics*, 75(1): 33–60.

The Blockchain Socialist (2022) ' "Cowboy bebop" was a warning', *FWB*, 14 July. Available from www.fwb.help/wip/cowboy-bebop-web3-bount ies-blockchain-socialist [Accessed on 15 March 2023].

Thompson, A., Winn, E., Oates, G., Esber, J., Jin, L., Kanter, M., Mannan, M., Poux, P., Hubbard, S., Moore, S., Deleveaux, S., Scholz, T.R. and Hum, Q.Z. (2022) 'Toward a more cooperative Web3', SSRN, 14 December. Available from https://papers.ssrn.com/sol3/papers.cfm?abst ract_id=4302681 [Accessed on 15 March 2023].

Vieta, M., Quarter, J., Spear, R. and Moskovskaya, A. (2016) 'Participation in worker cooperatives' In Smith, D.H. Stebbins, R.A. and Grotz J. (eds) *The Palgrave Handbook of Volunteering, Civic Participation, and Nonprofit Associations*. London: Palgrave Macmillan UK.

Wood, A.J. and Lehdonvirta, V. (2021) 'Antagonism beyond employment: How the "subordinated agency" of labour platforms generates conflict in the remote gig economy', *Socio-Economic Review*, 19(4): 1369–1396.

Yamori, N., Harimaya, K. and Tomimura, K. (2017) 'Corporate governance structure and efficiencies of cooperative banks', *International Journal of Finance & Economics*, 22(4): 368–378.

Yeung, K. (2008) 'Towards an understanding of regulation by design'. In R. Brownsword and K. Yeung (eds) *Regulating Technologies*. London: Hart Publishing, pp 79–107.

'Our Club, Our Community, Our Future': Co-operation, Deindustrialization and Motherwell Football Club's Journey to Community Ownership

David Stewart

Introduction

During the 1980s the Scottish steel industry experienced 'death by a thousand cuts' due to the ruthless free market restructuring of the UK economy implemented by Margaret Thatcher's governments, which culminated in the closure of the vast Ravenscraig steelworks in 1992. The town of Motherwell in Lanarkshire, with a population of c.30,000, stood at the epicentre of the Scottish steel industry. The demise of bulk steelmaking not only generated mass unemployment and economic dislocation in Motherwell, it presented a challenge to the identity of the town, which was renowned as Scotland's 'Steelopolis' (Duncan, 1991, p 1). The local football team, Motherwell Football Club (FC), emerged from this scarring process as the last remaining symbol of local identity and pride. Yet, a decade on from Ravenscraig's closure, faced with declining attendances, falling television revenues and a spiralling wage bill following a short period of large-scale investment from a high-profile owner-investor, the club entered administration. This chapter analyses how a community-centred campaign to save Motherwell FC from extinction in 2002 evolved into a supporter takeover through the Well Society, which resulted in Motherwell FC becoming the first top division football club in Scotland and the UK to be supporter owned in 2016.

The chapter, which constitutes the first published academic account of Motherwell FC's journey to community ownership, is undergirded by a historical approach which analyses the factors underpinning supporter cooperative formation in their local socio-economic environment with a view to enabling the recent past to offer insights into contemporary social and economic trends. Deindustrialization forms the key reference point in the chapter, which interprets Motherwell FC's adoption of supporter ownership as a reaction against the detrimental effects of market liberalism on the local community since the 1980s. Existing scholarship on deindustrialization, influenced by E.P. Thompson's seminal work on 'the moral economy of the English crowd', has linked the strongly collectivist reaction to deindustrialization in Scotland to the prevalence of a working-class 'moral economy' perspective, which prioritized 'economic security' and 'control of resources' (Thompson, 1971; Phillips et al, 2021). The mass unemployment, deprivation and erosion of social capital which arose due to the Thatcher governments' market liberal restructuring was interpreted as an attack on communal as well as individual security (Perchard, 2013; Gibbs, 2018; Ferns, 2019). This chapter works within this conceptual space but breaks new ground by expanding analysis of 'the moral economy of deindustrialisation' beyond the confines of industrial politics, labour market restructuring and workplace culture to incorporate football supporter culture, a form of collective working-class cultural expression capable of bridging the recent industrial past and deindustrialized present. It is a key contention of the chapter that due to the ingrained nature of the working-class moral economy perspective within industrial communities that it adapted to the contraction of industry and remained central to popular understanding of economic and social activity in those communities. The chapter, therefore, attributes the Well Society's achievement of supporter ownership to the endurance of a working-class 'moral economy' view of community in Motherwell. This sense of community was grounded in a shared industrial identity preserved through the bond between the supporters and the football club and which remained intact despite harsh experience of market liberal orthodoxy.

The existing academic literature on supporter ownership in Europe does not engage with deindustrialization in any depth and largely overlooks the recent trend towards supporter ownership in Scottish football. The literature tends to concentrate on the most well-established examples of European supporter co-operatives, such as Barcelona, Athletico Bilbao, FC St Pauli and the German '50 + 1 model', and their roles as focal points for regional identity, political activism and anti-commercialism (Walton, 2005; Totten, 2014). When supporter ownership has been examined in the UK, its application in the English lower leagues has been the predominant focus, leading to the Anglo-centric perception developing that supporter co-operatives are confined to the lower echelons of British football. Relevant debate has emerged regarding the merits of the supporter trust model as a route to fan ownership. Peter and David Kennedy conclude that supporter trusts are prone to manipulation by club owners and governments who view them as a vehicle to commodify working-class social relations in order to create the illusion of a socially inclusive, market-based society (Kennedy and Kennedy, 2008). In contrast, Sean Hamil and Stephen Morrow trace the roots of supporter co-operation to the Rochdale Pioneers and identify mutual methods as a progressive, democratizing force (Hamil and Morrow, 2008). According to Morrow, Andrew Adams and Ian Thomson, supporter ownership represents a means of safeguarding struggling Scottish football clubs but is not necessarily suitable for all clubs (Adams et al, 2017). Despite noting Motherwell as an example where supporter ownership has proved successful, they identify the need for greater research into relations between club's owners and supporters and the 'social worlds' occupied by them to determine the wider applicability of mutualism across Scottish football. The chapter responds to their call by applying a moral economy approach to analysing how memories of the decimation of the local steel industry during the 1980s–90s and the near loss of their club in 2002 combined to convince Motherwell supporters of the merits of supporter co-operation.

'Death by a thousand cuts': Thatcher and the closure of the 'Craig

Steelmaking defined Motherwell and the surrounding area from the 1880s. When Motherwell FC was established in 1886 the shareholders were drawn overwhelmingly from the steel companies in the local area. As John Swinburne explains, 'Trades such as smelters, blacksmiths, roll turners, foundrymen, steelworkers, bridgebuilders, bell furnacemen, platers, forge rollers, moulders, hammermen, riveters, fitters, boiler makers, all indicate that the new Motherwell Football Club and the vast expanding Steelworks were growing together' (Swinburne, 1985, p 1). Although steelworkers became less prominent among the club shareholders following the adoption of a limited liability company form during the early 1900s, the fortunes of the club and the local steel industry remained closely intertwined (Crampsey, 1986). By the late 1950s the town's Ravenscraig steelworks, one of the largest steelworks in Western Europe, spanning one square mile and employing 7,000 workers, symbolized the might and dynamism of Scottish steelmaking (Payne, 1979). Ravenscraig was established as part of post-Second World War UK regional policy, which sought to maintain full employment by providing public subsidies to diversify and modernize local economies dependent upon staple industries. Regional policy was integral to securing consent for industrial restructuring as it was negotiated in consultation with trade unions and tied to alternative employment opportunities, which respected the emphasis within the working-class moral economy on collective rights and economic security. Originally operated by the Motherwell-based steel magnates, the Colvilles, Ravenscraig transferred ownership to the British state when the steel industry was nationalized in 1967 (Ovenden, 1978). Nationalization was welcomed for securing the future of the steel industry and generated a sense of communal ownership in the local area. However, nationalization ultimately took decision-making over the steelwork's future out of local hands and centralized decision-making in Whitehall instead. This left the industry badly exposed after 1979 when Margaret Thatcher's governments set about reducing the size of the traditional industries as part of their market liberal restructuring. Aggressively challenging the working-class moral economy, they contended that regional policy subsidies and state ownership constrained the profitability of industry and did not produce 'real jobs' (The Right Approach to the Economy: 1977). Between 1979 and 1982 Ravenscraig's workforce was slashed from 6,400 to 4,400 and by the time production ceased in 1992 the workforce had been further culled to 1,800 (STUC General Council Minutes: October–November 1982; *Motherwell Times*: 25 June 1992). Due to the strength of opposition to its closure the steelworks experienced a long, drawn out and traumatic process of 'death by a thousand cuts'. Following the privatization of British Steel in 1988, its management asserted that Ravenscraig's future would be determined 'by market conditions' (Aitken, 1997, p 294). The plant's decimated workforce broke productivity records to ensure that Ravenscraig was operating at a profit in a valiant but ultimately unsuccessful attempt to keep the steelworks open. When the 'Craig's closure was announced in May 1990, British Steel refused to divulge the commercial reasons behind the decision and was unwilling to place the plant's main asset, its strip mill, on the market, frustrating desperate attempts to find an alternative owner (*Motherwell Times*, 24 May 1990; STUC General Council Minutes: August 1990).

The sense of disempowerment generated by this experience was exacerbated by the Thatcher governments' adherence to a unitarist view of the UK which not only opposed Scottish independence but rejected the possibility of Scottish self-government within the Union (Stewart, 2009). Industrial communities in Scotland, such as Motherwell not only experienced accelerating deindustrialization but were also shorn of electoral agency to change government policy on this matter due to the growing divergence between Scottish and English voters which resulted in Thatcher being returned to power with landslide majorities by virtue of her support in southern England while her policies were rejected by an overwhelming majority of Scots. As Rob Duncan describes the explosion of local unemployment rates, which soared from 10.8 per cent in December 1978, reached 18.8 per cent in 1986 and peaked at 20 per cent in 1992, generated a 'negative climate of fear and disillusionment, but also of rage and resentment, among steel workers, especially in the Motherwell area' (Duncan, 2009, p 211). According to the Industrial Chaplin at Ravenscraig, Rev. John Potter, 'it was not just the individual that was redundant, it was communities'; for them the 'loss of identity was a significant blow', with communities like Motherwell 'struggling to find a new purpose and identity' amidst the ruins of heavy industry (Ferns, 2020, p 129).

The 'Souness Revolution' and the spirit of 1991

Amidst this scarring process of industrial loss, the working-class moral economy was also shaken by the application of Thatcherite principles to Scottish football. Since the 1890s the Glasgow-based 'Old Firm', Rangers and Celtic, had used sectarianism to dominate the Scottish football market in both commercial and sporting terms. However, during the early to mid-1980s their stranglehold on the game was challenged by the 'New Firm' of Aberdeen and Dundee United. Rangers responded in 1986 by launching the 'Souness Revolution'. Led by the triumvirate of former Liverpool and Scotland captain Graeme Souness, David Holmes and from 1988 the venture capitalist David Murray, this project sought to restore Rangers' status as Scottish sport's leading sporting and commercial institution by redrawing the market boundaries of Scottish football to a European level (Jamieson, 1997). Murray, who had made his fortune in the steel distribution sector, shared the Thatcher governments contempt for the working-class moral economy, and pursued a strategy which threatened local control of Scottish football clubs and their very existence as community resources (Thatcher, 1994). High-profile English and European players were signed at great expense in order to enhance Rangers' competitiveness in European club football. Rangers' attempts to 'modernise' Scottish football through these methods constrained the competitiveness of the Scottish League and generated a widening financial gulf with their Premier League rivals, including Celtic. Asserting that the Old Firm were subsidizing the rest of Scottish football through their large travelling supports and attraction of commercial sponsorship, Murray argued that market forces should determine the future of Scotland's many small community-based clubs which he viewed as a barrier to greater commercialization and competition within Scottish football. 'I mean no disrespect to Motherwell, but our fans now expect more ... The Motherwells, Dumbartons and Partick Thistles of this world will have to find their own level' (*Scotland on Sunday*, 15 January 1989).

British Steel's management shared Murray's callous disregard for community. Ronnie Mercer, the former Director of Ravenscraig between 1985–1989, explains that British Steel head office tried to veto his attempts to invest in hospitality at Motherwell FC's Fir Park stadium. Despite protesting that he 'could see Fir Park's floodlights from his office window',

Mercer was urged to focus instead on Rangers who 'were a much bigger club with worldwide publicity' (Newell, 2019). A small club, c.20 miles from Glasgow, with a regular home support of 3–4,000, Motherwell had experienced great financial turbulence during the early 1980s due to a combination of relegation and financial mismanagement. The paternalistic business model pursued by Motherwell in order to address these issues jarred with the 'globalising' market liberal thrust of the 'Souness Revolution' and demonstrated the salience of the moral economy within Lanarkshire. Under the modest and prudent stewardship of local butcher, John Chapman, the club's finances were carefully nursed back to health through an emphasis on local youth development and the accumulation of transfer fee income from the sale of those players (*Scottish Football Today Annual*, 1988). Contrasting its community ethos with the aggressive sectarianism of the Old Firm and the commercialism of Rangers, Motherwell were promoted as an inclusive 'family club'. Solidarity with local steelworkers was displayed by incorporating Ravenscraig into the club crest in 1982 and by making Fir Park available to host rallies in support of the local steel industry, thus generating a strong sense of communal attachment to the club (Johnstone, 2021). Sensitive to the deteriorating industrial situation in the town, a children's supporters' club, the Claret and Amber Club, was established to facilitate subsidized entry to Fir Park, free tickets were distributed among the unemployed and subsidized supporters' buses were organized to maximize the club's travelling support (*Scottish Football League Review Season 1988–89*, 1989). The heightened sense of communality generated by this strategy peaked during Motherwell's 1991 Scottish Cup run which saw the club defy the odds to win the trophy in the shadow of the impending closure of Ravenscraig (Swinburne, 1991). The final against Dundee United, described as the 'Family Final', was watched by 30,000 Motherwell supporters, and the thrilling 4–3 victory was dedicated by the players and manager, Tommy McLean, to the local people (McLean, 2013). The scale of community mobilization generated by Motherwell's Scottish Cup win offered hope that the town could resist the demoralizing effects of deindustrialization and directly challenged the Souness Revolution's crude market liberal vision for Scottish football which denigrated the working-class moral economy. The 1991 cup win, therefore, underlined Motherwell FC's importance within Lanarkshire as a rallying point for community pride and symbol of local identity.

The rise and fall of the 'third force' strategy

As the 1990s progressed the trends initiated by the 'Souness Revolution' intensified. In an attempt to emulate the wealthiest clubs in England, the Scottish Premier League (SPL) severed ties with the Scottish Football League in 1997 in order to maximize television revenue and limit the redistribution of income across the Scottish leagues. During this period the business model followed by Motherwell under Chapman's tenure started to unravel due to the liberalization of the European transfer market through the Bosman ruling. By denying the club transfer fee income for players when their contracts expired and only offering 'compensation payments' to cover the departure of former youth team players, the Bosman ruling disincentivized investment in the club's youth system. With Chapman struggling to find the finance to compensate for reduced transfer fee income, the entrepreneur, John Boyle, who had recently sold Direct Holidays for a huge profit, agreed to take over the club in 1998. A Lanarkshire man, whose father had run a grocer's shop in the shadow of Ravenscraig, Boyle emphasized that his mission was to aid the regeneration of the former industrial community (*Motherwell Times*, 27 August 1998). There was a sharp contrast with Chapman's understated stewardship of the club, as Boyle channelled his flamboyant personality into the role of owner-investor. Boyle sought to compete with the Old Firm on their own terms by blending the market liberal methods pioneered by Rangers during the 'Souness Revolution' with pump priming of the local market. Record transfer fees were invested in high earning imports from England and entry prices were slashed as part of the 'Football for a Fiver' initiative as Boyle sought to make Motherwell Scottish football's 'third force' (*The Well*, 16 December 1998). Despite enjoying some initial success in boosting attendances, Boyle's massive investment did not translate into success on or off the park. According to former chief executive, Pat Nevin, Boyle had little understanding of how to run a football club and grew disillusioned as the losses started to mount and the media attention diminished (*Sunday Herald*: 14 September 2003).

In April 2002, Boyle's 'third force' strategy ended in dramatic fashion. Following the Old Firm's decision to veto the SPL's plans for its own subscription-based television channel, which left Motherwell with a budget shortfall of c.£1.8–c.2.1 million, Boyle plunged the club into interim administration and sacked 19 players in the process (*Motherwell Times*, 2 May 2002). The 'third force' strategy proved such a spectacular failure because the market liberal methods of the 'Souness Revolution' and a commitment to local community proved incompatible. The huge investment in player wages created a gulf with the club's support base many of whom were either unemployed or found themselves in low paid, insecure work as part of the deindustrialized Lanarkshire economy. Due to this, the supporters became increasingly alienated from the high earning, underperforming squad. The unravelling of the club's ailing finances was widely predicted by the supporters, but due to the nature of the owner-investor model they possessed no agency to influence the management of the club. The Motherwell supporters' website, FirParkCorner.Com, summarizes the situation succinctly: 'Essentially the reason Motherwell entered administration was to save a rich man from losing £12m rather than merely £9m from following through on contracts he had agreed to pay' (FirParkCorner.Com, 2012). Despite noting that 'there was little sympathy on offer' for the sacked players, they acknowledged that administration 'did hurt, in a much smaller way, a host of minor creditors and "normal people" lost their jobs too – something which should lie heavily on the conscience of the multi-millionaire who made the decision to put them at risk'. According to the website this 'left a stain on our history which can never be cleansed'. Therefore, Boyle's 'third force strategy' transgressed the moral economy by undermining the economic security of the club and exacerbated the effects of deindustrialization within Lanarkshire by further sapping community pride.

This in turn provoked a powerful moral economy reaction among Motherwell supporters focused on securing the future of the club as a community resource. This moral economy view identified the Old Firm's exploitation of sectarian divisions within the local community as central to undermining Boyle's attempts to widen the club's support base (*Waiting for the Great Leap Forward*, May 2002). Hostility towards the highly paid playing squad and the Old Firm was valuable in maintaining supporter unity, and this solidarity was channelled into the 'Well Worth Saving Campaign'. Prior to attending the press conference at which the club's entry to administration was announced, Boyle consulted with four supporters who were viewed as influential within the support base (Johnstone, 2021). Those supporters would become integral to organizing grassroots fundraising through the 'Well Worth Saving Campaign'. Despite grasping the urgency behind the fundraising effort, other supporters took a dim view of Boyle's chosen method of consulting the support base, which meant that the board 'knew the opinions of four fans when they could've had the views of four thousand! It seems that the club, yet again, are treating the punters with contempt' (*Waiting for the Great Leap Forward*, May 2002). This emphasis on greater inclusion and consultation crystallized into calls for a share issue to 'open the club up to the fans'. The chosen vehicle to articulate these demands was a hastily assembled Motherwell Supporters' Trust, committed to 'the full, accountable, democratic and constructive involvement of the supporters in the running and direction of the Club, including the principle of supporter involvement on the Board of Motherwell Football Club' (*Waiting for the Great Leap Forward*, August 2002).

However, the biggest stumbling block to achieving fan ownership was the £10 million debt owed by the club, which led the administrators to rule out the feasibility of a supporter takeover. Despite having its chairman, Martin Rose, appointed to the club board in September 2003, the Trust made little headway in enhancing its representation on the board or securing a meaningful shareholding in the club. Instead, the Trust concentrated on raising funds to keep the club alive while a new owner was sought

(Steelmen Online, 2009). Its major contribution in moral economy terms was to pressure Boyle to fulfil his obligations to the local community when another benefactor was not forthcoming. This meant that when Motherwell eventually emerged out of administration in 2004, Boyle remained as owner. Nonetheless, the Trust's experience reinforces warnings about the risks of supporters being exploited for commercial purposes by the club hierarchies they seek to replace (Kennedy and Kennedy, 2008). The outcome of the administration process was an awkward compromise which left the ownership of the club unchanged and the Supporters' Trust continuing to raise considerable funds while remaining devoid of a meaningful say in how the club was run. In the interim, having written off £8 million of debt owed to himself, Boyle continued to cut costs in order to reduce the club's dependence on his personal finances. This process brought him into conflict with season ticket holders in the Davie Cooper Stand who were required to relocate to another part of the stadium for matches against the Old Firm in order to maximize ticket revenue. Boyle's unbending market liberal stance soured relations with the club's hardcore support and damaged the credibility of the Supporters' Trust which proved powerless despite having representation on the club board (*Waiting for the Great Leap Forward*: September 2005).

Launching the 'Motherwell Revolution': the birth of the Well Society

In Spring 2011, with a buyer still not forthcoming, Boyle turned to the moral economy to break the stasis over the club's ownership by announcing plans to relinquish his 73 per cent shareholding and 'place it at the disposal of the local community'. While remaining open to approaches from any local owner-investors, Boyle explained that his preferred outcome was to 'sell ownership of the club – one member, one share, one vote – to those fans who wish to participate' (Boyle, 2011). Following consultation with the Supporters' Trust an industrial and provident society, the Well Society, was established to facilitate the move to supporter ownership. Work previously undertaken by the Supporters' Trust within the local community was to be continued under the auspices of a charitable body, the Motherwell FC Community Trust. Despite referring to this initiative as the 'Motherwell Revolution', Boyle adopted an incremental approach. Although the supporters were set the overall target of raising £1.5 million to secure Boyle's shares and generate a reserve to cover financial shortfalls, he initially asked the fans to raise £250,000 by March 2012 before the club would consent to handing over the running of the Well Society to them. The money was to be raised through a subscription scheme, with the minimum contribution set at £300 (*The Herald*, 13 March 2012). Boyle and the club's chief executive, Leanne Dempster, worked on the assumption that if most of the club's c.4,000 season ticket holders could be converted then supporter ownership would rapidly become a reality (*Wishaw Press*, 19 June 2013).

However, mixed messaging over the Well Society's purpose risked strangling it at birth. Some club directors, such as Andrew Wilson, had a clear moral economy vision of a 'membership cooperative' operating on a one member, one vote basis, which would over a period of a couple of years result in a fully elected club board (*The Herald*, 7 December 2011). Yet other club directors and Supporters' Trust representatives adopted a much looser and more capitalistic interpretation of community ownership which viewed the enhanced involvement of supporters and local businesses as a way of 'diversifying the funding base' (*Wishaw Press*, 2 March 2011; *Wishaw Press*, 13 July 2011). Indeed, Boyle's embrace of the moral economy remained open to question as he emphasized that in the short-term, at least, he envisaged the Well Society playing a key role in helping the club to manage any future cash flow difficulties which had until that point been handled by him. This generated contrasting concerns among the support base. Fans who were already frustrated by the Supporters' Trust's ineffective attempts to represent supporter interests on the club board feared that the board would take the fans' investment without offering the Well Society a meaningful say over club affairs. Meanwhile, others doubted the viability of the proposed fan ownership model due to the perceived incompetence of their fellow supporter representatives in representing their interests up until that point. Former Well Society marketing manager, Craig Hughes, explains that this section of the club's support 'believed that under fan ownership things would change drastically', and maintains that once they were reassured that the club would still be 'run properly' with the fans just having 'more of a say', they tended to be converted (Club Development Scotland, 2018). In reality, however, during these early stages many supporters remained sceptical on the grounds that they already contributed enough as season ticket holders, did not believe that Boyle would allow the club to fold or concerns that the club had too few supporters for the supporter co-operative model to be viable (Steelmen Online, 2012–2021).

Therefore, during the spring-summer of 2012 the Well Society grasped the opportunity offered by Rangers' dramatic liquidation to make the case for supporter ownership. Rangers' bankruptcy represented the ultimate failure of the market liberal orthodoxy which had gripped Scottish football since the 'Souness Revolution'. Having over-spent on players' salaries in a vain attempt to sustain regular Champions League qualification and negotiate entry to the English Premier League, the scale of debt generated by the club's reckless profligacy and cavalier accounting practices eventually resulted in Rangers being declared bankrupt (Morrow, 2015). On the field, Rangers' liquidation coincided with an upsurge in Motherwell's playing fortunes which presented the club with a unique opportunity to take Rangers' place in the prestigious Champions League qualifying rounds. However, it also posed a dilemma as with no realistic prospect of progressing to the lucrative Champions' League group stages the club was faced with the choice between allowing a rapidly formed Rangers 'Newco' to immediately 're-join' the SPL or to accept a steep fall in revenue arising from reduced gate receipts and the renegotiation of television broadcasting rights following the loss of what broadcasters considered to be the SPL's main asset: the Old Firm derby.

Motherwell's board heavily implied that refusal to admit the Rangers 'Newco' to the SPL would threaten the economic viability of supporter ownership (*Motherwell Times*, 20 June 2012; *Motherwell Times*, 27 June 2012). Well Society board member, Derek Wilson, argues that 'because they were worried about losing the revenue they [Rangers] brought to the league if that was a decision solely for chief executives and chairmen, it would have happened' (*Tribune*, 25 April 2021). However, the club kept faith with democratic, cooperative principle and agreed to consult Well Society members before taking a final decision. Wilson explains, 'Our members unanimously voted to keep them in the third tier. It caused a massive backlash from Rangers fans, but ultimately it was our fans making the decisions about what Motherwell should be doing – and saying there's a principle involved.' The way in which the club honoured the outcome of the ballot was highly significant as it demonstrated to the fans that unlike the Supporters' Trust, the Well Society would possess the agency to take key strategic decisions. According to Wilson this cultivated ownership consciousness by conveying the clear and simple message that through the Well Society, 'You know you can take these decisions. These decisions are in your hands' (Newell, 2019). Supporter ownership, therefore, came to be promoted by the Well Society as a way of empowering the supporters to resist the market liberal logic which had entrenched the Old Firm's dominance of Scottish football since the 'Souness Revolution' and redressing this inequity through the application of democratic, cooperative principle. This moral economy vision was reflected in the Society's recruiting slogan: 'Our Club, Our Community, Our Future'.

Finding the spark: supporter co-operation and industrial identity

Nonetheless, the most formidable obstacle to growing the Well Society's membership was the state of the deindustrialized Lanarkshire economy. Shorn of well paid, skilled industrial work and with unemployment and poverty rates well above the Scottish and UK averages, Motherwell was particularly badly exposed to the negative effects of austerity UK government policies following the banking crisis of 2007–2008 (Scottish Index of Multiple Deprivation, 2012). Although the supporters raised the capital to assume control of the Well Society on schedule, which secured a 15 per cent stake in the club and unlocked the opportunity to elect two representatives onto the club board, soon after question marks were raised over the capacity of the supporters to raise the remaining £1.25 million that Boyle stipulated would be required to secure majority ownership of the club (*Wishaw Press*, 4 April 2012). Well Society members adopted the moral economy view that they had 'a duty of care to support not only the football team, but the local community in these times of financial hardship' and initiated the organization of food bank collections on match days to show solidarity with the local community (*Motherwell Times*, 12 December 2014). Yet, as the Treasurer of the Central Branch Supporters' Association, Christopher Hutton, explained due to financial worries 'people that I've spoken to who haven't invested in it, they just don't see it as a long-term option' (*The Scotsman*, 25 November 2014). Therefore, during the spring of 2014 with Well Society membership plateauing around 1,250, having converted only a quarter of season ticket holders, and the club posting losses of £780,000 for the previous two years, Boyle lost patience and issued the Well Society with an ultimatum (*The Scotsman*, 22 May 2014). Boyle gave the fans six months to raise the £800,000 required to become majority shareholders or he would sell his shareholding to the highest bidder (*The Herald*, 25 April 2014). With the club rapidly running out of money and a London-based South American consortium expressing interest in buying the club, the Well Society's hopes of taking ownership of the club hung in the balance until the intervention of the Barbados based, Wishaw born multi-millionaire, Les Hutchison in December 2014 (*Scottish Daily Mail*, 16 May 2018). At the behest of his Motherwell-supporting daughter, Hutchison agreed to buy the remainder of Boyle's shares and provide the club with interest free working capital over a five-year period in order to move the club towards a financially self-funded footing and allow the supporters sufficient time to build the capital to take full ownership of the club (Motherwell FC, 2015).

Hutchison's motivations for supporting the Well Society were not football related and stemmed from his appreciation of the town's industrial past and his own personal story of business success. Hutchison had worked at British Steel, Motherwell Bridge and Anderson Strathclyde and emphasized that 'Bellshill, Motherwell, Carluke, Wishaw and those surrounding areas were frequently in the press because of British Steel, because of Motherwell Bridge, because of Anderson Strathclyde and so on, but now that they're gone the area is only ever talked about in the context of the football club' (Hutchison, 2015). He and the Well Society shared the view that rather than viewing the 'industrial devastation' of the local area as an insurmountable barrier to achieving fan ownership, the supporters should tap into the spirit shown by the local community in adjusting to these changes when making the case for supporter ownership. Tom Feely, a member of the Well Society board since its formation in 2012, identifies parallels between the football club and the steelworks as fixtures of everyday life and shared community identity. Having lost Ravenscraig and supporting industries, 'which were of course central to everything that went on here in the past and almost every person here either worked in that sector in the past or at least knows many people who did', he explains that the Well Society highlighted the potentially regenerative effects of community ownership as a way of 'bringing better days back to this area' (Feely, 2021). Then club captain, Keith Lasley, amplified this point when supporting the Well Society's campaigning: 'It's a tight-knit community in Motherwell and we've seen that in response to issues such as the steelworks closure. The whole community comes together and the football club is a place to do that' (*Daily Record*, 26 November 2015).

For former steelworkers the attraction of supporter ownership was both psychological and social. Membership of the Well Society filled some of the void left by the loss of skilled industrial employment and cemented their bond with former workmates: 'That's how we kept in touch wisn't it through going to see the football. We still do'. Supporter ownership 'just sort o' bonds you together' (Newell, 2019). The overriding message was that the economic security of the club and the local community were interlinked. Derek Wilson contends that 'if something like the steelworks was owned by the people then potentially it might still be up and running just now' (Newell, 2019). This emphasis on bringing the club under local, collective, democratic control in order to safeguard its future countered market liberal logic that fan ownership represented too big a financial risk for a small club in a former industrial community. Moreover, it greatly strengthened the case for community ownership by linking it to the town's industrial identity which was synonymous with collective solidarity. Indeed, when the last remaining steelworks in Motherwell, Dalzell slab mill, was faced with closure in the autumn of 2015 the Well Society rallied behind the campaign to save it by joining local marches and issuing the club's players with 'Save our Steel' T-shirts on match days, helping to stimulate Scottish government intervention to secure a buyer for the steelworks.

Solidarity of this sort made the Well Society's equation of supporter ownership with community ownership appear less abstract. It enabled the Society to argue that supporter ownership would hand control of the club to the local community which unlike a potential outside owner would have the best interests of the community at heart. As Well Society Board member, Markus Schieren, explains, supporter ownership is about 'not relying on any people who spend money in order to rule like those big billionaires, but get the club back to the people and let them support their own team' (Newell, 2019). The work of the Community Trust in supporting 37,000 local people through the provision of free meals for school children, dementia support and youth unemployment programmes was highlighted to demonstrate the egalitarian community ethos that could be developed under supporter ownership (Radio Clyde, 2015). Hutchison adhered to a moral economy approach in that he grasped 'the importance of the football club as a community asset'. Through his investment in the club, the Well Society was able to start addressing the main shortcomings of Boyle's plan for supporter ownership: the assumption that season ticket holders could afford to join the Well Society and the limited administrative support at the Well Society's disposal. Hutchison paid for the appointment of a general manager to organize a recruitment drive. This uncovered discrepancies in the Well Society's membership records which had resulted in some supporters discontinuing their subscriptions or only making one off payments (Steelmen Online, 2012–2021). Most significantly, Hutchison's input enabled the Well Society to lower the minimum annual cost of membership from £300 to £60 and restructure the payment method to facilitate monthly direct debit payments (*Evening Times*: 29 July 2015). A revised target of 2,000 members, paying an average of £10 per month, was identified as a marker of financial sustainability which once reached would trigger the shift to supporter ownership (*Scottish Daily Mail*, 17 March 2016).

By early 2016 the more inclusive membership structure and enhanced marketing and administration had helped to expand Well Society membership to c.1,700 (*Daily Record*, 17 March 2016). However, Hutchison's presence at the helm of the club was not unproblematic. His insensitivity to the harsh realities of the market liberal economy highlighted the class gulf between him and the local community. By urging supporters to cut back on a couple of cups of coffee a week in order to afford Well Society membership, Hutchison alienated low paid and unemployed supporters and risked undermining the Society's emphasis on community solidarity (*Scottish Daily Mail*, 17 March 2016). Furthermore, the media spotlight on Hutchison's wealth conflicted with the Well Society's efforts to develop ownership consciousness as it entrenched the pre-existing view among sceptical supporters that the adoption of supporter ownership might not be necessary with a person of Hutchison's business acumen in charge. Due to this, and despite the Well Society not having yet reached the benchmark of 2,000 members, in March 2016 Hutchison announced his intention to sell his stake in the club to the Well Society for £1 and for the club to transition to majority fan ownership by the end of that year. As part of the handover deal agreed in October 2016, and in keeping with the philanthropic nature of Hutchison's intervention, an agreement was reached that all money owed to Hutchison on loan repayments would be taken only from a percentage of transfer fee income for the first three years (*The Herald*, 29 October 2016). The response to Hutchison's departure and the advent of fan ownership was tangible. By February 2017 the Well Society had reached the 2,000-member target, and by the end of the following season, when the club reached both domestic cup finals, membership had further expanded to 2,500. At the time of writing Well Society membership now exceeds 3,500 members and incorporates the entire playing squad and management team (*Motherwell Times*, 13 February 2017; Motherwell FC, 25 November 2022). Derek Wilson explains this awakening to the benefits of supporter co-operation in emotive moral economy terms: 'having something that brings so much pride to the town and community ringfenced through that security, that it's owned by the people that it means so much to is maybe one of the reasons it's gonnae be a success and why we're gonnae keep fighting and make sure that the Well Society works' (Newell, 2019).

Conclusion

The chapter, therefore, reveals how historical analysis of the 'moral economy of deindustrialisation' can enhance understanding of the appeal of supporter cooperative forms of community ownership in former industrial communities. The intertwining of supporter co-operation with the working-class moral economy was part of a historical process stemming from the local community in Motherwell's experience of deindustrialization. Huw Beynon and Ray Hudson highlight the inter-relationship between 'the erosion of the historical identities' of former industrial communities and the associated diminution of 'sense of self' which has accompanied the loss of industry (Beynon and Hudson, 2021, pp 336–338). In effect, the fiercely contested transition from industrial to deindustrial society created a demand for new support structures to sustain the social fabric of the affected communities. This chapter contends that the Well Society emerged in response to this pressing social and cultural need. Supporter ownership represented a way for the local community to exert an element of democratic collective control over the town's destiny after a period of sustained disempowerment. The Well Society's emphasis on Motherwell supporters' shared industrial heritage facilitated the intergenerational transmission of working-class moral economy values in a way that reinforced community solidarity and identified supporter co-operation as a vehicle to enable the local community to move on from the loss of Ravenscraig while retaining its historic communal identity. The memory of the 1991 Scottish Cup win, achieved in the backdrop of Ravenscraig's closure, was used to highlight the bond between the club and the community and to identify the vibrant community solidarity that supporter ownership had the potential to generate. Motherwell supporters, therefore, became cooperators through a combination of local pride, a shared sense of working-class community and harsh experience of market liberalism.

When summarizing the ethos that guided the Well Society along the path to ownership of the club, Well Society board member Jason Henderson reflects that:

> first and foremost it is about that community spirit ... the history of the club, the history of the town with the steelworks and things like that. I think it's about that identity and community spirit. About coming together under the banner of something, and working together not just for the benefit of 11 players on a Saturday but for the benefit of the community. (Club Development Scotland, 2018)

The journey to fan ownership was a struggle for the Well Society which had to negotiate the challenges posed by the financial insecurity which gripped the deindustrialized Lanarkshire economy and the cynicism and apathy towards supporter ownership arising from this. Throughout this process the memory of the loss of the steelworks and an enduring sense of communal identity built upon pride in Motherwell's industrial past helped to sustain the drive towards supporter ownership. So too did the memory of administration and the near loss of the club. In that respect fan ownership emerged as a moral economy inspired reaction against market liberal orthodoxy and its harmful effects on the community's economic and social wellbeing since the 1980s.

From the outset, the Motherwell support was divided between those who felt unable to afford to participate, a sceptical hardcore and those who were committed to 'finding a way' to play their part by joining the Well Society and selling the vision of supporter ownership among their fellow supporters. The sceptics distrusted the motives of the club's owners, questioned the necessity of fan ownership and doubted the ability of the Well Society to run the club (Steelmen Online, 2012–2021). Converting those supporters proved a major challenge. Working in co-partnership with the club's owners proved vital to the moral economy approach but fuelled suspicion that the Society was not representative of the support base or sufficiently independent from the club's owners. Unwilling to attack the operation of the owner-investor model at Fir Park due to their reliance on the goodwill of the club's owners, the Well Society instead exploited the opportunity offered by the liquidation of Rangers to promote the merits of supporter co-operation. Rangers' plight not only reminded Motherwell supporters of the risks posed by the unaccountable owner-investor model which had led the club to the brink of extinction in 2002, it exploded the myth that market liberalism correlated with financial sustainability. The crisis enabled the Well Society to construct its own 'moral economy' vision by demonstrating the levelling effect that democratic cooperative principles could exert on decision-making within the club and Scottish football more widely. This led to a positive contrast being drawn between the Well Society's interpretation of the moral economy, which entailed harnessing community ownership to strengthen the economic security of the local community and reinvigorate communal pride, and the corrosive effects on community cohesion stemming from the Old Firm's exploitation of sectarianism for sporting and commercial gain. The campaign for supporter ownership, therefore, did not develop into a struggle to wrest control from the club's owners but was projected as a way of galvanizing community solidarity and rejecting subservience to the Old Firm.

The voluntary cooperative principle guided the Well Society throughout the journey to supporter ownership. The Society came to accept that the aim of converting all season ticket holders was unrealistic and concentrated instead on building a coalition of the willing. This emphasis on the voluntary principle informed the Society's commitment to inclusivity and was underpinned by understanding of the harsh reality of working-class life in the former industrial community. The Society recognized that unemployment, insecure work and low wages represented the main barrier to growing the membership. Food Bank collections aimed to forge a bond of solidarity with the local community by offering support to fans who were struggling to feed their families while condoning their inability to afford to join the Society. Under Hutchison's tenure there was shared recognition of the need to widen access to the Well Society by lowering membership costs in order to ensure the long-term financial viability of the supporter cooperative model (*Daily Record*, 15 December 2014). The lowering of the cost of membership and introduction of direct debit payments opened up membership to supporters who had previously felt excluded on financial grounds. This emphasis on voluntarism and inclusivity prevented a polarizing divide emerging within the club's small support base, which would have proved fatal to achieving supporter ownership. When Hutchison opted to sell the club to the Well Society earlier than planned, it enabled low-income supporters and sceptics, who recognized that it was 'now or never', to join without being stigmatized as late converts. Through this inclusive though paternalistic form of voluntary co-operation, the Well Society's takeover of the club in 2016 and subsequent expansion of its membership demonstrated the viability of supporter ownership as an alternative business model for small to medium-sized clubs competing in top division Scottish football.

Since 2016, fellow SPL clubs Heart of Midlothian and St Mirren have followed Motherwell's example in embracing community ownership, thus generating optimism regarding a 'structured transition' to supporter ownership in Scottish football. The Chief Executive of Supporters Direct Scotland, Alan Russell, attributes growing enthusiasm for community ownership to the prevalence of left-of-centre collectivist values within Scottish society (SD Europe, 2021). This case study links those values specifically to the working-class moral economy. The moral economy vision of supporter co-operation articulated by the Well Society reflected a distinct form of working-class mutuality, based around community institutions, and capable of reforming economic and social relations through its own associational activity (Yeo, 1988). The chapter contends that due to the ingrained nature of the working-class moral economy perspective within Lanarkshire, it adapted to the contraction of industry and remained central to popular understanding of economic and social activity. This case study, therefore, presents a challenge to the dominant scholarly view that the future of co-operation lies in post-industrial ethical causes and the delivery of public services by demonstrating the ongoing salience of voluntary co-operation in former industrial communities when it remains relevant to their social and cultural needs (Webster et al, 2016; Huckfield, 2021). Since the 1980s the presence of co-operatives in former industrial areas has declined in tandem with deindustrialization (Walton, 2009). As this case study of the former steel town of Motherwell demonstrates, supporter cooperative forms of community ownership can re-establish co-operation at the heart of former industrial communities and assist their adaptation to deindustrialization by tapping into their passion for football and histories of collective community solidarity. Supporter co-operatives, such as the Well Society, can help to fill the gap of industrial absence and retain a sense of place in communities previously defined by industrial activities. They possess the latent potential to challenge these communities' subjugation to market liberal orthodoxy and replenish working-class social capital. This raises the prospect of a distinct Scottish contribution to European supporter ownership in the form of a strong working-class strand of co-operation, shaped by the experience of deindustrialization, attuned to collective, democratic values and rooted in a moral economy view of community ownership.

References

Adams, A., Morrow, S. and Thomson, I. (2017) 'Changing boundaries and evolving organisational forms in football: Novelty and variety among Scottish clubs', *Journal of Sport Management*, 31(2): 161–175.

Aitken, I. (1997) *The Bairns O' Adam: The Story of the STUC*. Edinburgh: Polygon.

Beynon, H. and Hudson, R. (2021) *The Shadow of the Mine: Coal and the End of Industrial Britain*. London: Verso.

Boyle, J. (2011) 'Motherwell FC – farewell'. Available from www.youtube.com/watch?v=NK7zTpaCslo [Accessed on 20 June 2021].

Club Development Scotland (nd) 'Motherwell FC fan ownership one year on'. Available from www.youtube.com/watch?v=xhSyy4nwGZI [Accessed on 22 July 2021].

Crampsey, R.A. (1986) *The Economics of Scottish Professional Football*. Glasgow: Scottish Curriculum Development Service.

Daily Record, 13 February 2013.

Daily Record, 15 December 2014.

Daily Record, 26 November 2015.

Daily Record, 17 March 2016.

Duncan, R. (1991) *Steelopolis: The Making of Motherwell c.1750–1939*. Motherwell: Motherwell District Council Leisure Services.

Duncan, R. (2009) *Sons of Vulcan: Ironworkers and Steelmen in Scotland*. Edinburgh: Birlinn.

Evening Times, 29 July 2015.

Evening Times, 18 April 2018.

Feely, T. (2021) Email correspondence with author.

Ferns, J. (2019) 'Workers' identities in transition: Deindustrialisation and Scottish steelworkers', *Journal of Working-Class Studies*, 4(2): 55–78.

Ferns, J. (2020) '"The Iron Lady? She devastated the country": Former Scottish Steelworkers' narratives of unions, community and Thatcherism'. In Mullen, A., Farrall, S. and Jeffery, D. (eds) *Thatcherism in the 21st Century*. London: Palgrave Macmillan, pp 117–138.

FirParkCorner.Com (2012) 'Ten years on – a new attitude prevails'. Available from www.motherwell-mad.co.uk/feat/edx3/ten_years_on__a_new_attit ude_prevails_740546/index.shtml [Accessed on 4 March 2022].

Gibbs, E. (2018) 'The moral economy of the Scottish coalfields: Managing deindustrialisation under nationalisation c.1947–1983', *Enterprise and Society*, 19(1): 124–152.

Glasgow Caledonian University Research Collections: Archives, Scottish Trades Union Congress, General Council Minutes, October–November 1982, A Future for Steel – A Future for Scotland.

Hamil, S. and Morrow, S. (2008) 'The people's game?', *Scottish Left Review*, 47(2): 7–9.

Huckfield, L. (2021) *How Blair Killed the Co-ops: Reclaiming Social Enterprise from its Neoliberal Turn*. Manchester: Manchester University Press.

Hutchison, L. (2015) 'Les Hutchison talks about Well Society takeover'. Available from www.youtube.com/watch?v=U6HSJMeIVOQ [Accessed on 29 July 2021].

Jamieson, S. (1997) *Graeme Souness: The Ibrox Revolution and the Legacy of the Iron Lady's Man*. Edinburgh: Mainstream.

Johnstone, M. (2021) *The Weird and Wonderful World of Motherwell Football Collectables, Volume 1*. Aldridge: Curtis Sport.

Kennedy, D. and Kennedy P. (2008) 'Preserving and extending the commodification of football supporter relations: A cultural economy of Supporters Direct', *Sociological Research Online*, 12(1): 12–25.

McLean, T. (2013) *Football in the Blood: My Autobiography*. Edinburgh: Black and White.

Morrow, S. (2015) 'Power and logics in Scottish football: The financial collapse of Rangers FC', *Sport, Business and Management: An International Journal*, 5(4): 325–343.

Motherwell FC (2015) Official Newsletter email, 31 January.

Motherwell FC (2022) 'Well Society membership hits 3,500'. Available from www.motherwellfc.co.uk/2022/11/25/well-society-membership-hits-3500/ [Accessed on 27 November 2022].

Motherwell Times, 24 May 1990.

Motherwell Times, 25 June 1992.

Motherwell Times, 27 August 1998.

Motherwell Times, 2 May 2002.

Motherwell Times, 20 June 2012.

Motherwell Times, 27 June 2012.

Motherwell Times, 12 December 2014.

Motherwell Times, 13 February 2017.

Newell, J. (2019) 'Motherwell FC: We own the future', SwitchHit Productions. Available from www.bbc.co.uk/programmes/p078qllg [Accessed on 12 July 2021].

Ovenden, K. (1978) *The Politics of Steel*. London: Macmillan.

Payne, P. (1979) *Colvilles and the Scottish Steel Industry*. Oxford: Oxford University Press.

Perchard, A. (2013) '"Broken men" and "Thatcher's Children"': Memory and legacy in Scotland's coalfields', *International Labor and Working-Class History*, 84(1): 78–98.

Phillips, J., Wright, V. and Tomlinson, J. (2021) *Deindustrialisation and the Moral Economy in Scotland since 1955*. Edinburgh: Edinburgh University Press.

Radio Clyde (2015) 'Interview with Les Hutchison'. Available from www.youtube.com/watch?v=0lr4tz5dfsc [Accessed on 29 July 2021].

Scotland on Sunday, 15 January 1989.

Scottish Daily Mail, 17 March 2016.

Scottish Daily Mail, 16 May 2018.

Scottish Football League Review Season 1988–89 (1989) Glasgow: Scottish Football League.

Scottish Football Today Annual 2 (1988) Edinburgh: John Donald.

Scottish Index of Multiple Deprivation 2012. Available from https://simd.scot/#/simd2012/BTTTFTT/13/-4.0000/55.7850/ [Accessed on 31 May 2022].

SD Europe.eu (2021) 'Foresight not crisis: How Scottish football clubs are moving into fan ownership'. Available from www.sdeurope.eu/post/foresight-not-crisis-how-scottish-football-clubs-are-moving-into-fan-owners hip [Accessed on 18 May 2022].

Scottish Trades Union Congress, General Council Minutes, August 1990, Ravenscraig Works: Some Thoughts for the Shareholders of British Steel Plc.

Steelmen Online (2009) Available from www.steelmenonline.co.uk/forums/index.php?/topic/1473-mst-open-meeting/page/3/&tab=comments#comment-44517 [Accessed on 20 June 2022].

Steelmen Online (2012–2021) Available from www.steelmenonline.co.uk/forums/index.php?/topic/12411-the-well-society/&tab=comments#comment-327634 [Accessed on 28 February 2022].

Stewart, D. (2009) *The Path to Devolution and Change: A Political History of Scotland under Margaret Thatcher*. London: I.B. Tauris.

Sunday Herald, 14 September 2003.

Swinburne, J. (1985) *A History of the Steelmen, 1886–1986*, Motherwell: Motherwell Football and Athletic Club.

Swinburne, J. (1991) *Well Worth the Wait: The Story of Motherwell's Epic Cup Triumph*. Edinburgh: Mainstream.

Thatcher, M. (1994) *The Downing Street Years*. London: Harper-Collins.

The Herald, 7 December 2011.

The Herald, 13 March 2012.

The Herald, 25 April 2014.

The Herald, 29 October 2016.

The Right Approach to the Economy (1977) London: Conservative Party.

The Scotsman, 22 May 2014.

The Scotsman, 25 November 2014.

The Well – Match Programme, 16 December 1998.

Thompson, E.P. (1971) 'The moral economy of the English crowd in the eighteenth century', *Past and Present*, 50(1): 76–136.

Totten, M. (2014) 'Sport activism and political praxis within the FC Sankt Pauli Fan Subculture', *Soccer and Society*, 16(4): 453–68.

Tribune, 25 April 2021. Available from https://tribunemag.co.uk/2021/04/how-motherwell-is-leading-the-way-for-fan-owned-football [Accessed on 16 September 2021].

Vincent, M. (2016) 'How the DIY scene is different when you're Black'. *The FADER*. Available from www.thefader.com/2016/06/30/how-the-diy-scene-is-different-when-youre-black [Accessed on 8 December 2017].

Waiting for the Great Leap Forward, 44 (2002). Available from www.motherwell-mad.co.uk/news/tmnw/GLF44_BoomBust_50290/index.shtml [Accessed on 4 March 2022].

Waiting for the Great Leap Forward, 45 (2002).

Waiting for the Great Leap Forward, 57 (2005).

Wishaw Press, 2 March 2011.

Wishaw Press, 13 July 2011.

Wishaw Press, 4 April 2012.

Wishaw Press, 19 June 2013.

Walton, J. (2005) 'Football and the Basques: The local and the global'. In Magee, J., Bairner, A. and Tomlinson, A. (eds) *The Bountiful Game? Football Identities and Finances*. London: Meyer and Meyer, pp 143–161.

Walton, J. (2009) 'The post-war decline of the British retail co-operative movement: nature, causes and consequences'. In Black, L. and Robertson, N. (eds) *Consumerism and the Co-operative Movement in Modern British History: Taking Stock*. Manchester: Manchester University Press, pp 13–31.

Webster, A., Shaw L. and Vorberg-Rugh, R. (2016) 'Introduction'. In Webster, A., Shaw, L. and Vorberg-Rugh, R. (eds) *Mainstreaming Co-operation*. Manchester: Manchester University Press, pp 1–12.

Yeo, S. (1988) 'Rival clusters of potential: Ways of seeing cooperation'. In Yeo, S. (ed) *New Views of Co-operation*. London: Routledge, pp 1–9.

PART II

Bridges: Co-operative Culture and Education

7

Co-operation for Asset-Based Community Development: The Example of the Community Explorers Project at Leicester Vaughan College

Malcolm Noble

Introduction

Many contributions in this volume refer to the Preston Model which aims to use co-operation and co-operatives to build community wealth; significantly more nuanced delineations are available in the introduction. This chapter sits at an angle to this model, and is concerned with a Higher Education Co-operative using co-operative pedagogies to facilitate Asset-based Community Development (ABCD) in a project working with older people project which Leicester Vaughan College (LVC) completed in 2019. On one hand the Community Explorers project is quite different to many of the other examples in this volume; on the other it seeks broadly comparable goals, albeit in a different co-operative context. But using this example, in this chapter it is argued that cooperative pedagogy is particularly suited to projects seeking to build community capacity with adults generally, and ABCD. After discussing the Cooperative Identity and the bundle of cooperative pedagogies, it will consider the adaptability of coop pedagogies and their value in this kind of context. The chapter begins by exploring various terms and situating this work in the relevant literatures. The project itself is then discussed, finishing with reflections on how cooperative pedagogies were useful in building capacity in individuals within their communities. In doing this, the aim is to show

how cooperative pedagogy and Education Co-operatives can have broad uses for the movement.

Co-operative learning and related terms

It is necessary first to clarify some nomenclature. Cooperative learning and related terms might be used to describe several connected but quite different things, partly because cooperative education has a long history. First, it might refer to cooperative training, sometimes called Cooperative Education and Training (CET): gaining the skills needed to be an effective cooperator or other forms of training within co-operatives in order that those in them can function – essentially technical training within the movement, whatever personal benefits and capacities might accrue as a result. As a subset of this, it might also refer to other types of learning within the movement, which across the long history of a global social movement which has had broad educational aims since its earliest days, encompasses an enormous range of undertakings (Baloche, 2011; Woodin, 2011, 2017, 2019).

Second, cooperative learning can describe learning which takes place in any context using cooperative pedagogies. Third, and potentially linked, is a different technical usage to refer to a school of pedagogic thinking not connected to the values-based movement, typically with capital letters and without a hyphen, 'Cooperative Learning' (or CL) points to pedagogy-led or practice-led (Breeze, 2011, p 3); that orthographical convention is adhered to in this chapter to afford clarity. Finally, it might refer to learning which takes place in educational co-operatives; this is the site which the author contends hold the most radical possibilities.

With so many types of cooperative education, the literature on it is rather more piecemeal than might be expected. Some scholars have explored specific aspects of cooperative pedagogic approaches. Marie Huxtable and Jack Whitehead have shown the applicability of Living Theory research to any potential cooperative university, as part of a consideration of the application of cooperative values and identity in a higher education context (2018, p 23). An extensive literature on Cooperative Higher Education (CHE) has not generally been concerned with pedagogy, but rather with institutional formation and practicalities (a broadly comprehensive bibliography is Winn, 2021). This is an approach which sees learning environments and learners within them as generators of educational knowledge, establishing an important feedback loop between learning in cooperative contexts and pedagogy.

Most of the established literature on Cooperative Learning does not relate to the cooperative movement (see, for example, Topping, 1987; Gillies and Ashman, 2003). There are some exceptions to this. For examples, Alan Wilkins argues Cooperative Learning is an important part of co-operation, and applied can 'inherently contribute to initiatives than enhance community cohesion' (2011, p 12). Wendy Jolliffe looks at the application of Cooperative Learning in schools, making recommendations for what is needed to support teachers and schools seeking to do this (2011). There is much more work to be done to understand fully what makes learning in cooperative contexts different.

Articulations of what makes co-operatives different to other parts of the solidarity economy often focus on the collection of values and principles known as the Cooperative Identity, agreed by the International Co-operative Alliance, shown in Table 7.1. On the other hand, it is not desirable to over-privilege the traditional Rochdale-centred narratives focusing on formal co-operation, as this precludes other important informal cooperative traditions. Caroline Hossein has argued persuasively that we must consider that 'informal co-operatives known as "Susu" and "Sol" precursors to formal cooperative development and that these institutions are in fact the preferred financial institution for Caribbean people'. Long legacies are felt in the cooperative sector generally and within the Black Social Economy today as a result. Moreover, these African 'financial models were brought to the Americas by enslaved people, predating the European beginnings' (Hossein, 2021, p 172, but see also essays in 2018). Informal cooperative systems became necessary in Grenada and Haiti for example due to racist exclusion from mainstream financial services. Susus offered 'a means for people to save money with those they know and trust' and informal local banking co-operatives provided valuable services locally (2021, pp 180, 186). Alongside other Savings and Credit Cooperative Societies (SACCOs), these are important economic traditions which ought to be part of the narrative of the cooperative movement, bringing in African experiences fully to the story. This contextualization does not aim to claim any universalism of cooperative values, but to point to their resonance and relevance, and that co-operation should be understood broadly rather than limited tightly to the formal co-operative movement. Co-operation ought not to be short-hand for the social economy generally, and alignment with the values remains important. Alignment with the Cooperative Identity is perhaps the key thing to consider.

The application and the role of the Cooperative Identity in educational contexts has gained scholarly attention, particularly as it raises certain tensions between ethics and autonomy on one hand, and educational commitments and governance on the other. In schools, for example, there are significant, and possibly insurmountable difficulties in applying the full range of cooperative values and principles: pupils are too young legally to discharge governance functions and carry the fiduciary obligations of membership and directorship; thus in compulsory educational settings these tensions are sharp and restrained heavily by law and policy. Gail Davidge has explored these strains at some

Table 7.1: The co-operative identity

Co-operative values
Co-operatives are based on the values of self-help, self-responsibility, democracy, equality, equity, and solidarity. In the tradition of their founders, co-operative members believe in the ethical values of honesty, openness, social responsibility and caring for others.

Co-operative principles
1. Voluntary and Open Membership 2. Democratic Member Control 3. Member Economic Participation 4. Autonomy and Independence 5. Education, Training, and Information 6. Co-operation among Co-operatives 7. Concern for Community

Source: ICA (1995)

length (2014, 2017). The need to interpret the full suite of values and principles – rather than any partial selection has also been stressed. For example, Nigel Rayment is clear that 'their true power comes only when taken as a suite', even if application is not always straightforward (2011, p 23). Indeed, primarily considering higher educational contexts, where all participating will be adults – setting aside the relatively small likelihood of under-18 students applying to Higher Education Co-operatives, Cilla Ross and the author have argued that the Cooperative Identity needs to be translated to educational contexts. For example, good practices training and integrating new Members and Directors – what is known as on-boarding – will be needed given likely higher-than-average turnover of membership given student lifecycles (say six years for a part-time undergraduate degree). The firmly local, civic-facing nature of HECs points to easy meeting of the sixth principle. We note too, that the idea of member economic consideration must be reconstrued to consider the intellectual capital – or cultural capital as Bourdieu (1986) has it – provided by those teaching and researching (Noble and Ross, 2021).

Reviewing the literature on cooperative learning, Lynda Baloche noted a heavy post-secondary focus: 'including both vocational and university settings' with some 40 of 83 articles in her search being concerned with these contexts (2011, p 27). This points to the application and value of this material in post-compulsory educational contexts. All pedagogy is contextual, but there is clear value and potential in applying cooperative pedagogy in different contexts: in schools, post-secondary, and broad community settings. The application of cooperative values – if not pedagogies – in a local government context is discussed by Manley and Eseonu in Chapter 10.

Generally speaking, however, cooperative learning – that is learning in cooperative contexts – remains largely undertheorized, especially compared to a growing literature on CHE institutions and governance. Huxtable and Whitehead make a similar point (2018, p 23) and this trend has continued, as a cursory glance at Joss Winn's bibliography of writings on a cooperative university makes clear (2021). At the heart of much thinking about cooperative learning (from the values-based movement *with* hyphen), is the importance of the co-operative. Pablo Pérez Ruiz, both with Mike Shaw (2019) and with Teresa Macías (2018), reflect on the pedagogic function of membership of student housing co-operatives. Indeed, the broader cooperative educational ecosystem around education co-operatives is now receiving some scholarly attention – see for example the recent number of *Journal of Co-operative Studies* on Canadian campuses (Guillotte and Charbonneau, 2021). It would be dangerous to suggest that co-operation might be a magic bullet contra the neoliberal takeover of education, but it is also clear that it offers considerable potential.

Cilla Ross and the author have conceptualized cooperative learning in CHE in terms of how we learn as characterized as active and participatory, and by co-production; what we learn in terms of the broadest range of epistemologies and seeing the world, and where we learn: that the co-operative itself is a valuable pedagogic site (2020, pp 25–27). It follows that places which function as co-operatives – formal, *de jure* co-operatives formed as part of the Cooperative Movement, or more informal settings that run *de facto* along these lines – will become important sites of pedagogy in themselves. A project like the Community Explorers, which was run by a co-operative, in which participants were not necessarily members, but participated in learning spaces which had been deliberately configured cooperatively, is cooperative on multiple levels.

The formal cooperative context is important to understanding different kinds of cooperative learning: Alan Wilkins places an emphasis on the application of Cooperative Learning when it is as 'part of the cooperative movement' (2011, p 5). Learning which is provided by a co-operative should benefit educationally from that cooperative nature of its space. While all co-operatives provide education and training under the fifth principle, a growing number of 'Education Co-operatives' exist only, or primarily, to provide education (Noble and Ross, 2021, pp 3–6).

Education Co-operatives encompass a range of cooperative spaces dedicated to education. The most diverse group of these are Higher Education Co-operatives. Examples of these from the UK include Leicester Vaughan College of which I am a member, the Glasgow-based Centre for Human Ecology pursuing education for deep ecological change, the RED Learning Co-operative providing Trade Union education, and Hull's Feral Art School offering a range of art courses at high levels (Centre for Human Ecology, 2022; Feral Art School, 2022; The RED Learning Co-operative, 2022). Much greater in number are Cooperative Schools and Academies, with the caveat that they must function cooperatively (Davidge, 2017; Schools Cooperative Society, 2020). The material needs of students are met by a growing number of adjacent co-operatives which form part of a cooperative educational ecosystem: student housing co-operatives. In the UK, there are four successful student housing co-operatives in Edinburgh, Birmingham, Sheffield, and Brighton, with a national body, Student Coop Homes seeking to finance the expansion of this sector challenging exploitation of students by commercial landlords and universities (Birmingham Student Housing Co-operative, 2022; Edinburgh Student Housing Co-op, 2022; SEASALT Housing Co-operative, 2022; SSHC, 2022; Student Co-op Homes, 2022). Linked to these are student-run food co-operatives, of which Students for Co-operation list 12 active ones (Students for Co-operation, 2022).

The neoliberal takeover of public education in the United Kingdom has led, in the last decade or so, to some of the most interesting innovations in co-operation. Co-operatives have shown considerable capacity to respond to the neoliberal takeover of public education, with some success. First, the move to academies has been one way in which successive UK governments have dismantled local education authority control over education, with less accountability for public funds, soaring executive pay, a succession of scandals especially over very high levels of leadership and 'executive' remuneration and expenses, the awarding of contracts and other failures of governance (for examples see: Akehurst, 2018; BBC News, 2018; Sodha, 2018; Thomson, 2020; Andrews, 2021); 'Multi-Academy Trusts (Ofsted Inspection', 2021). The North American equivalent of this of this is charter schools. The Co-op Academies Trust has seen the Co-operative Group sponsor a growing number of academies, starting with two in 2010, and continuing to grow in size, with 26 by 2020 (Co-op Academies Trust, nd). However, the focus in these academies is not on co-operative pedagogy or learning. Other co-operative schools have sought to be more co-operative through the Schools Cooperative Society. Fundamental tensions remain because the pupils are minors and cannot be full participating members exercising full democratic autonomy.

Second, the emergence of CHE in the UK has been given considerable impetus in recent years. A long-held ambition of the movement, since the founding of the Co-operative College in Manchester at least, drawing inspiration and encouragement from Mondragon and other examples, a number of Higher Education Co-operatives have been working towards offering accredited degrees (Wright et al, 2011; Cook, 2013; Swain, 2017). The liberalization of HE policy since the Higher Education and Reform Act (2017) has apparently opened the door to alternative providers, but onerous regulatory restrictions leave questions over the extent to which it may immediately be possible for a federated cooperative university to be established. However, many Higher Education Co-operatives exist and have a range of educational and research offers.

In 2017 the author became a Founder Member of Leicester Vaughan College, a Community Benefit Society. LVC's long-term goal was, and is, to provide part-time degrees taught in twilight evening sessions, to enable students to have jobs and caring commitments during conventional working hours as well as studying part-time. It has been an active member of the Co-operative University Project previously led by the Co-operative College. One of the interesting aspects of Higher Education Co-operatives is that they provide a flexible and responsive space in which to undertake research projects and contracts, with an agility which would not be possible in mainstream universities, and on small scales which would not be economical with conventional overheads and full-economic-costing regimes. The potential of platform co-operatives to support enterprising researchers has been discussed elsewhere (Hall, 2019; Swann, 2019; a more general introduction to platform co-operatives is found in Borkin, 2019).

Co-operative pedagogies for asset-based community development in action

In 2019 LVC ran a community research project for Leicester Ageing Together (LAT) designed to address loneliness in older people by working with them to explore research questions of interest to them as they addressed needs they perceived in their communities through research. LAT was part of Ageing Better, a major strategic investment from the National Lottery Community Fund, together 'a seven[-]year, £87[-]million investment to improve the lives of people aged over 50 by addressing social isolation and loneliness within local communities' (The National Lottery Community Fund, nd). The project was a kind of action research, and targeting older people, very broadly and openly defined, and over six months, supporting them to interrogate issues of local concerns, so building community capacity generally, and supporting individual participants, 'Community Explorers', to become volunteers active in their communities. An end of project report *Learning Together* is available which documents much of the project and individual explorations undertaken within it, to make it appealing and to lower barriers to participation as explained next. There were three key aims of the project (Noble and Stones, 2020):

1. To empower people to use research in order to solve problems in their lives.
2. To encourage them to find ways to continue in doing this after the end of the project.
3. To realise their potential to act as a resource in solving community problems.

The project recruited Community Explorers through existing parts of the LAT project and its Community Connectors, as well as a host of community groups and centres. Centred around informal drop-in sessions, people could simply turn up to these over several months, with 1:1 supervision and small group research training to support individuals and pairs pursuing some approximately dozen projects. Modest financial support was available to meet research costs such as digital recorders and travel expenses. A formal – but very gentle – application process was available, helping identify themes, questions, and training needs. After the six months has passed a celebration event enabled participants to show off their findings, reflect on their work through collaging, and make connexions with each other. The project sought to achieve ABCD which sustainably builds community capacity by drawing on existing strengths (Morgan and Ziglio, 2007). With origins in public health, much interest in ABCD has been around its potential as 'a way of tackling the social determinants of health and reducing inequalities', particularly in the UK (Harrison et al, 2019, pp 1, 3).

Explorations

While the report gives fuller detail, brief summaries of various explorations indicate the broad range of topics pursued and the general approach taken to support them.

1. Visual Impairment Project saw one Explorer share their experience of visual impairment through a spoken-word performance. This took some work already completed and shared in English and Gujarati presentations. A very flexible approach designed to accommodate all meant that we worked with someone to share work already done and provide support to incorporate slides to enable inclusive performances, as well as arranging and helping to facilitate a number of performances to engage with various community groups.
2. A project run with members of WISCP (West Indian Senior Citizens Project) enabled them to explore what the community centre meant to them. We worked with Crafting Relationships, a social enterprise with expertise in running crafting and coaching sessions with a wide range of groups (Crafting Relationships, 2022). A specialist facilitated a session which saw members identify key words about what mattered to them about the WISCP, before proceeding to decorate three canvases with the words emblazoned: Friendship, Laughter, and Food. These now decorate the wall of the day centre.
3. Another existing group, Pukaar, ran two projects. The Trips project explored core issues for older people: mobility and accessibility – how

could members have their needs met to access out-of-town shopping centres, in so doing dealing with fundamental issues of logistics and access, feeding back to centre management as well as empowering them in respect of future explorations generally.

4. The Arts and Crafts project run by members from the same Pukaar group worked with existing capabilities to develop capacities. Several members of this group wanted to add to their existing sewing skills. Specific skills, specialist instruction, and practical assistance enabled participants to learn technical skills including button-holes, patchwork, and appliqué.

5. A City Ring project was framed around seeking a circular walking route around the city similar to the large Leicestershire Round, a 100-mile 'circuit of the county devised by the Leicestershire Footpath Association (LFA) to celebrate their centenary' (Long Distance Walkers Association, nd). The Explorer undertaking this had a clear idea in mind and with only very light touch support was able to make prompt progress.

6. Silverstrand Club sought to reinforce and renew their organization which seeks to meet the need of the Afro-Caribbean community in South Highfields in Leicester. The idea was to take the existing, popular, luncheon club and find new activities for the group and find new members – especially younger ones to diversify it. 1:1 support and indeed 2:1 helped members of the group work through and identify a next-stage research project, Hidden Histories.

7. Another Explorer was given training to go and collect nursery rhymes to foster intergenerational connexion, furnished with a recorder, and helped to create a small run of a chapbook of material collected. Individual attention and support made this possible.

8. A Health Project saw an Explorer seek to bring together older people to build an autonomous self-directed group explore health issues. The individual was well-connected and would draw on their own existing community connexions, but it could not be completed for personal reasons.

9. Crowdsourcing Accessibility Map. An enthusiastic but open-minded Explorer approached us in search of a project. Another potential Explorer had questions about how people with visual impairments and other disabilities could be supported to access city-centre amenities. Where might accessible public lavatories be found, or lower-stimulus shopping hours be found? Together a bottom-up approach would seek to find ways for information to be pooled within communities.

10. Individuals came forward from the Belgrave Knitters group seek support to visit a modern knitting factory and a framework knitting museum to make comparisons, working through practicalities including arrangements logistics, and finance. Another line of enquiry was to help

the group develop generally through community connexions. Members of the Pukaar group were presented with hand-knitted scarves as a gesture of visible friendship so building and strengthening links between the two groups.

The project facilitators were approached or sounded out by approximately 24 projects overall; others were not completed for personal reasons. Had the support element have run for longer it seems likely that more of these would have been completed.

Frameworks and contexts

The project's approach was structured in response to several frameworks, deriving from the contexts in which it operated. The Community Explorers project made a small contribution to LAT; LAT itself is one of 14 local partnerships funded by Ageing Better concerned with an ageing population. Ageing Better was one of a handful of major charities funded by the National Lottery. Since 2015, '[t]he Leicester Ageing Together partnership has been working since October 2015 to reduce isolation and loneliness in older people in Leicester' (Leicester Ageing Together, nda). Following risk factors to identify those areas where tackling isolation was a priority, LAT has concentrated on five key wards in the city: Belgrave, Evington, Thurncourt, Spinney Hills, and Wycliffe, as well as some city-wide priorities including the African Caribbean community. Our project occurred toward the end of the projected five-year lifespan of the partnership and it might be noted that this was a small exercise, and focused on legacy and sustainability of their approaches developed around their 'LAT Wellbeing model' (Table 7.2), based on an influential New Economics Foundation report (Aked et al, 2008).

Entering an established national project enabled us to draw on lessons learned, and best practice established elsewhere. A series of reports in 2018 identified barriers to volunteering, that 'there are significant inequalities in participation in formal volunteering', leading to 'gaps in the representation of people from some Black, Asian and Minority Ethnic (BAME) communities'; in contrast barriers to more informal contexts 'seem to be lower'. In other words, opportunities, enabling those more at risk of loneliness and isolation to participate, make a contribution and enjoy all the health and personal benefits attendant thereupon (Jopling and Jones, 2018, p 6). An informal, flexible structure lay at the heart of our approach, underpinned by a responsive, co-productive, co-operative pedagogy.

As adult educators, the project team brought an understanding of the emotional needs of adult learners in extramural Higher education throughout the student lifecycle – from recruitment to completion. Indeed, noted in the various Centre for Ageing Better reports 'how people felt' was an important

Table 7.2: The LAT Wellbeing Model

Theme	Detail
Take care of your body	Do things that make you laugh Be active Take exercise Get enough sleep Eat well and drink sensibly Get some fresh air
Take care of your mind	Talk about your feelings Take steps to handle stress Be mindful/take notice Self-acceptance Develop resilience Focus on optimism Increase your sense of gratitude Sense of wonder: take care of your spiritual self
Connect with yourself	'Who I am': reviewing your life Self-appreciation Self-compassion Focusing on what you value and believe Make meaning, join the dots Develop goals for the next phase of your life Self-belief: 'I can make things happen'
Connect with Others	Maintain and build your relationships Give to others Be a part of something bigger Make a contribution 'We are part of the solution'
Keep Learning	Learning project: trying out new things – or digging deep into past interests – on your own or informally with others; using a new gadget, trying a new recipe, watching a new-to-you TV programme, reading a new author, walking new routes Learning in groups: IT, family history, cooking, armchair aerobics, arts and crafts, rights and entitlements, etc. Exercise your creativity

Source: Leicester Ageing Together (ndb). This was part of the draft model prepared June 2018. The most recent version on the LAT website uses more user-friendly nomenclature but offers less detail. The older version is presented here as it is this which framed our approach.

barrier (see, for example, Bidley, 2018, p 6). Our relaxed approach saw volunteers supported as, and as if they were, adult learners, with their own rich life experiences valued through their learning journey, as they explored research topics.

For example, stemming from the cooperative approach the project team sought to offer the most flexible and open support package to those coming forward. Best practice established by earlier projects on researching with older people as co-investigators framed other aspects of this approach: that older people should identify the issue (Buffel, 2015, p 35); indeed the team went as far as to allow carte blanche to Explorers, and where some came forward without particular agendas, they were able to match them to those with research questions beyond their individual capacities. The heavier requirements of 'good communication skills' on volunteer specifications used in this project (Buffel, 2015, p 38) were not appropriate for this context, and aligned with this, research training was provided on a one-to-one and small group guided basis.

Three of the challenges Buffel (2015) identifies in using 'older residents as co-researchers' are pivoted to strengths in or addressed directly by cooperative pedagogical contexts. First, that 'it blurs boundaries between researcher, researched, academic and activist' (Buffel, 2015, p 85) aligns perfectly with cooperative approaches which seek to move beyond the automatic privileging expertise in order to produce more equitable and democratic contexts and which are underpinned by a commitment to pluralistic knowledges. The direct confrontation of power relationships in a cooperative classroom and the radical openness [about which the author has written elsewhere, in press], offers a space which can approach the fact that 'it constitutes a form of power and can reproduce the inequalities is seeks to challenge' (Buffel, 2015, p 85). It is not a magic solution, but at least by acknowledging these inequalities offers a more honest approach and leaves scope to begin addressing them. Finally, our adaptive and flexible approach to research training, by helping one or two Explorers at a time meant that the 'training, and opportunities for skills development, need be designed in such a way that it appeals to everyone involved' (Buffel, 2015, p 85) was achieved by default.

The project aimed to support individuals in their research: at its simplest, it was focused on helping individuals explore questions which mattered to them. On one hand, this aligned closely with LVC's adult education aims, and clearly had aspects of higher learning; but on the other, it could not be said to resemble conventional higher education.

The final package made available to community Explorers ran as follows. Recruitment of Explorers ran through posters displayed in various locations: the intended audience was over 50s, but nobody was asked their age, and nobody excluded on the basis of any characteristic including age. Nomenclature was decided with some care: the term 'research' was not used but rather questions '[w]ant to tell people about your community? [c] oncerned about local issues?] [a]re people in your community important to you? [d]o you have new ideas for your community?' (reproduced in Noble and Stones, 2020, p 8). Lexical selections then were made so as not to exclude or discourage, but to lower the threshold as much as possible to keep the door open to all, in perfect alignment with the cooperative value of open membership.

Whereas originally larger workshops had been anticipated, in the end, partly due to the diversity of projects and agendas which emerged, small group and individual support were the main characteristics. Open drop-in sessions offered informal mentoring and support. These were run in several locations, and usually saw two members of staff available for discussion. This enabled the team to cope with several Explorers at once, and also to bounce around ideas in an engaging way. Often, then, when there was only one Explorer present at a session, the team exceeded the tutorial model with 1:2 student: staff ratio.

Co-operative dividends

The cooperative pedagogical underpinnings of the Community Explorers Project manifested four key advantages which supported ABCD. First: from a position of openness the project enabled the broadest range of people to become Explorers. Second, as the corollary of this the small team focused very firmly on meeting individual needs and supporting individuals to succeed on their own terms. Again this meant that the team were able to support both individuals and groups. Third was allowing Explorers to identify what mattered to them. LVC had no agenda or theme for Explorers to follow. Not only were the research questions posed by Explorers but – with gentle guidance – the ways of exploring and enquiring and answering them were of their own device too. This fits not only with good practice for co-production but also naturally aligns with the fundamental tenets of ABCD. Fourth, following from this, the generous acceptance of epistemologies which forms part of cooperative pedagogy enabled a broad range of ways of knowing to be accepted, including arts-based enquiry and walking.

Moreover, this co-operative approach to ABCD facilitated all the mechanisms identified by Harrison and colleagues (2019) for successful ABCD. Community Explorers were supported in '[d]eveloping relationships' – with each other and within their communities. As these connexions were made, areas of common concern such as mobility or access enabled 'collective goals' to be identified. Harrison et al (2019) suggest '[e]ngagement with target population'; the team were able to work directly with small portions of populations which had been identified as priorities by LAT, and its flexible, granular approach enabled the team to engage even where only one interested person came forward. The ethical approach required by the Cooperative Identity meant that the project team were able to build 'trust and trustworthiness' in themselves with a view that this would frame behaviours generally – absolute candour about what the team could and could not do, for example. Explorers gained voices within their communities and several were accessing funds available through ward-level municipal funding or making demands of organizations, so providing '[e]ngagement with political powers' (Harrison et al, 2019, p 9).

At the end of the project in November 2019 a celebration event was held. As well as a festival of research it also incorporated some reflexion through a collaging session. In pairs and trios, across the different projects, Explorers reflected on their experiences by creating group collages using a range of images from existing print material (such as newspapers, magazines, promotional literature). To start, as a group, the team asked for words they associated with their experience of the project: challenged, communication, confidence, connected, curiosity, doubt, eagerness, enlightened, exploring (literally), friendship, healthy, heritage, insight, inspiration, inspired, liberation, surprised. It was obvious too that our low-threshold cooperative approach had enabled people to participate and follow up issues of interest to them, and left with capacity to respond to community concerns. It shows too, the extent to which Explorers had realized their potential to act as a resource in solving community problems.

Sustainability was also a key focus in the final stage of the project. In the immediate aftermath, a number of follow-up projects were delayed for a range of reasons related to the pandemic and its continuing effects. It is hoped than in 2023 these can be resumed, but it would be premature to discuss any of this in print. Next steps involve seeking funding to work in partnership with some organizations. A proposed heritage project will see cooperative pedagogies applied in a similar way to the Community Explorers project to support a community group rebuilding after COVID-19. During the project we focused on four steps to sustainability: by harnessing momentum within and around existing community groups, a focus on adding capacities in existing places for new and different things, by supporting individuals to gain the skills they need, and encouraging others to make their demands known and influence policy.

It is worth pondering the broader implications from the lessons in cooperative learning drawn from this small project. First, as a speculative point, the author increasingly thinks that all learning contexts could be modelled on co-operatives in terms of the ethics, democracy and flexibility. Elsewhere I have argued this is characterized by radical openness on the part of those facilitating teaching and learning (Noble, 2022). This project showed how cooperative learning could be used in relatively marginal spaces rather than formal learning environments as part of longer, structured and assessed programmes of study.

If educators and those facilitating learning or training outside formal cooperative contexts might benefit by drawing on cooperative pedagogies, then in turn it makes sense to ask what the implications are for cooperative learning from these broader applications. It points to a need for those studying co-operatives to look beyond the formal movement. Education was an early ambition for the cooperative movement, but it is arguably the least understood element of the Cooperative Identity. The radical implications of cooperative education and learning unfold rapidly when we think about co-operatives as communities of economic activity – in a broad sense, then ABCD has implications for the CET and indeed cooperative development more generally.

Cooperative education is a dynamic and rapidly developing part of contemporary co-operation in the United Kingdom. Beyond the immediate needs of the movement, cooperative values applied to education offer a practicable way to resist neoliberal managerialism and the dismantling of public goods. Cooperative schools and academies are one strand, and cooperative higher education is another by which the cooperative movement may grow and strengthen. The cooperative difference in education flows from the Cooperative Identity and cooperative pedagogies. A small project here has shown how this might be applied in community educational contexts, building community capacity, benefitting both individual and collective, so strengthening the capabilities to meet the profound social challenges which lie ahead.

Acknowledgements

The present chapter draws on the project report I wrote with Ann Stones (2020). The work on co-operative pedagogy has been largely developed with Cilla Ross, cited as appropriate. In both cases the intellectual property in these is shared. I am grateful to both for their customarily generous support in the preparation of this chapter. However, it remains my work, for which I take full responsibility. The Community Explorers project and report were commissioned by Leicester Ageing Together as part of the National Lottery Community Fund Ageing Better programme.

References

Aked, J., Marks, N. and Cordon, C. (2008) *Five Ways to Wellbeing: A Report Presented to the Foresight Project on Communicating the Evidence Base for Improving People's Well-Being.* London: New Economics Foundation.

Akehurst, N. (2018) 'Think Carillion was bad? Wait until you hear about the financial scandal engulfing our children's academies', *The Independent*, 31 January. Available from www.independent.co.uk/voices/carillion-academies-conservatives-deficit-financial-scandal-education-a8186751.html [Accessed on 25 March 2022].

Andrews, M. (2021) 'School academy trust rapped for lavishing more than £100,000 on boss's own companies', *Express & Star*, 31 July. Available from www.expressandstar.com/news/education/2021/08/06/academy-trust-rapped-for-lavishing-cash-with-bosss-own-companies/ [Accessed on 25 March 2022].

Baloche, L. (2011) 'A brief view of co-operative learning from across the pond, around the world, and over time', *Journal of Co-operative Studies*, 44(3): 25–30.

BBC News (2018) 'Academy chain accused of misusing government funds', BBC News, 10 September. Available from www.bbc.com/news/educat ion-45472189 [Accessed on 25 March 2022].

Bidley, T. (2018) 'Primary research into community contributions in later life: Local report for Castle Ward', Scarborough. Centre for Ageing Better, p 42. Available from https://ageing-better.org.uk/sites/default/files/2018-10/Scarborough-Primary-research-community-contribution.pdf [Accessed on 7 September 2022].

Birmingham Student Housing Co-operative (2022) Birmingham Student Housing Co-operative. Available from https://bshc.co.uk [Accessed on 16 May 2022].

Borkin, S. (2019) *Platform Co-operatives: Solving the Capital Conundrum*. Nesta/ Co-operatives UK. Available from https://media.nesta.org.uk/documents/ Nesta_Platform_Report_AW_v4_3.pdf. [Accessed on 7 September 2022].

Bourdieu, P. (1986) 'The forms of capital'. In Richardson, J. (ed) *Handbook of Theory and Research for the Sociology of Education*. New York: Greenwood, pp 241–258.

Breeze, M. (2011) 'Transforming education through co-operation: A force for change', *Journal of Co-operative Studies*, 44(3): 2–4.

Buffel, T. (ed) (2015) *Researching Age-friendly Communities: Stories from Older People as Co-investigators*. Manchester: The University of Manchester Library. Available from http://hummedia.manchester.ac.uk/schools/soss/ brochures/Age-Friendly-Booklet.pdf. [Accessed on 7 September 2022].

Centre for Human Ecology (2022) Homepage. Available from www.che. ac.uk/index.php [Accessed on 16 May 2022].

Cook, D. (2013) *Realising the Co-operative University. A Consultancy Report for The Co-operative College*. Available from https://josswinn.org/wp-cont ent/uploads/2013/12/realising-the-co-operative-university-for-disemm ination.pdf [Accessed on 8 June 2023].

Co-op Academies Trust (nd) 'Our Trust, Co-op Academies'. Available from www.coopacademies.co.uk/about-us/trust/ [Accessed on 16 May 2022].

Crafting Relationships (2022) 'About, Crafting Relationships'. Available from www.craftingrelationships.co.uk/about [Accessed on 16 May 2022].

Davidge, G. (2014) *For 'Getting It': An Ethnographic Study of Co-operative Schools*. Doctoral thesis. Manchester Metropolitan University. Available from http://e-space.mmu.ac.uk/843/ [Accessed on 2 January 2021].

Davidge, G. (2017) *Rethinking education Through Critical Psychology: Co-operative Schools, Social Justice and Voice*. New York: Routledge.

Edinburgh Student Housing Co-op (2022) 'Edinburgh Student Housing Co-op – affordable housing run by students'. Available from www.eshc. coop/ [Accessed on 16 May 2022].

Feral Art School (2022) 'About us'. Available from www.feralartschool.org/ about-us/ [Accessed on 16 May 2022].

Gillies, R.M. and Ashman, A.F. (eds) (2003) *Co-operative Learning: The Social and Intellectual Outcomes of Learning in Groups.* London: Routledge Falmer.

Guillotte, C.-A. and Charbonneau, J. (2021) 'Co-operation between Canadian universities and the co-operative sector', *Journal of Co-operative Studies*, 54(2): 3–4.

Hall, R. (2019) 'On platforms for co-operative knowledge production'. In Woodin, T. and Shaw, L. (eds) *Learning for a Co-operative World: Education, Social Change and the Co-operative College.* London: UCL Institute of Education Press, pp 118–133.

Harrison, R, . Blickem, C., Lamb, J., Kirk, S. and Vassilev, I. (2019) 'Asset-based community development: narratives, practice, and conditions of possibility: A qualitative study with community practitioners', *SAGE Open*, 9(1): 1–11.

Hossein, C.S. (ed) (2018*) The Black Social Economy in the Americas: Exploring Diverse Community-Based Markets.* New York: Palgrave Macmillan US (Perspectives from Social Economics).

Hossein, C.S. (2021) 'The legacy of cooperatives among the African diaspora', *National Review of Black Politics*, 2(3–4): 171–194.

Huxtable, M. and Whitehead, J. (2018) 'Living co-operative values in educational contexts', *Journal of Co-operative Studies*, 51(2): 19–28.

ICA (1995) 'Co-operative identity, values and principles'. Available from www. ica.coop/en/cooperatives/cooperative-identity [Accessed on 10 June 2021].

Jolliffe, W. (2011) 'Co-operative learning: Making it work in the classroom', *Journal of Co-operative Studies*, 44(3): 31–42.

Jopling, K. and Jones, D. (2018) *Age-friendly and Inclusive Volunteering.* Report, Centre for Ageing Better. Available from https://ageing-better.org.uk/ sites/default/files/2018-10/Age-friendly-and-inclusive-voluteering-rev iew.pdf [Accessed on 8 July 2023].

Leicester Ageing Together (nda) 'About us'. Available from www.leiceste rageingtogether.org.uk/about-us/ [Accessed on 3 April 2022].

Leicester Ageing Together (ndb) 'Ways to wellbeing'. Available from www. leicesterageingtogether.org.uk/about-us/wellbeing-/ [Accessed on 3 April 2022].

Long Distance Walkers Association (nd) 'Leicestershire round'. Available from www.ldwa.org.uk/ [Accessed on18 May 2022].

Macías, T. and Pérez Ruiz, P. (2018) 'Co-operation in action: The Edinburgh Student Housing Co-operative as a pedagogical space', *Journal of Co-operative Studies*, 51(1): 54–57.

Morgan, A. and Ziglio, E. (2007) 'Revitalising the evidence base for public health: An assets model', *Promotion & Education*, 14(2_suppl): 17–22.

'Multi-Academy Trusts (Ofsted Inspection)' (2021). Westminster: Hansard. Available from https://hansard.parliament.uk//commons/2021-09-08/debates/51981A3C-D4D5-42CA-B0B3-2005F371E255/Multi-Academy Trusts(OfstedInspection) [Accessed on 25 March 2022].

Noble, M. (2022) 'Co-operation not competition'. In Mahn, C., Taylor, Y. and Brim, M. (eds) *Queer Sharing in the Marketized University*. London: Routledge, pp 44–62.

Noble, M. and Ross, C. (2020) 'Bundling co-operative higher education: Towards a theory of co-operative learning', *Journal of Co-operative Studies*, 53(3): 25–29.

Noble, M. and Ross, C. (2021) 'From principles to participation: "The Statement on the Cooperative Identity" and higher education co-operatives', *Journal of Co-operative Organization and Management*, 9(2): 100146.

Noble, M. and Stones, A. (2020) *Learning Together: the LAT Community Explorers Project*. Leicester: Leicester Vaughan College.

Pérez Ruiz, P. and Shaw, M. (2019) 'The co-operative as site of pedagogy: The example of Edinburgh Student Housing Co-operative'. In Noble, M. and Ross, C. (eds) *Reclaiming the University for the Public Good: Experiments and Futures in Co-operative Higher Education*. Cham: Springer International Publishing (Palgrave Critical University Studies), pp 169–183.

Rayment, N. (2011) 'Co-operative learning: Values into practice', *Journal of Co-operative Studies*, 44(3): 15–24.

Schools Cooperative Society (2020) 'The Schools Cooperative Society (SCS)'. Available from https://csnetwork.coop/index.php/the-schools-cooperative-society-scs/ [Accessed on 2 January 2021].

SEASALT Housing Co-operative (2022) 'SEASALT Housing Co-operative'. Available from https://seasalthousingcooperative.com/ [Accessed on 16 May 2022].

Sodha, S. (2018) 'The great academy schools scandal', *The Observer*, 22 July. Available from www.theguardian.com/education/2018/jul/22/academy-schools-scandal-failing-trusts [Accessed on 25 March 2022].

SSHC (2022) 'Sheffield Student Housing Co-op'. Available from http://sshc.sheffield.coop/ [Accessed on 16 May 2022].

Student Co-op Homes (2022) 'Student Co-op Homes'. Available from www.studenthomes.coop/about/ [Accessed on 16 May 2022].

Students for Co-operation (2022) 'Food co-operative profiles, students. coop'. Available from www.students.coop/category/food-co-operative-profiles/ [Accessed on 16 May 2022].

Swain, H. (2017) 'Coming soon, a university where students could set their own tuition fees', *The Guardian*. 12 September.

Swann, T. (2019) 'Co-operative research and research co-operatives'. In Noble, M. and Ross, C. (eds) *Reclaiming the University for the Public Good: Experiments and Futures in Co-operative Higher Education.* Cham: Springer International Publishing (Palgrave Critical University Studies), pp 185–204.

The National Lottery Community Fund (nd) 'Ageing better'. Available from www.tnlcommunityfund.org.uk/funding/strategic-investments/ageing-better [Accessed on 16 May 2022].

The RED Learning Co-operative (2022) 'Meet RED'. Available from www.redlearning.coop/who-we-are [Accessed on 16 May 2022].

Thomson, P. (2020) *School Scandals: Blowing the Whistle on the Corruption of our Education System.* Bristol: Policy Press.

Topping, K. (1988) *The Peer Tutoring Handbook: Promoting Co-operative Learning.* London: Croom Helm.

Wilkins, A. (2011) 'Co-operative learning: A contextual framework', *Journal of Co-operative Studies,* 44(3): 5–14.

Winn, J. (2021) 'Co-operative universities: A bibliography', 31 August. Available from https://josswinn.org/2013/11/21/co-operative-universities-a-bibliography/ [Accessed on 21 January 2022].

Woodin, T. (2011) 'Co-operative education in Britain during the 19th and early 20th centuries: Context, identity and learning'. In Webster, A., Walton, J.K., Shaw, L., Stewart, D. and Brown, A. (eds) *The Hidden Alternative: Co-operative Values, Past, Present and Future.* Manchester: Manchester University Press, pp 78–95.

Woodin, T. (2017) 'Co-operation, leadership and learning: Fred Hall and the Co-operative College before 1939'. In Hall, R. and Winn, J. (eds) *Mass Intellectuality and Democratic Leadership in Higher Education.* London: Bloomsbury, pp 27–40.

Woodin, T. (2019) 'Useable pasts for a co-operative university: As different as light from darkness?' In Noble, M. and Ross, C. (eds) *Reclaiming the University for the Public Good: Experiments and Futures in Co-operative Higher Education.* Cham: Springer International Publishing, pp 23–43.

Wright, S., Greenwood, D. and Boden, R. (2011) 'Report on a field visit to Mondragón University: A cooperative experience/experiment', *Learning and Teaching,* 4(3): 38–56.

8

Engaging Universities in Capacity Building for a Co-operative Economy

Andrei Kuznetsov and Olga Kuznetsova

Introduction

In March 2013, the British financial sector was shocked by the news that one of the larger banks in the country, the Co-operative Bank, had accumulated losses of £600 million. Later in the year, it emerged that the Bank had a shortfall in its capital of about £1.5 billion, putting the bank on the brink of collapse. Until then, the Co-operative Bank plc had been 100 per cent owned by The Co-operative Group. The rescue operation required a major restructuring, following which the Co-operative Group's shareholding fell to 30 per cent. Later, in 2017, in the course of a second restructuring, the Group was forced to sell all its remaining shares, leaving the bank 100 per cent owned by private equity, mostly US hedge funds. The sad irony of the story was that the institution created to advance the principles of fairness, co-operation and mutuality had ended up in the hands of organizations that for many were the epitome of capitalist greed and exclusivity.

Much of the blame for the near collapse of the bank centred on the blatant incompetence of the directors putting in doubt the workability of the cooperative participatory principles, allowing unqualified people to sit on the board of a major cooperative company. The spotlight was on the Reverend Paul Flowers. As Chairman of the Co-operative Bank, he presided over the policies that had led the Bank to a catastrophe. An investigation by the Financial Conduct Authority found Flowers entirely unfit for the job, to which Flowers progressed through the elective processes of United Co-operatives. He had never worked in banking in any senior capacity when, in March 2010, he was put at the helm of the Co-operative Bank – a bank with £50 billion of assets, £36 billion of customer deposits and 4.7 million customers. However, there were people who saw the problem not in the principle but in its implementation. Rob Harrison, editor of *Ethical Consumer* magazine and an activist for the Save Our Bank campaign, argued that the implementation of cooperative principles in the management of mutual societies was predominantly a question of training and education: 'You need to spend lots of money on training people because they aren't necessarily going to turn up with all you need to manage a complicated company. And for me it would be far better to look at what is in place to train members to be effective directors' (*The Guardian*, 2013).

The Co-operative Bank debacle and the stark revelations of incompetence at the top level of management that followed was an early impetus for our interest in the relationship between business educators and co-operatives. It was spurred further by evidence in the literature that for an equivalent occupational group, people in co-operatives have a lower education level than their counterparts in stock companies. This was reported by Pestana and Gomes Santos (2003) who investigated Portuguese co-operatives, and later by Chevallier (2011) who looked at French coops. We have also noticed a glaring lack of educational programmes about and/or for co-operatives offered by UK universities, and the fact that coops are neglected in management and economics textbooks (Hill, 2000; Kalmi, 2007). Where university degrees in cooperative management are available, as in Canada, most programmes struggle to recruit the number of students required to be viable (Miner and Guillotte, 2014).

In 2018, the authors were awarded a research grant from the European Academy of Management that gave us resources to interview university tutors involved in cooperative studies as well as coop practitioners from Australia, Belgium, Canada, Fiji, Germany, Italy, New Zealand, Spain, and the UK. Based on the available evidence, our starting proposition was the existence of a disconnect between the institutions of mainstream business education and the cooperative movement. We sought to identify the reasons for this situation, its consequences and how it may be corrected. This chapter presents reflections on the debate in the literature and some of our findings.

Cooperative movement and education

Education is one of the original principles of the cooperative movement as formulated by the Rochdale Society of Equitable Pioneers in 1844. Education has since been confirmed as a pillar of the cooperative identity in the documents of the movement (ICA, 2017; for the time-line see: Myers, 2019). In 1995, education was established as one of the seven principles of the cooperative movement by its apex body, the International Cooperative Alliance: 'Cooperatives provide education and training for their members, elected representatives, managers, and employees so they can contribute effectively to the development of their cooperatives.'

The manner in which this principle is implemented today is largely determined by the place that cooperative movements occupy within societies based on the capitalist mode of production. This makes it, as noted by one commentator, at once the most important and yet often weakly implemented of the cooperative principles (Webb, 2020). The commitment of coops to equality, solidarity and democratic practices sets them apart from the privately owned businesses, which represent the mainstream of business organizations. It was probably inevitable, therefore, that co-operatives found themselves seen and even occasionally self-defining as some sort of an alternative to the capitalist firm, even though in the economy based on private property and run by market forces their freedom to be different is restricted. Characteristically, Karl Marx described the co-operative under capitalism as a firm in which workers are 'their own capitalists' (Marx, 1894/1981, p 571). However, the distinguishing features of the cooperative movement have been strong enough to create a sort of ideological chasm, separating it from other forms of capitalist firm.

Historically, because the cooperative project was such a new and original idea about how things should be done, when training their members in how to run the organization, co-operatives had to rely on their own educational process (Dawson, 1923) and not 'the formalised types of education from outside' (Jakobsen, 1995). Out of necessity, this process was mostly implemented as 'implicit education' through everyday operation and experience. Later, the movement has developed its own system of cooperative education with unique pedagogy and ideology (Woodin, 2011). However, the tradition of 'implicit education' has not lost its importance. During a fact-finding visit, we had conversations with members of the Mondragon cooperative corporation, and academics and students of Mondragon University, which is a part of this group. They all emphasized that, as far as the cooperative ideology and ethos were concerned, there was no mandatory indoctrination. Rather, the cooperators, including students at the university, were expected to pick up the values of the movement through their everyday experience of being a member (for the evolution of the Mondragon education model see: Wright and Manley, 2021).

Certain professional skills, however, cannot be mastered within an insular environment of an individual organization and the limited experience it offers, in particular if the organization is small in size, which is typical of many co-operatives. Managerial skills belong to this category. There is convincing evidence that professional managers who successfully rose through the ranks within firms, and at some point topped up knowledge acquired on the job by gaining a degree in business studies, subsequently outperform their colleagues without a degree. Using a sample of 416 CEOs from S&P

Global Ratings 500, Slater and Dixon-Fowler (2010) found a significant positive association between CEOs with MBAs and corporate performance, even after accounting for several firm- and individual-level characteristics. Importantly, this result is confirmed for microfinance institutions (MFIs), organizations that have certain similarities with co-operatives in that they share the quality of being of a hybrid nature as they pursue both financial and social institutional logics.[1] Empirical results (Pascal et al, 2017) indicate that MFIs with CEOs who have a business education perform significantly better, financially and socially, than MFIs managed by CEOs with other types of educational backgrounds.

Within the cooperative sector, member education tends to be somewhat inward-looking and insular by keeping its focus on the specifics of experiences within co-operatives (Emmanuel, 2007; Hannley, 2007). As a result, co-operatives may be disadvantaged in accessing (and by implication being able to adopt) the cutting-edge general management know-how. As a rare exception, *Otalora* – the Centre for Management and Co-operative Development in Mondragón – shows that open-minded and embracing programmes in business education do not cause a deficit or erode co-operative values (Wright and Manley, 2021). Yet, for many co-operatives the acceptance of 'outside' business education remains a challenge. In an exhaustive study of cooperative business education, Miner and Guillotte (2014) report conflicting attitudes in the movement even towards educational programmes that are customized for their business model. On the one hand, co-operators who pursue cooperative-focused business education find the relevance and impact of such programmes as tangible and significant. On the other, these programmes receive limited recognition and support from the cooperative sector as a whole. At the same time, it is fair to say that such dedicated university level programmes are few and far between. Cooperators who want to get an advanced degree in management rarely have a choice but to attend a standard course in one of numerous business schools. However, co-operatives and business schools seem to harbour mutual suspicions.

Co-operatives and mainstream business education

The cooperative movement has good reasons to be reticent in its attitude to business school orthodoxy. From the early days, business schools as the embodiment of advanced business education were growing and developing in response to demand predominantly from large investor-led corporations. As demonstrated by Chandler (1962; 1984), the need for business education and managerial knowledge arose from the transition from owners actively managing business to shareholder capitalism and multifunctional organizations run by professional managers. The history of the first two business schools in the UK, the London Graduate School of Business (LBS) and the University of Manchester Business School demonstrate the forces at play (Larson, 2009; 2020). British universities had traditionally been sceptical of management education on the grounds that it lacked an independent body of knowledge which clearly demarcated it from other disciplines in the social sciences and engineering that showed concerns with the aspects of management. According to Larson, commentators in the press often asked 'What exactly is management?', a question which those immersed in management or studying it struggled to answer. The initial aloofness on the part of universities was illustrated by their reluctance to finance business schools directly, looking instead to external funds from business. Industrialists, for their part, were keen promoters of expanding management education, contributing both ideas and funds. The Federation of British Industry played a leading role in promoting higher management education in the UK in the 1960s, concerned by the findings of a report that 82 per cent of managers in the country had no professional qualifications at all, including accounting, engineering, law and so on (Larson, 2009). Perhaps not surprisingly, there is no evidence in the literature that coops were consulted.

That globally the initiative was in the hands of industrialists, influenced the nomenclature of subjects and philosophy of business schools with long-term consequences. One was an ideological division between co-operatives and business schools regarding the purpose and role of managers in society. On one side are co-operatives, organizations that subscribe to uphold the values of equality and solidarity. On the other, business schools that are expected to teach their students how to win in a market that is fiercely and mercilessly competitive. It must be remembered that, from the days of the Pioneers, education was seen by co-operative thinkers not as an aim in itself, but as a mould for cooperative identity (Noble and Ross, 2021), a path for the betterment of human beings and a means to advance awareness of the members of the principles of fairness, democracy and equality. It is easy to see why co-operators may harbour doubts about entrusting the education of their members to business schools.

There is an extensive literature that is highly critical of business schools, arguing that economic theories and free market philosophy, which form the basis of much of the business school curriculum, have a detrimental effect on the values, attitudes and behaviour of business students (Leavitt, 1989; Ghoshal, 2005; Khurana, 2007; Parker, 2018; Starkey and Tempest, 2008). Critics point out that modern business education has an umbilical link with established economic theories that incorporate as their core elements the notion of individualism embodied in the concept of *homo economicus* with conceit and egoism as the driving force of economic and social progress. In a variety of interpretations and guises, these views have influenced much of the thinking about the teaching of mainstream economics, business and management. Similarly, the emphasis of economic theory on competition as the most efficient mechanism of the distribution of resources contributes to a worldview that places efficiency above equity. Together, these concepts and their derivatives create a model of society based on self-interest, instilling the belief that behaving selfishly is a winning strategy (McCabe et al, 2006). Research shows that exposure to business education does have an influence on individuals' ethical decision-making processes. Business students were found to be less inclined to consider the intrinsic worth, beyond the economic issues, of the others, in comparison to non-business students (Godos-Diez et al, 2015). Business schools are accused of providing education framed in terms of a winner-takes-all managerialism (Starkey and Thomas, 2019).

The incidence of cheating in exams among students seems to give some direct support to these allegations. McCabe and colleagues (2006) describe two research projects investigating cheating in US colleges. In the early 1960s, William Bowers revealed the results of an undergraduate survey which showed that business students as a group we are more prone to cheating than students in other disciplines (Bowers, 1964). Almost 40 years later, John McCabe replicated Bower's experiment with the same outcome. Of course, one should regard this data critically, especially since these studies did not include control for self-selection, that is, that individuals who enrol in business courses are already prone to fraud more than their counterparts in other programmes (Klein et al, 2007). However, the notion that cheating may be a bigger problem in business schools than elsewhere does not help allay concerns about the ethical focus of mainstream business education and its compatibility with the cooperative values.

Business schools and coops

There are very few business schools in the world offering customized programmes for and about co-operatives, and none in the UK. In the latter case, a plausible explanation is that, because universities in Britain are increasingly driven by the necessity of producing income to guarantee their own sustainability (Brown and Carasso, 2013), they simply do not see demand in the market for higher education justifying the expense of setting up and running such programmes.

The same explanation is valid for the lack of interest in co-operatives on the part of the authors and publishers of textbooks in business and economics. Kalmi (2007) in an exhaustive analysis of economics textbooks hypothesized that at least in part this was the result of a tradition in teaching economics established by influential textbooks by Samuelson, who completely ignored co-operatives and even excluded them from the list of business organizations in the 1970 edition. This may be true to an extent; however, the market for university textbooks is subject to the forces of competition, which must eventually be stronger than tradition. Other explanations are therefore needed.

One possibility is the long-standing conviction in certain academic circles that co-operatives have nothing to offer to enrich economic theory. The origins of this view can be traced back as early as the last decade of the 19th century and the writings of Maffeo Pantaleoni, a notable proponent of neoclassical economics (for debate see Gide and Foley, 1898). This opinion has not faded with the passage of time. In fact, according to Spencer Thompson, who dedicated considerable effort to investigating the issue in relation to worker co-operatives (Thompson, 2015; 2016), it remains central to modern theories of the firm. There are two main strands of theory explaining the existence of the firm. Contract-based theories argue that firms exist because they minimize transaction costs by internalizing certain market functions. Competence-based theories characterize the firm as a platform for accumulating productive capabilities that result in competitive advantages in the market. Although these schools offer a very different interpretation of the firm, they have, as Thompson points out, one common implication: both schools argue that co-operatives are generally inefficient and have no advantage over the traditional firm due to slowness of decision processes, the pluralism of objectives and a risk avoidance proclivity. This view mitigates against making co-operatives a focus of attention in standardized business courses that dominate teaching programmes of modern business schools, relegating them to a 'special interest' category. It does not help that in the eyes of market fundamentalists, whose philosophy has a great influence on what business programmes teach (Fernández-Gago and Martínez-Campillo, 2012), co-operatives are an outdated idea that ideologically leans too much to the left of a political spectrum as noted by Levi and Davis (2008) and Whyman (2012) among others.

Understandably, the negativity towards the coop model on the part of mainstream theorists provokes a defensive reaction on the part of the cooperative community. Johnston Birchall, a scholar and champion for the coop movement, formulated a question that was probably pondered by many cooperative thinkers: 'Why should we try to fit co-operatives into a conventional economic theory that is essentially hostile to them?' (Birchall, 2017, p 27). Birchall himself showed the way by determinedly developing what he called a theory of member governance. However, when claiming difference from the mainstream it is essential to avoid a negative attitude toward knowledge and ideas derived from a source external to the 'specialist' field (Antons and Piller, 2015). The temptation to regard conventional business education and knowledge as only marginally relevant can lead to disastrous developments such as that described at the beginning of this chapter. Birchall, for his part, stressed the importance of ensuring expertise on boards of directors and managing the costs of a participatory governance model. But the reality is that relations between business schools and the cooperative sector remain largely distant and indifferent. This is not in the interest of the latter, which needs sustained and disciplined academic analysis of its practices and strategies (Weiss, 1977; Davies et al, 2005).

Examples and lessons

The apparent deficit of collaboration between academia and co-operatives significantly weakens the ability of the cooperative model to showcase itself and influence mainstream business culture in promoting social objectives as well as commercial outcomes. When the UN announced the International Year of Co-operatives, it emphasized the importance of enlisting the academic and research community in mainstreaming the cooperative business model, especially to facilitate the spread of humanistic and social values practiced by co-operatives to all business endeavours (UN, 2013).

We interviewed academics teaching about and/or studying management in co-operatives, and practitioners working for co-operatives and their associations in nine countries over three continents, seeking their views on the disconnect between universities and the coops and what can be done to bridge it. A number of common themes have appeared.

Where universities do collaborate with cooperative economy and offer dedicated degree programmes, such as in Belgium, Canada and Italy, the initiative came from the cooperative side, whether individual large and prosperous co-operatives or an association representing smaller organizations, or a combination of the two. This is understandable, since cash-strapped universities are reluctant to launch courses, the sustainability of which may be uncertain. By making a financial commitment, the cooperative sponsor creates an opportunity for the university to expand its teaching and research portfolios. The role of the university is not entirely passive; nevertheless, as our interviews show, often it is the individual academics previously interested in cooperation who led the way. Through their research activities, they establish contacts with co-operatives and become a natural point of contact when coops start looking for partnership with the university sector. The role of individuals with the expertise and awareness of cooperative matters is very important because they provide a necessary stepping stone for possible wider collaboration between academia and coops.

There are reasons to believe, however, that fewer academics are involved in cooperative studies than in most other business and management disciplines. We analysed the proceedings of the 81st Annual Meeting of the Academy of Management (AOM) that took place in the summer of 2021. AOM is the largest scholarly association in the field of management, uniting faculty, students, and practitioners from more than 120 nations. It publishes a spectrum of journals which are among the most authoritative and prestigious in the field. During the 2021 meeting, in over 1,400 sessions more than 5,000 papers were presented. Of these, we found only a single session linked to the thematics of co-operatives and only one of four papers included in the session mentioned co-operatives in the abstract.

This highlights an important issue arising from our interviews. In order to expand the teaching offering for and about co-operatives, business schools need more faculty members willing to build their academic careers on topics related to co-operatives. These days, career prospects increasingly depend on one's publication record. There is a race to publish in the so-called 'top' journals. Mostly, these are established journals that have earned their reputation over many years by essentially contributing the building blocks of mainstream orthodoxy. It is not easy for cooperative scholars to have their work accepted there. For example, we were able to identify only three papers exploring aspects of cooperative organization that have appeared over the last 20 years in *Academy of Management Journal*, AOM's flagship publication. The neglect of cooperative topics may be attributable to the composition of various journal quality lists that often play a decisive role in performance metrics used by university management. Thus, only *Annals of Public and Cooperative Economics* features both in Chartered Association of Business Schools and the Australian Business Deans Council's journal quality lists, and its ranking is middling. Although there are specialist journals outside these lists, the perceived lack of prestige makes them less attractive as publishing opportunities in the eyes of aspiring academics. Career consideration by members of staff may be seen as a serious deterrent, making it more difficult for business schools to reach out to co-operatives.

Yet, it transpires from the interviews that building expertise in business schools is an important prerequisite for their collaboration with coops. Academics with experience of working with co-operatives pointed out that coops expect the university to come out with proposals about the content of the course rather than tell them what to put in it. One of the interviewees shared with us that the group of co-operatives that sponsored a programme at his university wanted it to be tailored to the specific needs of cooperative enterprises, but they were not sure what those needs were. In fact, in the opinion of this interviewee, a quality-approved programme from an established university was important for these co-operatives to strengthen their own legitimacy and confidence. We find this account very telling. It implies that co-operatives that have achieved some success and want to develop further commercially recognize the need for external evaluation and advice from specialists with state-of-the-art expertise rooted in the mainstream analysis of the functioning of the market. This is probably inevitable, considering that the prevailing institutional environment is generally geared to the dominant capitalist mode of organization, thus leaving co-operatives no choice but to integrate. At the same time, co-operatives care for their identity and are looking for knowledge that is relevant and adapted to their needs as well as the principles on which they are founded. To meet these requirements, teaching for coops must be led by academics who have good understanding of the cooperative enterprise and its needs, which brings us back to the current situation with expert capacity in coop studies. Efforts are needed by both cooperative organizations and the academic community to raise the profile of cooperative studies to make them an exciting career prospect for early career researchers if co-operatives are to benefit from knowledge creation in business schools.

Where business schools do offer courses with emphasis on co-operatives, it is done typically for a postgraduate student market. Structurally they are similar to a standard curriculum with coop-specific aspects embedded in the mostly conventional content. As we learned from the interviews, because of the paucity of relevant learning sources, case studies supplied by the students themselves are often used as educational tools. This kind of collaborative study may be particularly appropriate for cooperative education, in our opinion. It creates a learning environment in which co-operators can acquire mainstream knowledge without losing sight of the objectives and values of cooperative entrepreneurship. It also facilitates the spread of best practices, finding solutions to common problems, mutual support and networking between co-operatives, leading to greater confidence and efficiency of the cooperative movement.

Our interviewees stressed that to make progress in their studies it was highly desirable that students on postgraduate courses dedicated to co-operatives have some previous experience or a good understanding of how co-operatives function. Many emphasized that this placed a considerable constraint on the growth of postgraduate provision, because one of the traditional channels of student entry – progression from a bachelor's programme to a master's programme – was not working as would be the case with more traditional disciplinary specializations. Such a situation is mostly the consequence of what was described earlier in this chapter: the lack of information on co-operatives in business and management courses and textbooks makes them invisible to undergraduate students. As a result, few undergraduates develop an interest in cooperative studies or acquire sufficient knowledge to pursue the subject at an advanced level. As long as co-operatives are not mentioned, the majority of students show little interest in them. Hence, one can argue, the onus is on the cooperative movement to become more visible to help develop interest in the subject and encourage universities to respond by offering appropriate courses. This, of course, is linked to a wider issue that worries pro-cooperative academics who, like the Cambridge economist Ha-Joon Chang, point to the limited awareness of co-operatives given the substantial size of the sector (CoopNews, 2014). With few exceptions, the visibility of co-operatives both nationally and globally does not match their economic weight and role in society.

Moving forward

Now is an opportune moment for relations between business schools and co-operatives to change. A growing number of academics and public intellectuals argue in favour of market plurality and endorse the cooperative model as a breaker of market orthodoxy, capable of advancing more socially balanced economies, championing incorporation and building of democratic values into organizational structures and processes (Porritt, 2007; Stiglitz, 2009; Adler, 2014, 2019; Case and Deaton, 2020). In turn, the UN General Assembly credits the cooperative movement with a prominent role in achieving the Millennium Development Goals, while an EU-commissioned report recognizes co-operatives as a principal sector in advancing social economy long term (EU, 2012).

As was shown earlier in this chapter, one of the stumbling blocks in relations between business schools and the cooperative movement is ideological difference. Business schools are routinely accused of becoming 'the hired hands of business' (Khurana, 2007), of indoctrinating students in the values of individualism and a disregard of societal interests. This characterization of business schools unequivocally places them and co-operatives at the opposite ends of the ideological spectrum. But is it accurate? The last 20 years have seen a major shift in expectations on the part of civic society, first in the developed countries and later around the world, towards business in general and big corporations in particular. It has found its most visible manifestation in the spread of the concept of Corporate Social Responsibility (CSR). Corporations around the globe have found that their legitimacy in the eyes of the public and governments very much depends on their performance as responsible citizens, protectors of the environment and creators of societal value. Of course, this does not mean that the nature of business has changed; there are many voices accusing corporations of cynically using CSR for their own benefit as a tool to manipulate public perception. Nonetheless, the consequences for business education of this shift in business discourse and the actual policies of corporations have been enormous. Although the basic assumption of individualism as the foundation of the capitalist economy remains in place, it has now received a powerful and compelling counterbalance in the form of the ideals of CSR and their acceptance by the public, governments and firms as an imperative. Business education cannot ignore this. On the contrary, there is a strong feeling that business schools can and must play a central role in advancing these ideals through their curriculum, research and student and community engagement.

Numerous business schools declare their position by subscribing to the Principles for Responsible Management Education (PRME), a United Nations-supported initiative founded in 2007. The initiative counts over 850 business and management-related higher education institutions across 96 countries. It is a platform to raise the profile of sustainability in business and management schools and 'to ensure they provide future leaders with the skills needed to balance economic and sustainability goals, while drawing attention to the Sustainable Development Goals and aligning academic institutions with the work of the UN Global Compact' (UNPRME, nd). The signatories take it upon themselves to incorporate into their academic activities, curricula and organizational practices the values of global social responsibility, and to facilitate and support dialogue and debate among educators, students, business, civil society organizations and other interested groups and stakeholders on critical issues related to global social responsibility and sustainability. The Principles are designed to guide the effort of business schools to create positive change in students, staff, business partners and wider communities. The success of initiatives such as PRME indicates that there may be far more common ground between co-operatives and business schools in terms of values and purpose than is commonly believed. This may help to pull down one of the barriers in relations between the two. Another aspect that is likely to see change is cooperative-focused theorizing. The belief that the cooperative mode of organization is not interesting from a conceptual point of view has found itself under a two-prong attack. The COVID-19 shock has been a factor.

The pandemic has awakened theorists' interest in preconditions for business resilience. There is a strong opinion among analysts that the pandemic will rewrite the growth scenarios for all national economies, rendering the recovery of regions and wellbeing of economies and individuals dependent on solutions requiring co-operation and grassroot-level sources of resilience and initiative (OECD, 2020a, 2020b). Worker and social co-operatives in Europe have a well-documented record of being more stable employers and showing more resilience to crises than conventional enterprises of similar size, active in the same sectors and present in the same communities and regions (Birchall and Ketilson, 2009; Stiglitz, 2009; Roelants et al, 2012; Billiet et al, 2021). In addition, cooperative-type organizations have proven to be especially efficient in mobilizing and creating community assets to boost the sustainability of local economies. Coops have a recognized unique capacity to generate civic capital (Vieta, 2010). Under these conditions, the search for business models reflecting the need of a new balance between efficiency and resilience cannot ignore the experience of cooperative organizations, even if it means a revision of long-standing preconceptions. There are views, for example, that the features which organizational theorists for decades interpreted as deficiencies, for example, democratic procedures that slow down decision-making, result, in fact, in a higher economic stability of cooperative organizations (Chevallier, 2011).

In a similar vein, increasing interest in sociological factors of productivity and efficiency of labour prompts researchers to pay closer attention to the cooperative model. The accelerated automation and work precarity, 'global resets', such as the 2008 financial crisis, Brexit and the COVID-19 pandemic have affected the nature and organization of work, the physical, social and physiological dimensions of employment, related expectations and opportunities. All this has moved to the forefront of work relations concerns about moral leadership, care, wellbeing, equality, participation and accountability. There has been a growth of interest in organizational cultures that influence key drivers of productivity, such as development of human capital and knowledge building (Case and Deaton, 2020). Insights into cooperative employment can help address many of the current work-related challenges and spread the best of cooperative practice to the business mainstream in such aspects as work–life balance, participatory models, compensation and work security. In particular, the stability of internal social relations and solidaristic behaviour attract attention as a source of efficiency based on trust and loyalty, and a strong integration of the members of the work collective that such stability fosters, leading to greater knowledge accumulation and sharing.

It is naïve to anticipate or even advocate a major expansion of customized cooperative-centred programmes by business schools. Demand for them cannot be big, if only because in smaller co-operatives, which currently make up the vast majority, training for business literacy is normally sufficient for board members and managers do deal with the day-to-day tasks. It is a different proposition for a large organization, some of them multinational like Mondragon. There, boards of directors address complex economic and strategic problems. They are more likely to support their members in acquiring advanced degrees, also because they have resources to do so. Indeed, in our sample of universities with a postgraduate course on co-operation it was precisely large coops that initiated and sponsored their provision. However, this may not be a typical behaviour or a precursor of the future. Webb (2020) reports that in Canada cooperative graduate educational programmes offered by Saint Mary's University were met with strong resistance from many large co-operatives, who continued to send managers to standard MBA programmes. This may be a manifestation of a trend that we noticed during our research, where large co-operatives choose to take a pragmatic line in moving from finding a balance between economic self-interest and social goals to merging them, which secures economic sustainability without losing a cooperative purpose. While the prospects of postgraduate cooperative education may be uncertain, there is no doubt that business schools have to take radical steps to increase the awareness of undergraduates on business and management courses of co-operatives as a business form. This is necessary in the light of the sustained and profound criticism of the traditional models of capitalist organizations as responsible for deepening inequalities and for their inability to achieve greater social, economic and environmental sustainability. As organizations that prioritize social solidarity, organizational democracy and community-focused commitments, co-operatives fully deserve visibility in university programmes to arm students to deal critically and creatively with the challenges of our time.

Note

[1]   Institutional logics are socially constructed frames of reference that organizational actors use to infuse their work with meaning (Mangen and Brivot, 2015). They represent core cognitive principles and values that guide people at work.

References

Adler, P.S. (2014) 'Capitalism in question', *Journal of Management Inquiry*, 23(2): 206–209.

Adler, P.S. (2019) *The 99 Percent Economy: How Democratic Socialism Can Overcome the Crises of Capitalism*. New York: Oxford University Press.

Antons, D. and Pillers, T. (2015) 'Opening the black box of "Not Invented Here": attitudes, decision biases, and behavioural consequences', *Academy of Management Perspectives*, 29(2): 193–217.

Billiet A., Dufays F., Friedel S. and Staessens M. (2021) 'The resilience of the cooperative model: How do cooperatives deal with the COVID-19 crisis?' *Strategic Change*, 30(2): 99–108.

Birchall, J. (2017) *The Governance of Large Co-operative Businesses*. Manchester: Co-operatives UK.

Birchall, J. and Ketilson, L.H. (2009) *Resilience of the Co-operative Business Model in Times of Crisis*. Geneva: ILO.

Bowers, W.J. (1964) *Student Dishonesty and It's Control in College*. New York: Columbia University Press.

Brown, R. and Carasso, H. (2013) *Everything for Sale? The Marketisation of UK Higher Education*. London: Routledge.

Case, A. and Deaton, A. (2020) *Deaths of Despair and the Future of Capitalism*. Princeton, NJ: Princeton University Press.

Chandler, A.D. (1962) *Strategy and Structure: Chapters in the History of American Enterprise*. Boston: MIT Press.

Chandler, A.D. (1984) 'The Emergence of Managerial Capitalism', *Business History Review*, 58(4): 473–503.

Chevallier, M. (2011) 'The cooperatives' sources of efficiency: A catalyst for the emergence of localized norms', *Journal of Cooperative Studies*, 44(1): 31–40.

CoopNews (2014) 'A different point of view: Ha-Joon Chang'. Available from www.thenews.coop/85032/sector/different-point-view-ha-joon-chang/#.XXjWI0UgyqQ.wordpress [Accessed on 7 February 2022].

Davies, H., Nutley, S. and Walte, I. (2005) 'Assessing the impact of social science research: Conceptual, methodological and practical issues'. Available from https://esrc.ukri.org/files/research/research-and-impact-evaluation/international-symposium/ [Accessed on 8 March 2022].

Dawson, L. (1923) *Co-operative Education.* London: The Fabian Society.

Emmanuel, J. (2007) 'Critical issues in the life of a co-op'. In Emmanuel, J. and Cayo, L. (eds) *Effective Practices In Starting Co-ops: The Voice of Canadian Co-op Developers,* Gabriola Island, BC: New Rochdale Press, pp 73–96.

EU (2012) *The Social Economy in the European Union.* Brussels: European Union.

Fernández-Gago, R. and Martínez-Campillo, A. (2012) 'Teaching business management from a perspective beyond self-interest', *Innovar,* 22(46): 165–174.

Ghoshal, S. (2005) 'Bad management theories are destroying good management practices', *Academy of Management Learning & Education,* 4(1): 75–91.

Gide, C. and Foley, C.A. (1898) 'Has co-operation introduced a new principle into economics?' *The Economic Journal,* 8(32): 490–511.

Godos-Diez, J.L., Fernández-Gago, R. and Cabeza-García, L. (2015) 'Normative stakeholder management orientation: Business vs. non-business students', *Society and Economy,* 37(4): 477–492.

Hannley, L. (2007) 'Good governance' in Emmanuel, J. and Cayo, L. (eds) *Effective Practices in Starting Co-ops: The Voice of Canadian Co-op Developers,* Gabriola Island, BC: New Rochdale Press, pp 213–227.

Hill, R. (2000) 'The case of the missing organizations: Co-operatives and the textbooks', *The Journal of Economic Education,* 31(3): 281–295.

ICA (2017) 'The guidance notes on the cooperative principles'. Available from www.ica.coop/en/media/library/research-and-reviews/guidance-notes-cooperative-principles [Accessed on 7 February 2022].

Jakobsen, G. (1995) 'When education for cooperation leads to development in cooperatives: A study of educational processes', *Journal of Rural Co-operation,* XXIII (2): 105–118.

Kalmi, P. (2007) 'The disappearance of cooperatives from economics textbooks', *Cambridge Journal of Economics,* 31(4): 625–647.

Khurana, R. (2007) *From Higher Aims to Hired Hands: The Social Transformation of American Business Schools and the Unfulfilled Promise of Management as a Profession.* Princeton NJ: Princeton University Press.

Klein, H.A., Levenburg, N.M., McKendall, M. and Mothersell, W. (2007) Cheating during the College Years: How Do Business School Students Compare? *Journal of Business Ethics,* 72(2): 197–206.

Larson, M.J. (2009) 'The Federation of British Industry and management education in post-war Britain', *Cardiff Historical Papers*, 2009/1.

Larson, M.J. (2020) 'Re-imagining management education in post-WWII Britain: Views from government and business', *Management & Organizational History*, 15(2): 169–191.

Leavitt, H.J. (1989) 'Educating our MBAs: on teaching what we haven't been taught', *California Management Review*, 31(3): 38–50.

Levi, Y. and Davis, P. (2008) 'Cooperatives as the "enfants terribles" of economics: Some implications for the social economy', *Journal of Socio-Economics*, 37(6): 2178–2188.

Mangen, C. and Brivot, M. (2015) 'The challenge of sustaining organizational hybridity: The role of power and agency', *Human Relations*, 68(4): 659–684.

Marx, K. (1894/1981) *Capital*, Vol. III, Harmondsworth: Penguin Books.

McCabe, D.L., Butterfield, K.D. and Trevino, L.K. (2006) 'Academic dishonesty in graduate business programs: Prevalence, causes, and proposed action' *Academy of Management Learning & Education*, 5(3): 294–305.

Miner, K. and Guillotte, C.-A. (2014) *Relevance and Impact of Co-operative Business Education*. Quebec, CA: IRECUS.

Myers, J. (2019) 'Co-operative principles variations and adaptions', *Journal of Co-operative Studies*, 52(2): 33–36.

Noble, M. and Ross, C. (2021) 'From principles to participation: "The Statement on The Cooperative Identity" and higher education co-operatives', *Journal of Co-operative Organization and Management*, 9(2): 100146.

OECD (2020a). 'Coronavirus: The world economy at risk'. OECD Interim Economic Outlook, March 2020. Available from www.oecd.org/ber lin/publikationen/Interim-Economic-Assessment-2-March-2020.pdf [Accessed on 8 June 2023].

OECD (2020b). 'Tackling the Coronavirus (COVID-19): Contributing to a global effort'. Available from www.oecd.org/coronavirus/en/ [Accessed on 30 September 2021].

Parker, M. (2018) *Shut down the Business School: What's Wrong with Management Education*. London: Pluto Press.

Pascal, D., Mersland, R. and Mori, N. (2017) 'The influence of the CEO's business education on the performance of hybrid organizations: The case of the global microfinance industry', *Small Business Economics*, 49(2): 339–354.

Pestana, B.C. and Gomes Santos, J-C. (2003) 'Earnings and schooling of cooperative managers', *Annals of Public and Cooperative Economics*, 74(3): 349–364.

Porritt, J. (2007) *Capitalism as if the World Matters*. Abingdon: Earthscan.

Roelants, B., Dovgan, D., Eum, H. and Terrasi, E. (2012) The resilience of the co-operative model: How worker cooperatives, social cooperatives and other worker-owned enterprises respond to the crisis and its consequences. CECOP-CICOPA Europe. Available from www.ess-europe.eu/sites/defa ult/files/report_cecop_2012_en_web.pdf [Accessed on 9 June 2021].

Slater, D.J. and Dixon-Fowler, H.R. (2010) 'The future of the planet in the hands of MBAs: An examination of CEO MBA education and corporate environmental performance', *Academy of Management Learning & Education*, 9(3): 429–441.

Starkey, K. and Tempest, S. (2008) 'A clear sense of purpose? The evolving role of the business school', *Journal of Management Development*, 27(4): 379–390.

Starkey, K. and Thomas, H. (2019) 'The future of business schools: Shut them down or broaden our horizons?' *EFMD Global Focus*, 13(2): 44–49.

Stiglitz, J. (2009) 'Moving beyond market fundamentalism to a more balanced economy', *Annals of Public and Cooperative Economics*, 80(3): 345–360.

The Guardian (2013) 'The Co-op scandal: Drugs, sex, religion ... and the humiliation of a movement'. Available from www.theguardian.com/busin ess/2013/nov/23/coop-scandal-paul-flowers-mutual-societies [Accessed on 22 February 2022].

Thompson, S. (2015) 'Towards a social theory of the firm: Worker cooperatives reconsidered', *Journal of Co-operative Organization and Management*, 3(1): 3–13.

Thompson, S. (2016) 'Worker cooperatives in the theory of the firm: Marx and Veblen on technological determinism', *Journal of Economic Issues*, 50(4): 913–939.

UN (2013) 'Co-operatives in social development and the observance of the International Year of Co-operatives', *Secretary-General Report A/ 68/168*. Available from http://daccess-dds-ny.un.org/doc/UNDOC/ GEN/N13/402/80/PDF/N1340280.pdf?OpenElement [Accessed on 11 February 2022].

UNPRME (nd) 'What is PRME?'. Available from www.unprme.org/about [Accessed on 3 March 2022].

Vieta, M. (2010) 'The new cooperativism', *Affinities: A Journal of Radical Theory, Culture, and Action*, 4(1): 1–11.

Webb, T. (2020) 'Learning to manage the co-operative difference: Saint Mary's co-operative management education', *International Journal of Co-Operative Accounting & Management*, 3(1): 18–28.

Weiss, C.H. (1977) 'Research for policy's sake: The enlightenment function of social research', *Policy Analysis*, 3(4): 531–545.

Whyman, P.B. (2012) 'Co-operative principles and the evolution of the "dismal science": The historical interaction between co-operative and mainstream economics', *Business History*, 54(6): 833–854.

Woodin, T. (2011) 'Co-operative education in Britain during the nineteenth and early twentieth centuries: Context, identity and learning'. In Webster, A., Shaw, L., Walton, J.K, Brown, A. and Stewart, D. (eds) *The Hidden Alternative: Co-operative Values, Past, Present and Future.* Manchester: Manchester University Press, pp 78–95.

Wright, S. and Manley, J. (2021) 'Co-operative Education: from Mondragón and Bilbao to Preston'. In Manley, J. and Whyman, P.B. (eds) *The Preston Model and Community Wealth Building: Creating a Socio-economic Democracy for the Future.* London: Routledge, pp 48–64.

PART III

Growth: The Preston Model, Co-operation and Community Wealth Building

9

The Strange Death of Co-operative Britain? Comparing the Development of British Co-operation with Wider European Trends and Emerging Strategies for a 21st-Century Revival

Anthony Webster

Introduction

As the author wrote this chapter, he had an eye on BBC TV's *Digging for Britain* (BBC 2, 16/1/2022), one section of which covered an archaeological dig in Rochdale, revealing fascinating artefacts of Rochdale's industrial history. Celebrated TV commentator Alice Roberts commented upon Rochdale's 'small part' in the history of industrialization. One can only assume that she is unaware that the town bequeathed a model of democratic cooperative commercial organization which spread around the world. Having considered the importance of Rochdale Town Hall, it is a great pity she did not walk just 100 yards from the dig site to the building on Toad Lane which housed the first coop store (now a museum) for another, arguably more important, example of 'living' archaeology, and the origin of Rochdale's greatest contribution to global development. But she is not the first popular academic to ignore co-operation. The celebrated BBC TV Series *Turn Back Time: The High Street*, aired in 2010, used a reality format to examine the evolution of high street retail in the Somerset town of Shepton Mallet. No reference was made to the fact that the town had the largest and most successful cooperative society in the county. That the programme made great claims to be educational in intent makes the omission even more egregious.

Yet both instances allude to a gradual retreat of co-operation from British popular consciousness.

Until early in this century in Britain the word 'coop' frequently conjured up nostalgic memories of 'divi' numbers (member registration numbers used for recording purchases from the coop store by members so that dividends could be calculated) among a fast-disappearing older generation. For many elderly working-class people the coop symbolized a fixed point in daily life in the first half of the 20th century; the local store which rewarded loyal customer-members was a reliable fixture for several generations of working-class communities. But the nostalgia itself suggests an important story in the development of the British social economy. As the later 20th century wore on, such recollections became rarer, and the coop store was increasingly regarded as a fading feature of a disappearing industrial social landscape. However, the social economy, defined by the European Commission as 'a variety of businesses, organisations and different legal entities ... [that] share the objective of systematically putting people first, producing a positive impact on local communities and pursuing a social cause' (European Commission, nd) remained alive and buoyant. One of the fastest areas of growth were social enterprises (SEs), usually defined as organizations which are run as a business and generate profit to be used for socially useful goals, though there is no one, accepted definition (Ridley-Duff and Bull, 2011, p 79). Co-operatives are generally regarded as falling within the general category of social enterprise, but with distinctive features of democratic control by members (Ridley-Duff and Bull, 2011, p 62). Mutual organizations such as building societies also shared this democratic principle, though unlike co-operatives they do not have to subscribe to the values and principles set out in the ICA values and principles governing co-operatives (Parliamentary Website, 2012). As will be seen however, like coops, mutuals retreated significantly in the later 20th century. By contrast, social enterprises thrived, and by 2012 there were 68,000 social enterprises contributing £24 billion to the UK economy (Why Social Enterprise?, 2012). Social enterprises by then had become the preferred social economy model, and were actively promoted by government, working with organizations such as Social Enterprise UK which actively promoted the sector with the help of funding organizations such as Key Fund and Big Society Capital (Webster, 2017, p 127). By 2017 the number of UK social enterprises was estimated at 471,000, though calculated on a different basis to the earlier figures. Overall, SEs provided employment for 144,000 people, though this latter survey does not offer figures for SE turnover (Social Enterprise: Market Trends, 2017). Interestingly, co-operatives and mutuals are hardly mentioned in the report. A survey of social enterprises in 2021 showed that less than 20 per cent of the social economy sector defined themselves as co-operatives, and less 10 per cent saw themselves as mutuals; while 80 per cent preferred the term social enterprise (No Going Back: Social Enterprise Survey, 2021 by Social Enterprise UK, p 13). The social economy in the UK therefore shows a marked move away from the democratic cooperative and mutual forms which predominated in the late 19th century, towards the social enterprise which, while emphasizing social goals and benefits, tend not to have democratic control by a body of members. Huckfield argues that this was largely the work of the Blair administration, which tended to see co-operatives as rather 'Old Labour'. Huckfield shows that the 1970s and 1980s had seen a flourishing of co-operatives and local community organizations locally run and controlled, largely in response to the unemployment and hardship of the Thatcher era for areas of industrial decline. But Blair's government favoured a more business-oriented approach which was more in tune with the neoliberal *zeitgeist*. Social enterprises, usually controlled by a few individuals, not necessarily from or belonging to the local communities they served, increasingly came to be seen as deliverers of public services rather than agents of local community representation and autonomy. As a result, Huckfield contends that the new social enterprises have tended to become an integral part of the neoliberal order, delivering services at the lowest cost through competitive tendering, rather than positing an alternative, community-based and controlled alternative to neoliberalism (Huckfield, 2021). Increasingly reliant on state sources of finance, a process of financialization ensured that these social enterprises would be driven essentially by neoliberal principles, methods and management (Huckfield, 2020). Moreover, through agencies such as the British Council and other channels of British influence, this approach was exported to parts of the EU and the wider world (Huckfield, 2022).

This chapter explores the development trajectory of the UK social economy, from the beginning of the 19th century until the early 21st century, focusing especially on the role of co-operatives within it. As will be seen, the social economy moved away from a strong tradition of collective self-organization as exemplified by co-operatives, Friendly Societies and Building Societies, to, from the latter 20th century, the social enterprise format which largely eschewed membership and democratic structures, while retaining a firm commitment to social improvements, especially the alleviation of poverty and deprivation. An important element of this chapter is to consider how far the British experience reflected wider trends across Europe, and the extent to which it deviated from these, and if so – why?

In Britain it will be seen that while the relationship between co-operatives and mutuals and the state had been problematic, by the early 20th century there was cross-party enthusiasm and support for the social enterprise model; in the early 2000s the Labour governments of Tony Blair (PM 1997–2007) and Gordon Brown (PM 2007–2010) facilitated new legal forms for social enterprises; notably the CIC and the Charitable Incorporated Organization

(CIO), the former involving an asset lock to prevent the transfer of assets for purposes other than for the good of the community (Webster, 2017, p 136). David Cameron's Conservative-Liberal Democrat coalition government of 2010–2015 saw social enterprise as a key form to take over local authority services during the drastic reduction in public spending in the wake of the 2008 financial crisis. They, like Blair and Brown, became strong advocates of social enterprise. A central theme of the chapter will be why in Britain there was such a pronounced shift away from co-operation and mutualism in the sector, towards the altruistic yet less democratically structured social enterprise model. But first, a general overview of the main developments in the evolution of co-operation during the period will be provided, together with some comparison with European trends.

Patterns in the development of the British co-operation and comparisons with Europe 1800–2021

Activity aimed at social good was not of course solely a product of industrialization. Charitable activity, especially by the Church and related organizations, has a long history and indeed there has been legislation to permit and regulate charitable giving since the Charitable Uses Act of 1601. In Europe also, a long tradition of charitable giving was a legacy of the Middle Ages, most notably in the Dutch Republic, where the high concentration of elite involvement in charity has attracted a great deal of interest among historians (Van Voss and Van Leeuwen, 2010). In Greece, the widespread emergence of charities followed independence from the Ottoman Empire, and was led not only by the Orthodox Church, but also by wealthy merchant families such as the Onassis dynasty; though the move into social enterprise activity has been quite recent (Social Enterprises and their Ecosystems in Europe. Country Report: Greece, 2019). Of course, while many charities do not rely on commercial activity to fund charitable activity, this has become more common; the best example in the UK being Oxfam, which has partly funded activity since 1948 through its network of shops (History of Oxfam, 2015). Some charities have therefore effectively become part of the social economy.

Nonetheless, in Britain and Europe industrialization acted as a spur to the emergence of the social economy for two reasons. First, the geographical and social upheaval of rapid urbanization expanded towns and cities resulting in poor housing, overcrowding, localized food shortages and high prices due to a dearth of retail outlets, as well as a plethora of health issues. Self-organization was often the only option of communities pressed in these ways. Second, in the case of Britain, industrialization was accompanied by a shift in state ideology towards free market economics, a determination to minimize government spending and a much harsher and punitive regime for the poor exemplified by the new Poor Law of 1834. This ideological shift overturned well-established informal customs governing such important issues as bread prices, as market forces were allowed to exert themselves. One reaction was a rash of food riots across the country from the late 18th century, but examples of self-organization to address the problem by other means were arguably more significant. An important initiative was the 'Hull-Anti-Mill Society' established in 1795, which involved the purchase of corn and the milling of flour. At least 46 such societies emerged during the early years of the 19th century, particularly in areas where there had been food riots (Bamfield, 1998, p 17). Other self-help groups such as Friendly Societies to provide support during sickness or old age also began to be formed. K.D.M. Snell has argued that the sense of alienation and loss of social/family support experienced by many of the predominantly young people who moved to the new industrial jobs in the burgeoning towns and cities was an especially powerful spur to co-operation between people who were lonely and stripped of the social and domestic supports of wider family (Snell, 2012).

This trend in Britain towards self-organization was also supported by powerful intellectual forces, including luminaries such as Robert Owen, Dr William King and the Christian Socialist movement, all of whom lobbied for and engaged in experiments in cooperative communities as an alternative to mainstream capitalist society. But while this influence was significant, the overwhelming momentum for self-organization came from industrial workers, usually among such occupational groups as cotton operatives and miners, and in this sense its roots are similar to those of British trade unionism. The formation of the Rochdale Pioneers in 1844, one of the earliest consumer co-operatives in the UK marked a highly important moment in the development of the UK social economy. With its principles of member democracy, dividends-based member/customer loyalty, as well as commitments to education and high quality made the Pioneers sensationally attractive. Not only did the Rochdale Society grow rapidly in membership and turnover, the ideas and principles on which it was based spread rapidly across the UK, where safe and affordable food was a priority. By 1900, there were about 1200 consumer cooperative societies across the country, with almost 1.2 million members; and individual membership continued to grow well into the 20th century, peaking at 11.9 million in 1965 (Wilson et al, 2013, p 400). In addition, the movement created a political leadership, in the form of the Co-operative Union (CU), and its own wholesale organizations in England and Scotland (Co-operative Wholesale Society [CWS] and Scottish Co-operative Wholesale Society [SCWS]). The latter organizations rapidly grew into large and sophisticated operators with their own factories, ships, banking facilities and global supply chains (Webster, 2019). These were formidable organizations which enabled British retail co-operatives to capture a substantial share of the British market, which it held until after the Second

World War. By 1951 it still held 12 per cent of the domestic retail market in all goods, and 17.1 per cent of the food market (Wilson et al, 2013, p 237). The movement had played a key role in the war effort between 1939 and 1945, becoming a major procurer of wheat on the international market, and a leading body in the implementation of rationing. The British consumer cooperative movement bestrode the social economy like a colossus, with its huge membership and large market share. Consumer co-operation was not only the backbone of the social economy, it was also a national institution.

There were both similar and divergent trends in the development of co-operatives across Europe. Most European countries also saw an increase in cooperative and mutual formation in the wake of the rapid economic change. There were certainly commonalities, especially in the ubiquity of consumer cooperative growth across the continent in the later 19th century. The German movement was not only a response to the impact of industrialization; there was also a conscious effort to copy the Rochdale model, and by 1900 the country had 568 societies, with half a million members – just about a third of the size of the English consumer movement (Prinz, 2017, p 266). In Italy, by 1910, of 4,960 co-operatives, 1,652 were consumer co-operatives (Battilani, 2011, p 164). Certainly the Rochdale model was consciously copied across Europe, and the emergence of the International Co-operative Alliance in the 1890s ensured that the Rochdale principles became universally accepted as those which should govern the cooperative movement globally. One consequence of this was a conscious effort to imitate the British consumer movement, especially in the early years after the end of the First World War, which saw new consumer co-operatives spring up. The English CWS in fact supported some of these with loans, notably the Polish Warsaw CWS (£200,000), the Polish CWS (£100,000), the Finnish CWS (£20,000) and the Romanian CWS (£400,000) (Webster, 2019, p 107).

But elsewhere in Europe it was not always the consumer model which led the way for co-operation. One of the most striking examples was Denmark, where agricultural co-operatives, led by the creamery co-operatives, provided the basis of national recovery after defeat in the war with Prussia in 1864. Creamery co-operatives encouraged rigorous training in the latest agricultural technologies among member farmers and demanded the highest standards in the quality of milk supplied for butter production (Henriksen, 1999; Henriksen and O'Rourke, 2005; Henriksen et al, 2011). They pioneered winter dairying and developed marketing so successfully that their share of the UK market grew from 13.5 per cent between 1880 and 1884 to 40 per cent between 1910 and 1913 (Higgins and Mordhorst, 2008, p 188). In Ireland there were efforts to imitate the Danish model under the leadership of Horace Plunkett. Though only partially successful, the cooperative sector did play a significant role in the evolution of Irish republican national identity in the 20th century (Doyle, 2019). In Italy, by

1910 the 1,652 consumer co-operatives were outnumbered by 2,070 credit unions of various types (Battilani, 2011, p 164). Germany's cooperative movement was also initially linked to agriculture, though this time through credit unions providing finance for farmers, along the lines pioneered by Friedrich Wilhelm Raiffeisen. Urban based credit unions subsequently emerged on the model developed by Hermann Schulze Delitzsch. These provided the basis for the growth of other cooperative models, so that by 1933 there were 50,000 co-operatives with 9 million members (Zamagni, 2017, p 9). France became the early leader in the growth of worker co-operatives – though this was by no means the largest sector – and by 1904 there were 358 French worker co-operatives (Zamagni, 2017, p 9). Perhaps the most unique model is the Mondragón consortium which emerged in the Basque Country of Spain from the early 1940s. This involved the creation of a system of interlocking co-operatives covering sectors such as industrial production, retailing, finance and even a cooperative university, with a variety of cooperative forms including worker and stakeholder co-operatives (Molina and Walton, 2011). What has been created is a sophisticated system of interdependent co-operatives – a coherent cooperative economy which has inspired imitation overseas, including the US and even the UK (Webster et al, 2021).

Neither were co-operatives always a response to the challenges of industrialization. In those areas of Europe where industrial change was less rapid or all encompassing, co-operatives were formed to meet other needs. In Sweden, for example, consumer co-operatives emerged not only to address the requirements of emerging industrial towns, but also of isolated rural communities lacking retail facilities. The outcome was a much more cohesive and centrally controlled Swedish consumer movement, without the fractious relations which characterized those between the British wholesales and local societies. Consumer co-operation in Britain grew during a period of intense industrialization and was concentrated in the new towns and cities, where they encountered severe competition and hostility from private stores. British societies, desperate to keep prices low and dividends high, were less inclined to buy solely from their cooperative wholesales, creating friction between societies and the cooperative wholesales, and arguably a much more market-sensitive consumer movement than in Sweden (Friberg et al, 2012, pp 250–252).

In Britain, what followed the Second World War was a dramatic turn of fortunes which, by the first 20 years of the 21st century, had seen co-operation retreat in its position in the social economy, to be replaced by the looser, frequently less democratic social enterprise model. By the early 2000s these were proliferating rapidly with the general approval of politicians across the party spectrum. Co-operatives were generally obscured by these developments, and consumer co-operation – notwithstanding a brief rally in commercial performance and reputation between the late 1990s and 2013 – declined in market share, membership and both commercial and ethical reputation. By 1981 market share had been reduced to just 12 per cent, and eventually settled to about 8 per cent by 2010, following the recovery of the early 2000s (Wilson et al, 2013, p 301; Friberg et al, 2012, p 257). The financial crisis which hit the new Co-operative Group in 2013, which resulted in the selling of key assets such as the Co-operative Bank, and major reforms in the governance of the organization, further damaged the reputation of co-operation as a model. One consequence of this long-term decline was the effective airbrushing of co-operatives out of British popular culture and history.

There were also similarities and differences in the long-term trajectory of British and European consumer co-operation. The differences are especially significant. Whereas the Second World War represented a high point in British cooperative fortunes, it was a very different story for many parts of mainland Europe. In both Germany and Italy co-operation was suppressed from the 1920s and 1930s respectively, and the war in mainland Europe was destructive of other European cooperative movements, both through the physical impact of war and the subjection of cooperative movements to Nazi domination (Battilani, 2017, pp 595–597; Brazda et al, 2017, pp 284–287; Lambersens et al, 2017, p 109; Zamagni, 2017, p 9). The period after the war also saw major challenges to European consumer co-operation, in some cases resulting in outright failure; notably with Konsum Österreich in Austria (1995) (Brazda et al, 2017, p 293), Co-op AG in Germany (1989) (Ekberg, 2012, p 1009) and widespread failures in France in the 1980s (Lambersens et al, 2017, pp 114–115). As in the UK, the emergence of well-funded powerful private competitors played an important role in this.

However, the post-war story of European consumer co-operation is not one of universal decline. In some countries, steps were taken which stemmed decline, and even reversed it. Ekberg contrasts the striking failure of the German movement in the 1980s with the success of the Norwegian model in advancing both membership and market share (Ekberg, 2012, p 1013). Moreover, the success was also replicated in the other Nordic states of Sweden, Finland and Denmark, a phenomenon which Ekberg attributes to the skill with which the Nordic consumer co-operatives adapted to the demands of the retail market, most notably in developing self-service, supermarkets and effective supply chains (Ekberg, 2017, pp 724–725). Though the British consumer movement declined for much of the post-war period, there was a renaissance in the 2000s, following the reforms initiated by Graham Melmoth, CEO of the CWS and the creation of the Co-operative Group. These were, unfortunately not to prove the decisive turning point hoped for (Wilson et al, 2013).

It is important to note that in Britain and various parts of the world co-operation was not the only democratic model in decline. New legislation in the 1980s facilitated the conversion of mutual organizations into investor-led firms, and resulted in the demutualization of a substantial section of the mutual sector. By 2022 the only substantial building society to have survived was the Nationwide, which began life in the 19th century, ironically enough, as the Co-operative Permanent Building Society. In Eastern Europe, the USA, Canada and Australia, there were similar demutualizations, though in Europe it was mainly a phenomenon of the former communist states of Eastern Europe (Battilani and Schröter, 2012). Why then this spectacular fall from grace of the democratic model of social economy in Britain?

The strange death of co-operative Britain? Some key factors

While it might seem easy to correlate the decline of co-operation in the UK with its commercial retreat some international comparisons are instructive. Italy's cooperative movement was all but wiped out following Mussolini's rise to power in 1923, yet it recovered spectacularly after 1945. The problems of the French retail movement in the 1980s did not prevent the consolidation and recognition of a new wave of French worker co-operatives. Furthermore, the success of the Mondragón cooperative cluster even during the unpromising and potentially hostile Franco period was evidence of the robustness of the model. The decline of the British cooperative and democratic enterprise model as a key element of the social economy was the result of several distinctive and interlocking factors as well as commercial retreat.

First, it is important to recognize a distinctive imbalance in the British cooperative movement from the later 19th century. Consumer co-operation rapidly rose to a dominant position within the British movement. While worker co-operatives emerged, especially from the 1870s, they did not share in the success of the consumer movement. There were some valiant but catastrophic failures, notably the Ouseburn Engine Co-operative on Tyneside. This created a growing conviction among many in the consumer movement that cooperative production needed to be under its control, rather than left to workers themselves. This might be by individual societies, the wholesales, or even through consumer societies holding key positions on the management committees of worker co-operatives, as was the case with the Hebden Bridge Fustian Manufacturing Society (Bibby, 2015, p 56). This view was consolidated by the consequences of the CWS taking over failing worker co-operatives in the 1870s (especially coal mines) which resulted in it having to write off £32,000 in related debts in 1881 (Wilson et al, 2013, p 80). The upshot was a deep antipathy towards worker and producer co-operatives within the consumer movement, exacerbated by the rise of the wholesales as major producers in their own right. Non-retail co-operation never really recovered from this in the UK, and such societies remained relatively few and often viewed with suspicion. Attempts to promote worker co-operatives, such as by the Labour Governments of 1974 to 1979 were made but enjoyed only limited success. There were success stories, such as the enduring Suma Wholefoods co-operative in Yorkshire, but these were rare, compared to other European countries. As a result, when British retail co-operation went into decline in the later 20th century this tended to discredit the whole idea of co-operation itself; there were few countervailing success stories. Indeed, some long-standing components of the cooperative movement chose to actively dissociate themselves from co-operation itself – thus the Co-operative Permanent Building Society rebranded itself as the Nationwide Building Society at the end of the 1960s. Indeed there were serious consequences for popular perceptions of what a co-operative is or might be. There was a tendency for coops to be seen solely as a supermarket chain, with little difference from its rival private operators. Indeed, among younger generations unfamiliar with cooperative membership and the 'divi', awareness of co-operation became almost non-existent. Many European countries hosted a much more diverse range of co-operatives, including worker co-operatives and credit unions. The comparative underdevelopment of British worker co-operation is evident from some basic statistics. In 2016, there were 25,000 worker co-operatives in Italy, 17,000 in Spain, 2,600 in France, but a mere 500–600 in Britain (Pérotin, 2016, p 240).

A second problem for the British movement was its political position. The rise of local coop stores from the 1850s incited the active opposition and fury of private retailers, which manifested itself as boycotts by wholesalers, anti-cooperative propaganda, and lobbying for anti-cooperative legislation. The upshot was a considerable level of antipathy among capitalist political interests, especially on the right of the Conservative Party. By the 1980s, when the Conservative Party had shifted to the right and had begun to embrace an emergent neoliberal orthodoxy, it was easy to dismiss co-operation as an outmoded and socialistic form of organization, destined for extinction, and it prompted moves to speed that process in the new legislation which facilitated demutualization. But the problems were not only on the right. Trades Unions tended to view consumer co-operatives as just another employer willing to exploit workers, a suspicion only reinforced by consumer cooperative resistance to worker membership of their organizations. Those socialists such as the Fabians, who would be influential in the development of the ideology of the Labour Party regarded the state, rather than self-organized bodies such as co-operatives, as being the main instrument for creating a socialist society. This intellectual side-lining continued even after the formation of the Co-operative Party in 1917 and an uneasy alliance with

Labour was established with it in 1927, resulting in the sponsorship of some Labour MPs by the cooperative movement. But Whitecross's and Manton's research on the evolving ideology of the Labour Party in the 1930s and 1940s reveals little serious commitment to an enhanced role for co-operatives either in the development of a socialist economy, or in the retail trade (Manton, 2007; 2008; 2009; Whitecross, 2016). This indifference to co-operation was also evident in the attitude of Tony Crosland, the Labour politician, when he served on the Co-operative Independent Commission between 1956 to 1958. He regarded the structure of the cooperative movement as outdated and was rather dismissive of its traditions of democracy. Moreover he strongly advocated that British consumer co-operation should imitate the fast emerging private retail sector in its practices and strategies (Black, 2009; pp 45–47). Little wonder then that in the early 1980s a substantial number of Co-operative Party members, disillusioned with the scepticism about co-operation in the Labour Party, defected to the newly created Social Democratic Party; though the Party remained loyal to Labour (Stewart, 2011). Of course, political allegiance and rivalry also shaped the development of the European movement, but generally relations between parties of the left, trade unions and co-operation seem to have been much more harmonious than was the case in Britain. Indeed, Many European cooperators displayed a high degree of pragmatism in their political dealings. Perhaps the epitome of this was the success of Mondragón in the deeply unpromising context of Francoist Spain. In contrast, British co-operation had long-standing enemies and fair-weather friends. This meant that there were few voices advocating or defending co-operation when times turned hard in the later 20th century. Social enterprise, by contrast, was perceived as carrying little ideological baggage, was more compatible with the demands of neoliberal political economy and was thus more comfortably supported across the political spectrum. So, in the difficult economic circumstances of the early 21st century, the social enterprise model was widely embraced by all political parties as leaders of the social economy.

However, an important and third factor was undoubtedly the inability of British consumer co-operation to adapt to the rapidly changing world of post-war Britain. The rise of chain stores such as Tesco, Sainsburys and so on, which were handsomely supported by capital, proved difficult for 1,000 independent cooperative societies to cope with. In addition, while membership held up well into the 1960s, several studies revealed declining participation in meetings and decision-making (Walton, 2009). The active membership tended to be older, and arguably less willing to adapt to the changing retail market. The upshot over the next 40 years was a long list of failing cooperative societies being merged with others or taken over by the CWS or its erstwhile sub-department Co-operative Retail Services (CRS), which effectively became a rival organization to CWS. Then in 1973 the

Scottish CWS bank failed, resulting in the takeover of the Scottish CWS by the English CWS. A long period of failure, declining market share, loss of a clear cooperative identity, and sadly some damaging examples of corruption and scandal all served to undermine commercial and political confidence in the British consumer cooperative movement – and therefore the idea of co-operation itself, as understood by most British people. A nadir appeared to have been reached when, in 1997, an attempt was made to demutualize the CWS, and though it was unsuccessful, the general attitude to the coop in the financial press was that it was an outdated institution (Wilson, 2011, pp 26–27). Melmoth successfully implemented major structural reforms in the aftermath of the crisis, creating the Co-operative Group, but much of his work was undermined by the near collapse of the Co-operative Bank in 2013, which nearly brought the Group down with it, and reaffirmed the doubts of many about the validity of the cooperative model (Webster et al, 2016, pp 280–282). While this was a stronger record than the disastrous failures of co-operation in Germany and Austria, it does not compare well with the success of the Nordic model (Ekberg, 2017).

British co-operation: the future?

While much of this might give rise to pessimism about the future of the movement, there are several developments which offer encouragement that a renaissance might be possible, and there are some important initiatives in Europe which might offer a way forward.

In Britain, two developments over the last 15 years offer a glimmer of what might become a template for future cooperative growth. First, in 2006 government policy to revive underperforming schools lessened the control of local authorities over schools by facilitating the creation of Foundation Trusts which could run schools. This provided a perhaps unexpected opportunity for co-operation. Out of this the first Co-operative Foundation Trust was established in 2008 at Reddish Vale Technology College in Stockport (*Guardian*, 26 July 2012). Others soon followed and the trend was given impetus by the Coalition government's Academies Act of 2010, which effectively create an 'independent school state sector'. Supported first by the Co-operative College, which assisted in the establishment of the Co-operative Schools Network (CSNet) and the School Co-operative Society (SCS) in 2009 (SCS website; CSNet website), the movement acted swiftly to take advantage of the new situation. These support institutions played a leading role in the flourishing of cooperative schools across Britain, either as Foundation Trusts or Multi-Academy Trusts. By 2021 there were some 277 educational coops – many Multi-Academy trusts, with a turnover of £560.1 million (Co-op

Economy, 2021, p 9). These accounted for over 1,000 in schools in the UK (Cambridge University Faculty of Education). The adoption of a 'multi-stakeholder' model of organization has been pivotal in the growth of school co-operatives, enabling representation of employees, students, parents and other key local interests in the governance of the schools/trust. This development mirrors similar trends in Europe, where stakeholder co-operatives have been seen as a way of reconciling employee interests with those of clients, notably in the emerging Italian social co-operatives, a development assisted by legislation making such organizations easier, to be formed. This legislative accommodation has also been evident in Portugal and France; while the Mondragón consortium includes many multi-stakeholder co-operatives (Novkovic, 2020, pp 224–226, 229). There is little sign of new legal initiatives to accommodate multi-stakeholder co-operatives in the UK. As with so much other cooperative development, however, media coverage of cooperative schools has been limited. A second area of progress has been in local regeneration. Here the City of Preston has led the way. The 'Preston Model' is described and explained elsewhere in this volume, and the main point here is that it has won imitators, notably in Rochdale (Webster et al, 2021), and offers a radically new strategy for local regeneration which is winning support across the UK. But for all its talk of 'levelling up', the Johnson, Truss and Sunak governments have shown only limited interest, perhaps regarding its origins in a local Labour administration as ideologically suspect.

Developments in Europe point to other opportunities which might be seized in Britain. The progressive casualization of labour under neoliberal policies, the rise of the 'gig economy' and the emergence of the internet as an arena of economic activity have all created new economic circumstances for which co-operation offers solutions to new problems. The digital world has been an especially exciting field for new co-operatives providing internet-related services as well as mainstream ones via the online world. 'Platform Co-operatives' have been actively encouraged by local and national government in major European cities such as Tallinn and Barcelona, especially in the wake of the COVID-19 pandemic; and while progress has been made in the UK, especially in Glasgow, this has largely been left to the private sector (Calzada, 2020, pp 14–15). There have also been some inspired responses to the casualization of labour in Europe. In Finland, co-operatives have emerged which provide self-employed entrepreneurs with essential services to enable them to pursue their businesses, while at the same time remaining fully independent (Puusa and Hokkila, 2020). Also, France, since the mid-1990s, has seen the emergence of Business & Employment Co-operatives, similar to the Finnish example in that these consist of individual entrepreneurs who join the co-operative to secure new partnerships with other entrepreneurs in projects, as well as access training and commercial information (Boudes, 2020). Certainly the potential for co-operatives of various kinds to improve the lot of precariously employed workers in the gig and informal economies has been widely recognized, though progress in the UK to date has been slow (Eum, 2020).

Clearly one of the main issues facing British co-operation is political: the seeming indifference of politicians and the British state to co-operation as an option to increase employment and diminish inequality. This was even true of the Blair/Brown Labour administrations which, as shown, tended to favour alternative social enterprise models. In contrast, there are numerous examples in Europe of both state and legislation operating to encourage co-operation in a conscious way. In respect of multi-stakeholder co-operatives, as shown, Europe has been much more supportive of legislative changes which make it easier to establish and sustain them. There are other contrasting approaches. In Italy, for example, since the mid-1980s the 'Marcora Law' and the associated state apparatus established an efficient and supported system for enabling worker buyouts of businesses, especially those in danger of failure (Vieta, 2020). In Britain, no such effective state apparatus exists, and support for co-operatives and worker buyouts are largely left to non-state agencies such as Co-ops UK, the Plunkett Foundation and the Employee Ownership Association. There remains a weakness in terms of political will to encourage co-operation in Britain, rendered even more debilitating by fading public awareness and understanding of co-operatives. While consumer co-operation survives in Britain, and new co-operatives continue to emerge in education, finance and industry, they remain small, few and largely uncelebrated. Whether this is reversible remains to be seen, but strong leadership both within the movement itself and the British state would appear to be essential; and in the latter this seems to be absent. Where co-operation has been most effective it has aspired to create a system of interlocking and mutually supporting co-operatives. This is true of Mondragón in Spain, and also the Trentino cooperative complex in Italy (OECD Trentino Case Study, 2014, p 60). In the UK, notwithstanding the long-standing role of the Co-operative Union (now Coops UK), such an integrated system has never been achieved; rather rivalry and acrimony between different types of co-operatives has tended to prevail. This is why the Preston Model is so refreshing, representing as it does an attempt to create a discrete cooperative system. Without major political change, a renewed effort to build a truly systemic cooperative sector and a concerted effort to raise popular awareness of cooperative models, it is hard to be optimistic. What was once a colossus on the British commercial and political scene has almost disappeared from popular British consciousness. Little wonder that *Digging for Britain* missed the truly important contribution made by Rochdale to the modern world.

References

Bamfield, J. (1998) 'Consumer-owned flour and bread societies in the eighteenth and early nineteenth centuries', *Business History*, 40(40): 16–36.

Battilani, P. (2011) 'The creation of new entities: Stakeholders and shareholders in nineteenth century Italian co-operatives'. In Webster, A., Shaw, L., Walton, J.K., Brown, A. and Stewart D. (eds) *The Hidden Alternative: Co-operative Values, Past, Present and Future.* Manchester: Manchester University Press, pp 157–176.

Battilani, P. (2017) 'Consumer co-operation in Italy: A network of co-operatives with a multi-class constituency'. In Hilson, M., Neunsinger, S. and Patmore G. (eds) *A Global History of Consumer Co-operation since 1850.* Leiden: Brill 2017, pp 584–613.

Battilani, P. and Schröter, H.G. (2012) 'Demutualization and Its Problems'. In Battilani, P. and Schröter H.G. (eds) *The Co-operative Business Movement, 1950 to the Present.* Cambridge: Cambridge University Press, pp 150–174.

Bibby, A. (2015) *All Our Own Work: The Co-operative Pioneers of Hebden Bridge and Their Mill.* London: Merlin.

Black, L. (2009) '"Trying to sell a parcel of politics with a parcel of groceries": The Cooperative Independent Commission (CIC) and consumerism in post-war Britain'. In Black, L. and Robertson, N. (eds) *Consumerism and the Co-operative Movement in Modern British History.* Manchester: Manchester University Press, pp 33–50.

Boudes, M. (2020) 'Labour transformation and institutional re-arrangement in France: A preliminary study of a Business and Employment Co-operative'. In Roelants, B., Eum, H., Eşim, S., Novkovic, S. and Katajamäki, W. (eds) *Co-operatives and the World of Work.* London: Routledge, pp 205–219.

Brazda, J., Jagschitz, F., Rom, S. and Schewidy, R. (2017) 'The rise and fall of Austria's consumer co-operatives'. In Hilson, M., Neunsinger, S. and Patmore, G. (eds) *A Global History of Consumer Co-operation since 1850.* Leiden: Brill, pp 267–295.

Calzada, I. (2020) 'Platform and data co-operatives amidst European pandemic citizenship'. *Sustainability*, 12: 1–22.

'Co-op Economy 2021: A report on the UK's co-operative sector'. Available from www.uk.coop/sites/default/files/2021-06/Economy%202021_0.pdf [Accessed on 17 April 2022].

Doyle, P. (2019) *Civilising Rural Ireland: The Co-operative Movement, Development and the Nation-State, 1889–1939.* Manchester: Manchester University Press.

Ekberg, E. (2012) 'Confronting three revolutions: Western European consumer co-operatives and their divergent development, 1950–2008', *Business History*, 54(6): 1004–1021.

Ekberg, E. (2017) 'Against the tide: Understanding the commercial success of Nordic consumer co-operatives'. In Hilson, M., Neunsinger, S. and Patmore, G. (eds) *A Global History of Consumer Co-operation since 1850.* Leiden: Brill, pp 698–728.

Eum, H. (2020) 'Work and employment in the informal economy and new forms of work: How can the co-operative model be the answer?' In Roelants, B., Eum, H., Eşim, S., Novkovic, S. and Katajamäki, K. (eds) *Co-operatives and the World of Work.* London: Routledge, pp 90–106.

European Commission (nd) 'Internal market, industry, entrepreneurship and SMEs'. Available from https://ec.europa.eu/growth/sectors/proximity-and-social-economy/social-economy-eu_en [Accessed on 26 April 2022].

Friberg, K., Vorberg-Rugh, R., Webster, A. and Wilson, J.F. (2012) 'The politics of commercial dynamics: Co-operative adaptations to post war consumerism in the United Kingdom and Sweden, 1950–2010'. In Battilani, P. and Schröter, H.G. (eds) *The Co-operative Business Movement, 1950 to the Present.* Cambridge: Cambridge University Press, pp 243–262.

The Guardian (26 July 2012) 'Co-op schools: Is the future of education co-operation?'. Available from www.theguardian.com/social-enterprise-network/2012/jul/26/co-op-schools-future-education [Accessed on 17 April 2022].

Henriksen, I. (1999) 'Avoiding lock in: Co-operative creameries in Denmark 1882–1903', *European Review of Economic History*, 3: 57–78.

Henriksen, I. and O'Rourke, K.H. (2005) 'Incentives, technology and the shift to year long dairying in nineteenth century Denmark', *Economic History Review*, 58(3): 520–554.

Henriksen, I., Lampe, M. and Sharp, P. (2011) 'The role of technology and institutions for growth: Danish creameries in the late nineteenth century', *European Review of Economic History*, 15: 475–493.

Higgins, D.M. and Mordhorst, M. (2008) 'Reputation and export performance: Danish butter exports and the British market, c1880–1914', *Business History*, 50(2): 185–294.

History of Oxfam (2015). Available from www.oxfam.org.uk/about-us/history-oxfam/ [Accessed on 26 April 2022].

Huckfield, L. (2020) 'The financialization of community development: the role of social finance', *Community Development Journal*, 56(3): 100–118.

Huckfield, L. (2021) *How Blair Killed the Co-ops: Reclaiming Social Enterprise from its Neo-liberal Turn.* Manchester: Manchester University Press.

Huckfield, L. (2022) 'UK financialization of public service delivery goes global', *Canadian Journal of Nonprofit and Social Economy Research*, 13: 34–52.

Lambersens, S., Artis, A., Demoustier, D. and Mélo, A. (2017) 'History of consumer co-operation in France: From the conquest of consumption by the masses to the challenge of mass consumption'. In Hilson, M., Neunsinger, S. and Patmore, G. (eds) *A Global History of Consumer Co-operation since 1850*. Leiden: Brill, pp 99–120.

Manton, L. (2007) 'Playing both sides against the middle: The Labour Party and the wholesaling industry 1919–1951', *Twentieth Century British History* 18(3): 306–333.

Manton, L. (2008) 'The Labour Party and retail distribution, 1919–1951', *Labour History Review*, 73(3): 269–286.

Manton, L. (2009) 'The Labour Party and the Co-op, 1918–58', *Historical Research*, 82(218): 756–778.

Molina, F. and Walton, J.K. (2011) 'An alternative co-operative tradition: The Basque co-operatives of Mondragón'. In Webster, A., Shaw, L., Walton, J.K., Brown A. and Stewart, D. (eds) *The Hidden Alternative: Co-operative Values, Past, Present and Future*. Manchester: Manchester University Press, pp 226–250.

'No going back: Social Enterprise Survey 2021' by Social Enterprise UK 13. Available from file:///D:/Paris%20conference%20Feb%202022/SEUK-SOSE-Report-DIGITAL-1.pdf [Accessed on 17 April 2022].

Novkovic, S. (2020) 'Multi-stakeholder co-operatives as a means for jobs creation and social transformation'. In Roelants, B., Eum, H., Eşim, Novkovic, S. and Katajamäki, W. (eds) *Co-operatives and the World of Work*. London: Routledge, pp 220–233.

OECD Report 2014: 'The co-operative model in Trentino – Italy: A case study'. Available from www.oecd.org/cfe/leed/150202%20The%20 cooperative%20model%20in%20Trentino_FINAL%20wi [Accessed on 4 June 2022].

Parliamentary Website (2012) 'Mutual and co-operative approaches to delivering local services – Communities and Local Government Committee Contents'. Available from https://publications.parliament.uk/pa/cm201213/cmselect/cmcomloc/112/112.pdf [Accessed on 26 April 2022].

Pérotin, V. (2016) 'What do we really know about workers' co-operatives?' In Webster, A., Shaw, L. and Vorberg-Rugh, R. (eds) *Mainstreaming Co-operation: An Alternative for the Twenty-First Century*. Manchester: Manchester University Press, pp 239–260.

Prinz, M. (2017) 'German co-operatives: Rise and fall 1850–1970'. In Hilson, M., Neunsinger, S. and Patmore, G. (eds) *A Global History of Consumer Co-operation since 1850*. Leiden: Brill, pp 243–266.

Puusa, A. and Hokkila, K. (2020) 'Co-operatives of independent workers in Finland'. In Roelants, B., Eum, H., Eşim, S., Novkovic, S. and Katajamäki, W. (eds) *Co-operatives and the World of Work*. London: Routledge, pp 188–204.

Ridley-Duff, R. and Bull, M. (2011) *Understanding Social Enterprise: Theory and Practice*. London: SAGE.

Snell, K.D.M. (2012). 'Belonging and community: Understandings of "home" and "friends" among the English poor 1750–1850', *Economic History Review*, 65(1): 1–25.

'Social enterprise: Market trends 2017'. Department for Digital, Culture, Media and Sport; Department for Business, Energy and Industrial Strategy. Available from https://assets.publishing.service.gov.uk/government/uplo ads/system/uploads/attachment_data/file/644266/MarketTrends2017re port_final_sept2017.pdf [Accessed on 17 April 2022].

'Social enterprises and their ecosystems in Europe. Country report: Greece 2019'. Available from file:///C:/Users/Tony%20Webster/Downloads/ Social%20enterprises%20and%20their%20ecosystems%20in%20 Europe.%20Updated%20country%20report%20Greece%20(2).pdf [Accessed on 26 April 2022].

Stewart, D. (2011) '"A party within a party?" The Co-operative Party-Labour Party alliance and the formation of the Social Democratic Party, 1974–1981', in Webster, A., Shaw, L., Walton, J.K., Brown, A. and Stewart, D. (eds) *The Hidden Alternative: Co-operative Values, Past, Present and Future*. Manchester: Manchester University Press, pp 137–156.

Van Voss, L.H. and Van Leewen, H.D. (2010) 'Charity in the Dutch Republic: An introduction', *Continuity and Change*, 27(2): 175–197.

Vieta, M. (2020) 'Saving jobs and businesses in times of crisis: The Italian road to creating worker co-operatives from worker buyouts'. In Roelants, B., Eum, H., Eşim, S., Novkovin, S. and Katajamäki, W. (eds) *Co-operatives and the World of Work*. London: Routledge, pp 162–187.

Walton, J.K. (2009) 'The post-war decline of the British retail co-operative movement: Nature, causes and consequences'. In Black, L. and Robertson, N. (eds) *Consumerism and the Co-operative Movement in Modern British History*. Manchester: Manchester University Press, pp 13–30.

Webster, A. (2017) 'The third sector: Co-operatives, mutual, charities and social enterprises'. In Wilson, J.F., Toms, S., de Jong, A. and Buchnea, E. (eds) *The Routledge Companion to Business History*. New York: Routledge, pp 123–138.

Webster, A. (2019) *Co-operation and Globalisation: The British Co-operative Wholesales, The Co-operative Group and the World Since 1863*. London: Routledge.

Webster, A., Shaw, L., Vorberg-Rugh, R., Wilson, J.F. and Snaith, I. (2016) 'Learning to swim against the tide: Crises and co-operative credibility – some international and historical examples'. In Webster, A., Shaw, L. and Vorberg-Rugh, R. (eds) *Mainstreaming Co-operation: An Alternative for the Twenty-First Century*. Manchester: Manchester University Press, pp 280–304.

Webster, A., Kuznetsova, O., Ross, C., Berranger, C., Booth M., Eseonu, T. and Golan, Y. (2021) 'Local regeneration and community wealth building–place making: Co-operatives as agents of change', *Journal of Place Management and Development*, 14(4): 446–461.

Whitecross, A. (2016) 'The wasted years? The Co-operative Party during the 1930s'. In Webster, A., Shaw, L. and Vorberg-Rugh, R. (eds) *Mainstreaming Co-operation: An Alternative for the Twenty-First Century*. Manchester: Manchester University Press, pp 131–150.

'Why social enterprise? A guide for charities' (2012). Available from www. socialenterprise.org.uk/wp-content/uploads/2019/05/Why_Social_Enter prise_1-1.pdf [Accessed on 17 April 2022].

Wilson, J.F. (2011) 'Co-operativism meets city ethics: The 1997 Lanica takeover bid for CWS'. In Webster, A., Shaw, L., Walton, J.K., Brown, A. and Stewart, D. (eds) *The Hidden Alternative: Co-operative Values, Past, Present and Future*. Manchester: Manchester University Press, pp 16–36.

Wilson, J.F., Webster, A. and Vorberg-Rugh, R. (2013). *Building Co-operation: A Business History of the Co-operative Group, 1863–2013*. Oxford: Oxford University Press.

Zamagni, V. (2017) 'A worldwide historical perspective on co-operatives and their evolution'. In Michie, J., Blasi, J.R. and Borzaga, C. (eds) *The Oxford Handbook of Mutual, Co-operative, and Co-Owned Business*. Oxford: Oxford University Press.

10

How Far Can the Co-operative Character Extend? The Sense of Co-operation and Co-operative Councils

Julian Manley and Temidayo Eseonu

Introduction

It might be naturally assumed that the cooperative character – by which we mean organizational characteristics that are defined by cooperative principles and values – must necessarily be limited to cooperative organizations, whose rules require that such principles and values be embedded in the organization's governance. This chapter asks to what extent is it realistic to suggest that the cooperative character could also be part of a non-cooperative organization such as a local council of elected representatives? This is the interesting case of the growth of local councils around the UK who are self-denominating as 'cooperative councils' and committing themselves to cooperative ways of working by joining the Co-operative Councils Innovation Network (CCIN). Inherent in this discussion is a seeming link between CWB and co-operatives or, if not cooperative businesses, the connection to a feeling or 'sense of co-operation' within councils and the communities that they serve and between councils belonging to the CCIN. A sense of co-operation is a rather vague and somewhat abstract notion, so what is this 'sense', if it exists, and does it have any value? This chapter is also an enquiry into the validity and authenticity of this notion. Finally, a discussion of a network of cooperative councils must also bring with it the recently revived concept of 'new municipalism', analysed and usefully summarized by Thompson (2021).

This chapter, therefore, begins with a discussion of the turn to new municipalism and the balance or tension between a vision of a future that is both socially radically transformative on the one hand and practical and achievable on the other. This aspirational, some would say utopic, vision projects an alternative to capitalism through a system of mutual support, altruism for the common good, equality, equity, renewed democracy and the removal of hierarchies (Bookchin, 2005). At the core of this socio-economic transformation is an approach, embodied by the CCIN, that highlights the apparently irreconcilable, even bipolar opposites of co-operation and competition. The central question that arises from this conflict is how can co-operation function in the context of competition? In the UK and elsewhere, different versions of crisis, but all in the context of the failures of capitalist scenarios of competition, have been a trigger for co-operation: austerity politics in Preston (Preston Model), the housing crisis in Barcelona (Barcelona en Comú), racial discrimination in Mississippi (Co-operation Jackson), with each geographical location providing its own version of a cooperative society. Initial reactions to crisis often focus upon practical responses to immediate problems, which is why practice often seems to come before theory (Russell, 2019). While each locality may have its own distinctive and different crisis, most of them are responding to common difficulties linked to inequality, poverty, unemployment and disempowerment – in other words problems which are frequently endemic in the neoliberal order. Thus, a common sense of existential crisis underpins many local cooperative initiatives, as Russell describes in his analysis of the 2017 'Fearless Cities' summit convened by Barcelona en Comú (2019). One feature which connects many of these local models together is a 'sense of co-operation', which also binds the CCIN together. This 'sense' takes precedence over party political affiliation, as stated by the CCIN. A similar outlook is evident in the Barcelona example, which sees itself as involved in 'a different kind of battle from the past. It's not a battle for themselves, for their identity – we are communist, we are anarchist, we are ... no. It's a battle directly from the people ... I fight for commons' (Russell, 2019, p 13). The spirit of 'new municipalism', as described here, aspires to reach out to everybody in the framework of a common purpose and its 'newness' includes – in theory, at least – a liberation from party political affiliations.

The two faces of new municipalism: visionary

A sense of co-operation is what binds together an otherwise disparate movement under the banner of 'new municipalism'. The 'libertarian municipalism' of Murray Bookchin is an important component of platform municipalism (Thompson, 2020, p 328) but Bookchin's influence is also visible in visionary and apolitical versions of municipalism. In Bookchin's rather amorphous vision – it is its amorphous quality that lends it to the possibility of embracing different political ideologies – 'capitalism ... has almost completely absorbed the class war' (Bookchin, 2005, p 57). If true, then the ideologies that represent the capitalist struggle can no longer exist. Furthermore, according to Bookchin, the capitalist economy in its perpetual growth can only die when confronted with ecological limits (not unlike the ecological limits of Raworth's 'doughnut economics' (Raworth, 2017)). Bookchin goes on to claim that libertarian municipalism 'must be based on a participatory democracy, rooted in a politics of gradual confederalism – the step-by-step formation of civic networks that can ultimately challenge the growing power of the nation state' (Bookchin, 2005, p 57). These sound very similar to the principles of CWB, the creation of the Cooperative Councils Innovation Network and the sense of co-operation that frames the movement. Bookchin reaches for inspiration in the 'organic society' (or 'preliterate'), as if the new society will be able to reach to some original sense of purity in relationships to move beyond the self-destruction of the neoliberal condition. The meaning and significance of this 'organic society' are too sprawling and complex to be adequately explained in this chapter. Importantly, one of the key features of such a society, according to Bookchin, is a 'cooperative spirit', which he is at pains to emphasize is beyond social co-operation, that is to say the actual systems of governance. This 'spirit' appears to resonate with the idea of 'sense' as discussed in this chapter. For Bookchin, the cooperative spirit of organic societies is 'too primary to be adequately expressed in the language of western society' (p 115). Co-operation in this case is embedded in practice, described by Bookchin as a 'kinship relationship [with nature] ... a relationship more primary than our use of the term *love*' (p 115, original italics). Even if 'love' might appear rather exaggerated in the present discussion, Bookchin's use of the word is clearly intended to emphasize the intangible, spiritual nature of relationships as being fundamental to co-operation and necessary for the future survival and thriving of societies. Perhaps this comes close to a sense of co-operation, where relational and sensed practice comes before thought and theory. It is only through 'love' that political ideologies can be overcome for the common good.

The two faces of new municipalism: emergency response to crisis

Austerity policies in the UK implemented since the 2008 global financial crisis saw the removal of fiscal equalization[1] between local authorities, leading to severe financial difficulties for many councils but particularly for more deprived urban authorities (Hastings et al, 2017; Davies et al, 2020). Reduced central funding played a significant role in local authorities determining their spending priorities and programmes delivered to citizens in the face of increased demand for public services and welfare payments (Taylor-Gooby,

2012; John, 2014; Gamble, 2015). In the face of these acute challenges, many local authorities have been addressing the impacts of reduced funding by changing their governance strategies and by engaging with local stakeholders to deliver effective governance (Lowndes and Gardner, 2016;). In some cases, such as in Preston, this has led to a gradual reconceptualization of the nature of socio-economic governance, with a growing emphasis on co-operation among willing stakeholders and communities, as well as attempts to create worker-owned co-operatives and associated support organizations, such as the beginnings of a network of co-operatives – the Preston Cooperative Development Network (PCDN) – and the founding of an educational and training centre for co-operatives – the Preston Cooperative Education Centre (PCEC) (Manley and Whyman, 2021). The well-publicized successes of the Preston Model have been contagious, and the sense of co-operation has rapidly spread around the different cities in the UK and can be seen in the national programmes of the devolved nations of Wales and Scotland, thereby scaling up the local to the national and resonating with Russell's concluding remarks (Russell, 2019) on the need to understand new municipalism according to the politics of scale, one that views the state as a 'form of social relations' (in Russell, 2019, p 20), resonating with Bookchin's 'kinship relationships'. In Scotland, this turn to a sense of co-operation in place, allowing the local to be weaved into the state of relationship, is already underway in public consultation (Place Design Scotland, 2023). Of the three ambitions of the Scottish Government for future legislation, which includes creating employment opportunities and connecting land and property to local communities, is the explicit reference to co-operation: 'Promoting co-operative, social enterprise and employee-owned businesses to ensure that more wealth which is generated locally stays local' (Scottish Government, 2023). This is the context of the rapid development of the CCIN, where social relations in the form of co-operation are bringing councils together in a network of co-operation.

Councils in co-operation

Developed in 2012, when a group of local authorities across the UK launched the CCIN, the network has continued to grow. CCIN is intended to be an active hub for members who wish to reclaim the traditions of community action, community engagement and civic empowerment that can transform communities (CCIN, n.d). The CCIN website conflates co-operation and cooperative development with CWB in the section on 'Growing the Co-op economy', which is what gives the councils a conduit for integrated cooperative development and with it, adherence to cooperative principles and values. In this model, work with communities to create and retain local wealth, which was the first achievement of the Preston Model, is inextricably linked to co-operation in ways that the original CWB project in Preston did not contemplate. This is because the focus for Preston was an immediate response to economic crisis, with little attention given, at first, to the social impact, value relationships, participatory democracy and the proactive importance of community (Manley and Whyman, 2021). The fact that Preston City Council is now one of the many council members of the network that combines CWB and co-operation demonstrates the growing recognition of the importance of cooperative values in underpinning CWB, a development that was inspired by the recommendations of the 2016 report to Preston City Council 'Co-operative Activity in Preston' (Manley and Froggett, 2016). It was following this Report to Preston City Council that co-operation began to be actively weaved into the Preston Model, as evidenced by the adoption of the Report's recommendations by the council, in particular the creation of the PCDN.

Cooperative councils, values, principles and the co-operative character

The CCIN has a membership of over 100 councils, and includes other organizations among its members. This extraordinary coming together of cooperative councils, and its continued growth, appears to point to a genuine common cause and approach to local democracy and a desire to both reward the local and share experiences in a network of council endeavours, turning the local to the beginnings of a national project which is not bound or guided by central government.

Without being co-operatives, the council members of the CCIN subscribe to the principles and values of the cooperative movement and have devised a modified version of its principles to meet the needs of local government. While it cannot be assumed that because a council is a member, it behaves like a co-operative, there is a clear intention to move in that direction, often through a process of learning from practice and examples from other councils. The cooperative character of these member councils is defined by the values of self-help, self-responsibility, democracy, equality, equity and solidarity, as stated on the CCIN website. These are the same values defined as key cooperative values by the ICA. The conflation of 'cooperative' and CWB through the sharing of these values makes it possible for council members of the CCIN to call themselves 'cooperative'. The CCIN website adds 'ethical' values to the shared cooperative values. These are 'honesty, openness, social responsibility and caring for others' (CCIN). In addition to these two sets of values are CCIN principles, which are given a special importance for the council members of the CCIN by being required to be evidenced in council publications related to any work that is regarded as cooperative in nature and quality. These principles are: social partnership, democratic engagement, co-production, enterprise and social economy, maximizing social value, community leadership and a new role for councillors, the CCIN offers new models for meeting priority needs, with an emphasis on innovation, learning from bast practice and living up to what is promised ('walking the talk'). These principles differ greatly from those of the ICA, which naturally are directed to the governance of cooperative business organizations: (1) Voluntary and open membership, (2) Democratic member control, (3) Member economic participation, (4) Autonomy and independence, (5) Education, training and information, (6) Co-operation among co-operatives, (7) Concern for community. Principle (7) does indeed encapsulate many of the CCIN principles, since all of the CCIN principles have at their core the ICA principle of concern for community. In addition, the very existence of CCIN itself arguably embodies the principle of co-operation among co-operatives However, as a list of principles, the differences between the ICA and the CCIN are notable. In this difference is a recognition that councils are not themselves co-operatives. An important nuance in this difference is the idea that despite not being co-operatives, councils can nevertheless 'cooperate'. There is an analogy in the business world of co-operatives. Many agricultural co-operatives for example, consist of members who are not in themselves co-operatives. Thus, for example, the first CCIN principle of social partnership is described as strengthening 'the *co-operative* partnership between citizens, communities, enterprises and Councils' (CCIN, our italics). The CCIN principles are in fact mostly focused on co-operation as a quality of process and to be applied among communities, often as a means of promoting participatory democracy. This, if authentically and effectively applied (as suggested in the final principles of 'walking the talk'), is akin to the transformation of power and politics in communities in ways that resonate with the transformative aspirations of CWB (Manley and Whyman, 2021). The commitment to participatory democracy is explicitly stated in the second CCIN principle: 'We will support the active engagement of the full range of residents in decision-making and priority setting' (CCIN) and constitutes a real challenge to the representational democracy that councils actually represent through their elected councillors. Again, this is explicitly recognized in the sixth of the CCIN principles: 'We will explore ways for councils to act as a platform for helping the community to contribute to local outcomes, and to re-think the role of councillors as community connectors, brokers and leaders' (CCIN). The reconceptualization of the role of councillors as 'community connectors' and facilitators is truly revolutionary and also problematic within the current democratic system. To properly adhere to this principle implies a necessary eventual change in systems of local governance also implied in the application of CWB to localities. This, then, brings the thinking back to 'new municipalism' and draws the CCIN closer to the radical movements that gathered in Barcelona in 2017. Indeed, it could be argued that there is something especially radical about the combining of cooperative councils into a national network, which brings the local into the national, or, to use Russell's discussion of the local and the state, bringing the 'politics of proximity' into a 'politics of scale' (Russell, 2019). In 'proximity' and 'scale', and where 'politics' is relational, there is also the element of social capital (Bookchin's 'love' or this chapter's 'sense') as applied to networks by Saz-Gil and colleagues (2021). There is a 'proximity' in the local CWB network linking like-minded stakeholders defined as 'bridging social capital' which is augmented to 'scale' through the Cooperative Councils network, akin to 'linking social capital' (p 5).

A case study: the drive for change

The following is a small case study of an anonymized CCIN member council ('the Council') which contributes data illustrative of the situation of a typical 'cooperative council' as theoretically described earlier.

The Council had lost almost half of its budget due to the austerity measures implemented by central government, severely impacting its ability to deliver public services. According to Gray and Barford (2018), the burden of the largest cuts between 2010 and 2015 was shouldered by local government, particularly for those urban local authorities which relied heavily on grants from central government. Budget cuts during the prolonged period of austerity enacted by successive governments in the UK since 2010 have been a key driver in the restructuring of local government approach to budget and spend. In response to the cuts, local authorities, such as the Council in question, have needed to find different and innovative ways to deliver services to their residents (Lowndes and Gardner, 2016). In an interview, one of the political representatives of the Council in 2011 identified austerity as a real drive in the restructuring of the relationship between the Council, citizens and communities. As part of this urgent need for change, the Council became interested in the ideas and concepts held by the Co-operative Party, with which it already had established ties:

'It seemed to me that, as well as being Co-op in name, it would be good to look at ways in which we could actually make our political representation at local government level count more ... The spirit of the time, for me, was that we'd had this massive financial shock which had imposed all sorts of restraints on the capacity of governments to deliver things. The agenda was crying out for a different approach ... cooperation is an idea whose time has come back. A very old idea, very much applicable to the prevailing challenges of the time. Which as I said, were that the public finances were shot, the private sector economy was severely set back by the global financial crisis. It was a policy and values-based response, in many ways, to the financial crisis.' (Council representative, 2011)

For the Council, then, there was immediate recourse to the already established Co-operative Party within the Council at the time. The initial policy thrust as influenced by the Co-operative Party was for the mutualization of local public services where residents in that municipality became members of cooperative services. However, there was a feeling in the Council as a whole that not all public services were appropriate for mutualization. There was, however, widespread support for the general idea that cooperative values could drive policy where public mutualization was impractical.

The purpose and key driver for becoming a cooperative council for the Council was to get better value for money by doing what its residents wanted, in other words bringing residents closer in a more participatory fashion, to the Council's policies. The Council began to act in accordance with the idea that delivering services based on cooperative values could change the relationship between decision-makers and residents. Overall, and in the general way that innovative ideas become hatched, there was a sense that it was more important for cooperative values to underpin policies and services rather than relying solely on the mutualization of services as a response to austerity.

The birth of the Council as a cooperative council was, therefore, a merging of political will with a policy response to austerity. Importantly for the Council in question, this adherence to values was a safeguard against the trap of privatization. Since the underlying ideology for becoming a cooperative council was values-based, it could never become a way towards privatization or making citizens personally responsible for service delivery:

'We had to spend a lot of time basically saying, no. This is a different offer ... This is not about privatization. This is about doing things differently from a values-based perspective. If that leads to efficiencies or greater effectiveness in the delivery of services, great. But its principal aim was the idea that Co-op values could be applied to delivery of public services, at all levels.' (Local MP)

Such 'doing things differently' for the Council is specifically aligned to the generation of enhanced participation of citizens and communities, one of the main aims of the CCIN. The Council has stated a commitment to 'developing a co-operative future: one where citizens, partners and staff work together to improve the borough. We want all members of the community to play an active part in building our co-operative borough. This means everybody doing their bit' (Council policy document). An example of this move towards participation is the establishment of the right of community call-in, where residents can submit questions which are responded to as one of the first agenda items at every full council and district meeting. Further examples are the participatory budgeting programmes – which enables residents to have a say in how an allocated budget is spent by voting for their favourite community project – and a youth council being assured of their constitutional rights, through the roles and responsibilities of a youth mayor, deputy youth mayor and chair of youth council which have been written into the council's constitution.

The Council has various other initiatives that see residents and service users actively informing decision-making. An example is the social care service, redesigned by using the lived experiences of services users, parents and carers and services for children with disabilities and life-limiting health conditions. This redesign started with an event for practitioners and families to ask for their thoughts on what service design works best for their needs. It emphasized creating a vision that all stakeholders, people who either have got children or are working in, or influence, or spend money in the social care system in that municipality, could own. Following this, a governance structure was set up and populated by representatives of families, children and practitioners.

These innovations were partly forced upon the Council and yet at the same time are perceived as positive change, as described next:

'Part of the driver for doing things differently is that standing still is not an option, and the economic and ... so many of the issues facing many of the boroughs around you know economic downturn, challenges with reductions in the public sector, health under pressure, immense pressure ... changing communities, and all of that led us to the point where we knew we needed to start to evolve the co-operative ethos into something that would produce tangible results for us, that would support and bring about some resilience to our communities. So, no matter what policies, what happens, we've got in place a framework that can help us to support and stand with communities and not do it to them.' (Senior Officer)

The Council in question is clear, as explained in the CCIN website, that the motivation for change to a cooperative council is about values and behaviours rather than about the creation of cooperative businesses (although this is also a feature of the CCIN principles):

'We've got so much need in our borough and also, when we talked about co-operative councils, we didn't mean necessarily about co-operative enterprise or creating co-operatives. It's more ... about cooperation and about collaboration and working with people.

Particularly the community in the voluntary sector, creating a new relationship with communities, with partners. That was the driver, more than about a co-operative, although that was probably on the spectrum.' (Council Officer)

In line with the CCIN principle of promoting social value for communities, the Council implements CWB policies that are cooperative in the sense that CWB is seen as cooperative. According to the Council's report on its social value framework, it funds over half of all goods and services in its local economy with plans to increase this in the future. Just over 70 per cent of the Council's suppliers have created employment opportunities in the borough, and the Council aims to increase the social value element further. Local partners also have a social value agenda and have agreed to have a stronger emphasis on employing local people, including the borough's poorest and most under-represented areas. For example, one anchor institution is investing in skills and good quality jobs; a local hospital has pledged to increase the number of residents they employ, along with increasing average wage earnings. In an 'inter-cooperative' fashion, the hospital is working closely with a local educational institution to identify how young people can gain the skills to help them develop hospital careers. The local police has also made great strides in employing new recruits from across the Council's community remit. The Council itself is a Living Wage employer and encourages its suppliers to pay the Living Wage too.

Bringing co-operatives and co-operation to the forefront of the Co-operative Councils Innovation Network

Although at present the cooperative nature of the CCIN is embedded and implicit, there are ongoing efforts at time of writing to bring co-operation to the forefront of the CCIN project. With the support of South Ribble Borough Council and others, Kirklees Council is leading the development of a Council's Cooperative Development Toolkit, with the aim of establishing 'a framework that supports the identification of opportunities to improve the local cooperative development context and move towards action' (CCIN) and recognizing that this remains a difficulty in the development of specifically cooperative enterprises in the CCIN. For councillors like Cllr Aniela Bylinski of South Ribble, joining the CCIN is closely linked to this cooperative agenda, what Bylinski calls a 'passion for shared decision making and ownership' (personal communication). As in the beginnings of the development of the Preston Model, this CCIN project is drawn to the Mondragon experience, and in November 2022, nine CCIN councils participated in a study visit to Mondragon. The visit brought home the reality of practical action related to co-operation, with a certain element of disbelief, perhaps, brought down to earth by the facts of the Mondragon experience, as highlighted in the following observations from CCIN visitors on the study trip (quoted in Hadfield, 2022, np):

> [The Mondragon experience is] a direct challenge to the widely held belief that co-operatives can't operate and compete within the economic mainstream. (Simon Grove-White, Oxford City Council)

> The factory we visited could have been in Kirklees. (Jonathan Nunn, Kirklees Council)

> I would like to see South Ribble nurture a co-operative environment. (Aniela Bylinski, South Ribble Council)

> From a local government perspective, it's a way forward in developing a more inclusive and democratic economy when the national government don't seem to have any interest. (Sean Laws, Sunderland City Council)

With these attitudes in mind and the backing of the network, the cooperative toolkit for the CCIN could be a useful first step in turning cooperative aspiration and cooperative principles and values in the context of CWB into realities on the ground for cooperative councils. It is possible to imagine in this development the beginnings of a truly national network of local councils bringing new municipalism to the UK as a whole.

Conclusion

To Thompson's (2021) three examples of new municipalism – 'platform, autonomist and managed' municipalism – the developments in the UK CCIN project adds a networked dimension to the third definition, 'managed municipalism'. It also suggests a possible future merging of 'autonomist' and 'managed', should the efforts of each council in the network successfully achieve true participatory democracy, as desired in the CCIN principles. Additionally, the CCIN project goes some way to investigating Russell's (2019) concern with scale, providing a model in development that maintains the local while networking councils across the UK, scaling up to national without being state focused or centrally organized.

Sennett (2013) suggests that the nature of modern life, with its casualized labour, growing dependence on remote communication and individualized culture – in other words the capitalist system – make cooperative behaviours and skills more difficult to promote. This is why the CCIN project remains an experiment for the present. Although the Mondragon experience has stood the test of time even while working within a system that is distinctly uncooperative, it has also felt the strains of existing in a cooperative system within a capitalist system, as demonstrated in the criticism it has received for using a small percentage of employees instead of worker-members as a buffer zone against times of economic strain (that is to say, employees can be made redundant while worker-members cannot) and in the expansion in Asia and elsewhere of Mondragon co-operatives, except not as co-operatives but as ordinary (capitalist) companies abroad. For co-operation to flourish, therefore, it seems that there are two options, either the system itself undergoes a significant transformation (which is not impossible, given the strain and crises of recent years and the emergence of the post-growth and/or degrowth agendas) or a Mondragon-style cohabitation with capitalism becomes an acceptable alternative.

The other alternative that emerges in the CCIN project is to continue emphasizing the cooperative principles and values without necessarily going down the path of the creation of cooperative businesses. As Crome and O'Connor (2016) say, the cooperative character implies a strong ethical commitment to cooperative values and behaviours, a conscious capacity to reflect on one's own behaviour from a moral as well as a practical point of view. For them, cooperative character is in itself a virtue, a moral commitment to working with others for the general benefit of the community (Crome and O'Connor, 2016, pp 32–33).

To make the cooperative character a reality in the local context, van Oorschot et al (2013) suggest three pillars for change. These are: drive for change, economic capacity and organizing capacity. A strategy aiming to promote local cooperative economies is a legitimate, even a noble option, and local authorities can provide conducive environments for co-operative enterprises through the availability of resources and opportunities. They can also promote opportunities for participation in the governance of the municipality. As a network of like-minded 'cooperative' councils, local cooperative governance opportunities can start to acquire a national timbre. In these roles, councils can be drivers for change in ways that seek the best outcomes for their residents. Councils have an organizing capacity to mobilize residents, local businesses and organizations, support participation, and count on residents to deliver services. While their economic capacity has been significantly reduced due to austerity measures, they can seek alternative and innovative ways for viable models to deliver public services. Despite a significant literature associating the future of healthy governance with networks and networking, it is too early to say if the capitalist paradigm can possibly be replaced by some form of cooperative networking. For some, it is impossible to categorize networking as being separate from hierarchy (as Bookchin forecasts) and the market. It may be that there is no networking without coercion and the exercise of power, and there is no hierarchy without some form of networking (Davies, 2012). Nevertheless, if the crises of our times are identified as having roots in systemic problems associated to a capitalist system that has run its course, then it may be that the CCIN project is a precursor of what a different system might look like.

Note

[1] Fiscal equalization is the transfer of financial resources from central government to local governments to mitigate regional differences in fiscal capacity and expenditure needs (Dougherty and Forman, 2021).

References

Barnett, N., Griggs, S., Hall, S. and Howarth, D. (2022) 'Local agency for the public purpose? Dissecting and evaluating the emerging discourses of municipal entrepreneurship in the UK'. *Local Government Studies*, 48(5): 907–928.

Bookchin, M. (2005) *The Ecology of Freedom*. Edinburgh: AK Press.

CCIN/Co-operative Councils Innovation Network (nd) Our statement of values and principles. Available from www.councils.coop/about-us/val ues-and-principles/ [Accessed on 1 April 2022].

Crome, K. and O'Connor, P. (2016). 'Learning together: Foucault, Sennett and the crisis of the co-operative character', *Journal of Co-operative Studies*, 49(2): 30–42.

Davies, J.S. (2012) 'Network governance theory: A Gramscian critique', *Environment and Planning A: Economy and Space*, 44(11): 2687–2704.

Davies, J.S., Bua, A., Cortina-Oriol, M. and Thompson, E. (2020) 'Why is austerity governable? A Gramscian urban regime analysis of Leicester, UK', *Journal of Urban Affairs*, 42(1): 56–74.

Dougherty, S. and Forman, K. (2021) 'Evaluating fiscal equalisation: Finding the right balance', *OECD Working Papers on Fiscal Federalism*, No. 36, OECD Publishing, Paris.

Gamble, A. (2015). 'Austerity as statecraft', *Parliamentary Affairs*, 68(1): 42–57.

Gray, M. and Barford, A. (2018) 'The depths of the cuts: The uneven geography of local government austerity', *Cambridge Journal of Regions, Economy and Society*, 11(3): 541–563.

Hadfield, M. (2022) 'Co-op councils head to Mondragon for lessons in economic revival', Coop News. Available from www.thenews.coop/165 969/topic/business/co-op-councils-head-to-mondragon-for-lessons-in-economic-revival/ [Accessed on 19 February 2023].

Hastings, A., Bailey, N., Bramley, G. and Gannon, M. (2017) 'Austerity urbanism in England: The "regressive redistribution" of local government services and the impact on the poor and marginalised', *Environment & Planning*, 49(9): 2007–2024.

International Cooperative Alliance. Available from www.ica.coop/en/coope ratives/cooperative-identity [Accessed on 18 February 2023].

John, P. (2014) 'The great survivor: The persistence and resilience of English local government', *Local Government Studies*, 40(5): 687–704.

Lowndes, V. and Gardner, A. (2016) 'Local governance under the conservatives: Super-austerity, devolution and the smarter state', *Local Government Studies*, 42(3): 357–375.

Manley, J. and Froggett, L. (2016) 'Manley, J. and Froggett, L. (2016) 'Co-operative activity in Preston', report written for Preston City Council by the Psychosocial Research Unit, UCLan, Preston. Available from www.academia.edu/75083620 [Accessed on 15 March 2023].

Manley, J. and Whyman, P.B. (eds) (2021) *The Preston Model and Community Wealth Building: Creating a Socio-economic Democracy for the Future*. London: Routledge.

Place Design Scotland (2023) 'Views sought on community wealth-building'. Available from https://placedesignscotland.com/views-sought-on-community-wealth-building/ [Accessed on 16 March 2023].

Raworth, K. (2017) *Doughnut Economics: Seven Ways to Think Like a 21st-Century Economist*. London: Random.

Russell, B. (2019) 'Beyond the local trap: New municipalism and the rise of the fearless cities.' *Antipode*, 51: 989–1010.

Saz-Gil, I., Bretos, I. and Diaz-Foncea, M. (2021) 'Cooperatives and social capital: A narrative literature review and directions for future research', *Sustainability*, 13(2): 534.

Scottish Government (2023) Available from https://placedesignscotland.com/views-sought-on-community-wealth-building/ [Accessed on 16 February 2023].

Sennett, R. (2013) *Together: The Rituals, Pleasures and Politics of Cooperation*. London: Penguin.

Taylor-Gooby, P. (2012) 'Root and branch restructuring to achieve major cuts: The Social policy programme of the 2010 UK Coalition Government', *Social Policy & Administration*, 46(1): 61–82.

Thompson, M. (2021) 'What's so new about New Municipalism?' *Progress in Human Geography*, 45(2): 317–342.

Thompson, M., Nowak, V., Southern, A., Davies, J. and Furmedge, P. (2020) 'Re-grounding the city with Polanyi: From urban entrepreneurialism to entrepreneurial municipalism.' *Environment and Planning A: Economy and Space*, 52(6): 1171–1194.

van Oorschot, K., de Hoog, J., van der Steen, M. and van Twist, M. (2013) 'The three pillars of the co-operative', *Journal of Co-operative Organization and Management*, 1(2): 64–69.

11

Community Wealth Building in Preston: Successes and Challenges of Co-operation in Action

Ioannis Prinos

Introduction

Both the 2008 economic and, more recently, the COVID-19 crisis have sparked much debate regarding systems of alternative socio-economic organization, new conceptualizations of economic development, as well as democratic participation and governance. The types and necessity of economic growth are being re-examined (Novkovic and Webb, 2014; Raworth, 2018; Trebeck and Williams, 2019), and worker-owned co-operatives have been enjoying a resurgence as a response to new forms of employment associated with work deficits such as lower and irregular earnings, reduced social protection and deteriorating working conditions (Deller et al, 2009; Erdal, 2011). This chapter looks at an alternative approach to economic organization, namely CWB and, in particular, the 'Preston Model' (PM). From the early 2000s, CWB has emerged as a potent approach to local economic development, where local economies are reorganized so that wealth is not extracted from the local area, but broadly held and income is recirculated (Haskel and Westlake, 2017). The PM is spearheaded by Preston City Council (PCC) and inspired by co-operative principles of economic democracy, focusing on leveraging social value and economic growth through the utilization of local economic assets, wide community participation, economic resilience and sustainability, job market fairness and environmental awareness (Manley, 2017).

Resonating with 'new municipalism', and in contrast with cost-benefit analyses guiding local economic development, an alternative paradigm is being formed, where economic democracy, a local adherence to a participatory cooperative ethos, social value and community benefit criteria and goals are at the forefront (Gilbert, 2020). More specifically, this model attempts to enhance the generation and retention of wealth within the local area, by combining the strengths and commitments of various local economic and social actors. This includes harnessing the potential of local 'anchor institutions' (major wealth creators, spenders and employers with long-standing historical ties and presence in the area such as universities, hospitals, local authorities, among others); stimulating public–private sector partnerships; engaging with civil society and the third sector; and encouraging the development of networks of worker-owned cooperative businesses. These coops will then 'plug' into the opportunities created by the economic activities of the anchor institutions in terms of goods, services and skills, enhancing the sustainability and resilience of the local economy.

In keeping with CWB's core tenets, the PM aims at a plural ownership of the economy. The goal is to make financial power work for local places by focusing on local investment, emphasizing social value and economic democracy before profits, creating fair employment and just labour markets, encouraging the progressive and locally focused procurement of goods and services and developing the socially productive use of land and property, through widening the access of communities to local public assets (Prinos, 2021). This focus indicates that the attention given to social value, democracy and cooperative values is as important as strictly economically driven change. In a post-growth, post-COVID-19 society, these appear to be equally significant to the potential benefits of more businesses being configured as cooperative and/or employee-owned, and the Preston CWB initiative is a good example of that.

For the PM, embedding cooperative values in the strategies of local organizations and businesses, as well as infusing these principles into a local cultural ethos linked to cooperative education and training, is of paramount importance to its long-term sustainability and success (Bird et al, 2021). I argue that co-operation in its broadest sense, as a 'way of being' and an attitude, can be fundamental for overcoming the potential problems of being limited to scattered committed individuals in management positions or politicians 'driving' the project. The idea of co-operation can lead to the empowering local communities to embark on successful grassroots cooperative endeavours on their own. As such, co-operation is viewed as being just as important as the (much needed) economic planning and implementation of programmes for the creation of networks of cooperative businesses that the PM espouses. This notion reinforces previous findings where it was shown that the eventual longevity and success of the PM, may depend on 'informal' personal relationships, community ownership and – as of yet – quite vague feelings of pride, public service, identity and of 'buying in' to a 'higher cause' by people in Preston (Prinos and Manley, 2021).

Still, CWB's impact hasn't yet reached the most vulnerable social groups in Preston. In interviews, most practitioners from the voluntary third sector felt that the delivery of support and services to disadvantaged communities was lacking. They further claim that while there is a lot of 'grandiose talk' about co-operation, community engagement and social value they have not seen any practical applications, neither have they been included in the planning and decision-making related to the PM. This chapter aspires to look at the PM holistically, examining both its evident successes in laying the foundations for reorganizing the local economy in a more democratic manner rooted on worker-owned co-operatives and community-oriented anchor partnerships, as well as the barriers preventing it to reach its full potential. It argues that it is in the associated tensions arising between the model being a 'top-down' rather than a 'bottom-up' approach that the overall direction of this 'brand' of CWB and the resurgence of a 'true', community-encompassing cooperativism in Preston will be negotiated and ultimately decided. Local stakeholders and anchors have certainly 'started the conversation', but the progress towards building a truly sustainable co-operative economy embraced by the local community remains slow. The realization (or not) of the PM's transformative goals of connecting society and economic practice into a holistic strategy for the betterment of local communities based on co-operation and democratic participation will be determined on how this process ultimately unfolds.

The Preston Model and co-operatives: background and roots in Mondragón and Cleveland

The turn towards CWB, inward investment, cooperative principles and 'out of the box thinking' by Preston local authorities in 2011 was prompted by a huge £700 million private investment and regeneration scheme for the city that fell through (Hanna, Guinan and Bilsborough, 2018). Nevertheless, the seeds were planted during the acquaintance of PCC officials with the 'Mondragón experience' in the Basque Country, and the 'Cleveland Model' in the US. This created the impetus to experiment with a strategy focused on local growth within a more democratic, resilient and participatory economy, based on improved co-operation, a local ecosystem of cooperative businesses, public-private sector partnerships and community engagement to revitalize the city's economic prospects (Manley, 2021). In its early stages, the PM's main goal was to retain and reinvest in the area a much larger percentage of the locally produced wealth.

This was achieved primarily by altering the procurement strategies of local anchor institutions (PCC, Lancashire County Council, Community Gateway Association, the University of Central Lancashire (UCLan), Preston's College, Lancashire Constabulary and the local NHS Hospital) to favour local suppliers and contractors. Since then, what has become known as 'the Preston Model', has gone on to include a rather expansive web of interventions and a wide range of progressive policies for socio-economic transformation hinging on co-operation and cooperative principles. These include the growing adoption of the 'Living Wage' by anchors and the induction of social value in their business practices; programmes for providing seed-funding for the start-up of cooperative businesses that could cover local anchor demand or for upskilling local labour; the induction of social and environmental criteria in public contracting; and the use of local council assets by the community, including addressing housing needs and creating incubation spaces for new co-operatives. Most notable are the creation by volunteers of a development network for co-operatives, a co-operative itself, the Preston Cooperative Development Network (PCDN); a regional community and cooperative bank which will finance and support the development of independent SMEs and budding co-operatives in Lancashire; and Preston Cooperative Education Centre (PCEC), which are still in progress at the time of writing.

The Preston anchor partnerships and the focus on the development of new worker-owned co-operatives, especially in deprived areas and marginalized communities, have been heavily influenced by the Cleveland Model. Cleveland, like Preston, has been suffering from blue-collar job displacement, unemployment, underdevelopment, inequality and lack of investment for many years. Its CWB approach also arose from the pressing need to find ways to regenerate a dying local economy (Alperovitz et al, 2010). In 2005, the Cleveland Foundation, assisted by the Democracy Collaborative (DC) research institute, identified several local anchor institutions to partner on a CWB program, focusing on procuring locally and with the goal of creating worker-owned co-operatives that met the identified gaps in the institutions' procurement and contracting. Like the PM, the Cleveland Model attempts to guide the local economy beyond both traditional capitalism and traditional socialism by encouraging the expansion of public activity and procurement and the creation new local cooperative businesses, stimulating a form of cooperative and democratic governance that is rooted in the community: the Evergreen worker-owned co-operatives (Alperovitz et al, 2010). Studies have shown that these initiatives have been quite beneficial, especially for deprived communities, in getting people back into employment and education, featuring an increasing percentage of green jobs and green businesses, while providing much needed structure and stability to Cleveland neighbourhoods (Howard et al, 2010).

Similarly, the PM aspires to create a collaborative, participatory 'virtuous cycle' of economy and community joined together through democratically owned mechanisms of cooperative socio-economic organization. 'Cooperative' not only in the sense of the actual type of firms involved (worker co-operatives), which is of course a key component of this economic strategy, but also in terms of a significant shift in the general attitude towards economic development and organizational governance by local workers, managers, political authorities and communities. A detailed examination of the PM's macro-economic impact in the area is beyond the scope of this chapter. Nevertheless, so far, the initial outcomes from the application of CWB in Preston have been very encouraging, especially the major increase of the overall spend within Preston's economy and the intense interest of anchors to support the creation of worker-owned co-operatives (Manley and Whyman, 2021).

Both the Cleveland Model and the PM have been inspired by the much earlier Mondragón experience. Since the first Mondragón co-operative was formed in 1956 in the aftermath of the Spanish Civil War, the Mondragon Co-operative Corporation has become a €12 billion umbrella corporation, with over 110 worker-owned co-operatives and numerous subsidiaries and benefit societies, distributed across various industries, from finance and retail to IT and food (Thomas and Logan, 2017). Democratic practices are embedded in this system, with the 'one person, one vote' fundamental cooperative rule determining all key corporate decisions, and the general worker assembly of every cooperative business, being the sole body that appoints and recalls the governing and social councils as well as managers and directors (Heales et al, 2017). Furthermore, the Mondragón co-operatives feature a non-competitive approach of mutual support among themselves, emphasizing increased resilience and flexibility during the 2008 financial crisis when resources were shared and employees were shifted as needed between the co-operatives, avoiding layoffs (Arando et al, 2010). With reference to the PM and its Mondragón influences, Manley (2017, p 1), argues that 'If there are opportunities for making a success of life in Preston, a place where people have a sense of identity and belonging, then social capital is potentially increased; pride of place is enhanced; a sense of citizenship is developed; and democracy becomes relevant and vital.'

Building sustainable ecosystems of co-operatives in Preston and Cleveland

There are valuable lessons to be learned for creating an alternative, democratic economic strategy for growth in Preston and Cleveland, emerging both from their similarities and their differences. In contrast with Preston, in Cleveland, philanthropy and the third sector have played a central role in the setting up of development agendas and coalitions that would promote new economic strategies on a large scale, through 'top patronage' (Howard et al, 2010). The largest Cleveland philanthropic institution, the Cleveland Foundation, promoted the Evergreen Cooperative Initiative and asked DC to assist key stakeholders in the envisioning of innovative strategies in the field of economic and community development. Likewise, PCC commissioned a report concerning the potential viability of co-operatives (Manley and Froggett 2016) and also the first major analysis of local spend by Preston anchor institutions from the Centre for Local Economic Solutions (CLES). DC proposed the leveraging of the purchasing needs of anchor institutions, the development of a network of worker-owned co-operatives geared towards meeting those procurement needs and the utilization of green economy opportunities, given the sustainability commitments of local educational and medical anchor institutions in the 'University Circle' area.

So, the PM is 'driven' and led primarily by the local city council, in contrast to the philanthropic sector in Cleveland. Nevertheless, the two initiatives feature comparable goals. They focus on marginalized and vulnerable social groups and aim to develop the local economy around worker-owned co-operatives. In partnership with major local anchor institutions, the vision is to create sustainable, environmentally friendly economic growth and improve social conditions and outcomes for local communities. This shows how successful coop development can be approached from different avenues, depending on the socio-economic characteristics of every area. CWB is not just a rigid 'step-by-step' economic guide but can be achieved through variable and flexible community development strategies.

The Cleveland approach led to the creation of three different co-operatives: the Evergreen Cooperative Laundry, offering laundry services to a wide range of local institutions, the Ohio Solar Cooperative, installing and maintaining photovoltaic arrays on institutional, government and commercial buildings, and the Green City Growers Cooperative, running a greenhouse producing large quantities of lettuce and of herbs all year-round though hydroponic agriculture (Howard et al, 2010). Apart from putting great emphasis on environmental sustainability through the reduction of energy and water consumption, each of these co-operatives is obligated to pay 10 per cent of its pre-tax profits back into a fund to help seed the development of new co-operatives. Thus, each business has a commitment both to its workers through living wage jobs, affordable health benefits and asset accumulation, as well as to the wider community.

The PM also emphasizes such alternative forms of governance that characterize co-operatives, creating strong links to local communities and institutions. However, Preston diverges from Cleveland by taking a page from the Mondragon book for the development of resilient coop businesses which will be successful economic entities without depending on philanthropy or only the 'patronage' of anchors and public funding. In this context, the PM is attempting to tie cooperative work with education through the PCEC (https://prestoncoopeducationcentre.org/), founded in 2021 as a union–co-operative. This speaks to the understanding that the development of successful and sustainable cooperative businesses goes hand in hand with the creation of a robust cooperative culture and community ethos. PCEC's development has also been assisted by LKS consultancy work, bringing invaluable Mondragon experience and perspective into play (LKS, 2020). Governed by the members, worker–owners, staff and students, the PCEC intends to provide education and training in co-operatives and co-operation, leading to a regeneration of democratic and cooperative ways of working for Preston and beyond, and supporting people in the creation of new co-operatives.

In addition, the PCDN has also been set up as a co-operative with some funding from the Open Society Foundations (OSF) and PCC, to help new local groups start their own worker co-operatives through advice and training (business consultancy, financial planning and forecasting, paying the registration and legal costs of setting up a coop, setting up book-keeping systems, and so on). Examples of worker co-operatives the PCDN was involved in the development of, are the Preston Digital Foundation, specializing in digital services across Preston and Lancashire operated by UCLan students, and the cooperative network of taxi services North-West Black Cabs. The Larder, a food cooperative cafe, provides locally sourced sustainable farming products by networking with other community organizations to decrease food poverty. A co-operative operating in construction is also in the works, linked to investment plans by the PCC in building a new civic cinema (Bird et al, 2021). UCLan researchers have been handling the evaluation, knowledge exchange and learning aspects of these processes to better assess their impact, as well as facilitate the operationalization of this knowledge in the scoping, further planning and implementation of the PM. It could be argued, therefore, that its strategy on co-operative development is transferrable to other areas, but without necessarily utilizing the same methods. Rather than being a 'one size fits all model', CWB has to be flexible, with each individual stakeholder and each partnership of different social actors needing to adapt it to respond to the particular local contexts, needs, requirements, and the overall social, economic and cultural characteristics of a certain area and population.

The Preston Model as a hazy force for socio-economic transformation

The analysis in this section will utilize some examples taken from a series of interviews the author undertook in Preston between 20 July 2019 and

20 March 2021. One of the main differences between the PM and other past economic regeneration projects is that almost all participants identified the value of its local focus as being 'made by people in Preston for people in Preston'. The following comments indicate this belief in its potential to provide genuine, local solutions:

'the Big Society came up from London and there wasn't actually anything realised; in the end, nobody could see a difference, much less a positive influence in their lives, while the PM has helped local economy, pushed for the living wage and unemployment is reduced; probably it's not the only cause of that, but it has helped; and that's the real difference right here, for Preston.' (Participant C, Local Coop 1)

So, in contrast with strategies like the 'Third Way' or the 'Big Society Agenda' (both often mentioned in conversations with respondents), the PM is not something seen as a performative political agenda coming 'from London' by the central government, far removed from the realities of life in the North-West of the UK. Therefore, the PM appears to be succeeding in 'persuading' local people, that it is something that can spur positive change for the local community. There is a certain 'honesty' and an element of being 'genuine' in its intentions that respondents seem to attach to it, identifying with it as something positive; something to be proud of being a part of. This emotion is attached to that of belonging and pride of being 'allied' with a 'virtuous cause'.

However, sometimes, these positive sentiments about the PM's potential, don't coincide with the belief that it has achieved significant and tangible beneficial changes for the community: 'the high street after 6pm in the winter is still a very rough place, isn't it?' (Participant E, Anchor Institution 5 [quote taken from Prinos, 2021]).

Concrete examples of this include the perception that problems of homelessness and criminality have not been substantially improved by PM initiatives, and the urgent need to deal with these and other pressing social issues:

'the less affluent areas in Preston remain so; marginalised people don't really have better housing now, neither have their social services or healthcare markedly improved, so I'm not sure; it has been good for the city, but it's difficult for me to isolate something and say this is because of the Preston Model.' (Participant F, Anchor Institution 1)

Hence, many respondents don't latch on to CWB and the PM as a policy, a set of measures, a detailed economic plan or legislative piece having a significant effect on the pressing social and economic issues in Preston. At the same time, they identify with it as something that – in principle – is striving for the 'betterment of the local community'. In that respect, it also appears that there are group and organizational identification processes (Aharpour and Brown, 2002) active here, clashing with this apparent lack of public awareness about CWB's impact in Preston. Respondents associated with the local anchor institutions often presented themselves as opposed to 'the outside' (represented by the researchers). They positioned themselves and their respective organizations in the centre of this hopeful PM narrative, talking about positive changes in Preston and being invested in its potential, regardless of its dubious tangible impact.

Still, the portrayal of 'their organisations', the anchors, as 'drivers' and even as precursors of this shift towards CWB, cooperativism and democratic, community-focused economic strategies, is telling. Manley and Aiken (2020) in their discussion of dreams and the imagining of new cooperative relationships highlighted that it is aspirations and not facts or results that often become both the driving force and the essential function of such projects. Like the PM, alternative economies are bound to start small, begin as dreams and aspirations, focusing on areas free markets leave out, incorporating the excluded and unemployed, re-establishing environmental diversity and maintaining sustainable economic practices that might, momentarily, reduce monetary gain, but allow for social cohesion, co-operation and democracy to grow (Castells, 2014). Thus, they enable more participatory, emancipatory, democratic, cooperative and community-oriented economic practices (Bretos and Errasti, 2017). In that sense, the PM carries with it the potential for new social imaginaries and subjectivities to emerge (Castoriadis, 1987). Therefore, it is not only tangible and concrete outcomes that are valued, but directions and aspirations: 'I wouldn't say that we changed, this is not a policy mandate; but because of the influence of the Preston Model, perhaps issues like pursuing social value have now become more predominant, having more weight behind them' (Participant I, Anchor Institution 6).

This participant doesn't perceive the PM as a set of policy measures, but nevertheless strongly identifies with it as something striving for the 'betterment of the community'. Other respondents don't even consider the sociocultural influence of the PM. The following participant, as a third sector practitioner, is much more interested in the 'practical', echoing a criticism of the PM and its inability to make a 'real change' in vulnerable people's lives and wellbeing; in their income, housing, employment, access to health, education, and social support services. Furthermore, access into collaborative projects for smaller voluntary organizations is highlighted, along with the issue of seemingly everything hinging upon contacts and individual relationships, rather than structural reforms:

'Sure, we hear about the PM and it's a great buzzword, but I can't really say I've seen any of it. If I go to one of our service-users and talk to them about community wealth building, they'll probably answer with something like [expletive]. These policies by these massive institutions have nothing to do with us and the people we work with. If I didn't know that person in PCC, I wouldn't know about any of that. So, why are we talking about Preston Model successes? For us, often success is someone is still alive, a year later.' (Participant P, Local third sector organization 2)

Such responses indicate that hopeful aspirations of the PM and its massive potential are set against a background of people in Preston struggling to identify changes or simply not knowing about them. For example, outside of the anchor institutions, almost nobody had even heard of a Preston cooperative bank. The PM appears to be influencing a growing, but still relatively 'closed circle' of individuals involved with it, such as senior managers, procurement officers, directors of finance, academics, and others within the anchor institutions. Its ideas about cooperativism, collectivism and participatory democracy don't appear to be 'spilling out' to the day-to-day life of Preston communities and its impact seems to be less than its promise (Prinos, 2021).

Politics, anchor leadership, community ownership and the Preston Model

The political leadership of CWB in Preston is perceived in different ways by the participants. Some see it as a potential problem, since the PM will inevitably be linked to the political party the city council majority belongs to, and the frequently toxic political party rivalry will impair and distort decision-making. Nuance will be lost, the effectiveness of initiatives and interventions overlooked, and ideas discarded, because they are associated with the opposing party or ideology. Others consider the association of the PM with the PCC as a boon, since the clear political backing implies that at least for the foreseeable future, there will be substantive personnel and resources dedicated to developing these approaches. Furthermore, there are concerns about the sustainability and further evolution of CWB in Preston, due to its dependence on political leadership:

'My problem with that (PCC and major anchors leading the PM) would be how to make sure it's not just a firecracker; that these efforts continue even with a Tory PCC. The trick is to sustain it. We now have a good contact with (mentions an anchor institution) and can be a part of some things, but if I didn't have this contact, as a smaller organization, we wouldn't know that we could be represented in this network and bring our own perspective into the mix.' (Participant O, Local third sector organization 1)

The sustainability of the PM is clearly questioned here, as is the view that recent developments in Preston have mostly to do with interpersonal, individual relationships of engaged and committed people who are working together with a shared mentality of co-operation. Therefore, it can be understood that if these relationships are not preserved (that is, people move, change jobs, and so on), organizations wouldn't be as committed to these alternative CWB approaches.

It can be argued then, that the degree of structural embeddedness in organizational and business culture in Preston is also open to question:

'to give you an example, UCLan people talk about the PM but have they ever worked with us or even acknowledged the massive problem of sex working among their student population? No. I'm sorry to be negative, but I hear all these things happening like the social value framework now, but the NHS cares only about how to look good. We are never included, and we'll never see any money to make the difference that we know we could.' (Participant Q, Local third sector organization 3)

This third sector participant is arguing about how 'top-down' PM initiatives are virtually excluding community and voluntary organizations and that for large anchor institutions such as the university and NHS, the PM is more of a public relations activity related to anchors putting on a 'socially caring face', rather than a substantive effort for actual social change and economic democracy.

Such comments echo the criticisms of other place-based regeneration schemes such as 'new localism' or 'municipal socialism' which have been compared to the PM (Hanna et al, 2018). Namely, that such approaches of economic revitalization often become vehicles for maintaining current power relations and strengthening established institutional players rather than generating a capacity for the addition of new players and ideas (Imrie et al, 1995). Or, that local regeneration partnerships legitimize a pre-existing strategy of the local authority and preserve pre-existing power relations, thus structurally excluding community groups (Hall and Nevin, 1999; Raco, 1999).

So, it seems that political intervention is recognized both as a 'driver' of CWB in Preston, but also as a barrier for efforts to attain grassroots traction with smaller organizations and tangibly affect the most vulnerable parts of the community. The PM can enable social capital to be created through community-oriented goals, the pursuit of social value in economic initiatives and business strategies and place-based as well as organizational identification processes (Prinos and Manley, 2021). However, knowledge of its intricacies and goals mostly remains in the purview of individuals directly involved with the local anchor institutions and political leadership, rather than the wider community, while actual tools for enabling participatory democratic practices involving the latter in the creation of resilient worker-owned co-operatives, are still not in place.

Closing the gap between 'the dream' and reality in Preston

Prinos and Manley (2021) claim that the PM is

> being primarily driven not by formal, political mandates or strict economic planning, but by the social value of organically developing informal social relations, enabling the emergence and alignment of positive emotions, mindsets and attitudes related to pride, place, identity, and the participation to this alternative socio-economic initiative, for the 'greater good' of the local community. (p 6)

In this chapter, it was indicated that while this indeed appears to be the case, at the same time, there are existing tensions between the major anchors and political authority leading the project and smaller local social actors, while the most vulnerable parts of the wider community are not 'seeing the impact'. These conflicting complexities of the PM may nevertheless – despite its contradictions – still represent a broad rethinking of co-operatives and the organization of a culture of co-operation in the community.

The support for local independent SMEs rather than external corporate investment, and the creation of the cooperative community bank are key aspects of this process. The establishment of PCEC and PCDN, the drive for the creation of an ecosystem of cooperative businesses filling the gaps identified in the local procurement of products, services and skills are deemed as important tools (but still just 'tools') in a much wider project. In order for cooperative principles to take root into the local community, it is perhaps not so much about the benefits that cooperative enterprises bring to a local economy and community (though these should not be underestimated), but about the exercise and the process of the building of that environment. That in itself is invaluable, as local authorities, anchor institutions, businesses and the community sector learn to cooperate, co-ordinate and knowledge-share. This boils down to the progress that has been made by committed individuals forming these relationships, adopting this cooperative, community-focused mentality, finding ways around the rigid financial mandates of cost-benefit analyses and therefore, infusing their departments, businesses and organizations with a 'cooperative spirit', but not necessarily the actual, legal form of a co-operative.

Many respondents did recognize the need for CWB to develop more grassroots characteristics and involve the local community, civil society and the third sector going forward, even though little seems to have been done in terms of actually creating more formal and stable channels for cooperative action. Moreover, the cooperative values at the core of the PM are not easily spreading through the local community, beyond these 'closed circles' of anchor management and local authorities. In that respect, the sociocultural impact that perhaps the major PM proponents first envisioned when inspired by Cleveland and especially Mondragón, is – as of yet – slow to manifest itself.

It is possible that the answer to the frustration and anxiety expressed by parts of our sample concerning the PM's sustainability, its somewhat exclusionary, 'expert' nature, its political elements and low impact to the lives of those who seemingly need it the most, has more to do with current UK politics and prevailing economic imperatives such as the dominance of the neoliberal paradigm and private corporate investment rather than a more communal, participatory, cooperative focus. After all, the transition from standard capitalist businesses into worker coops in the context of such place-based regenerative efforts is possible, but not without major difficulties in terms of having the necessary legislative, regulatory and financial regimes in place to support this (Lockey and Glover, 2019), and that's currently the case in the UK. Furthermore, the PM has been less than ten years in development; its main ideological 'progenitor', Mondragón's cooperative economy and community, almost 70. The Mondragón communities are marked by deep, familiar and cooperative ties between people that often involve a high degree of personal intimacy, moral commitment, social cohesion and continuity in time (Arando et al, 2010). And while Mondragón operates in the same globalized, neoliberal market economy paradigm as Preston does, the Mondragón community has been bound by similar principles that the Preston CWB model still only strives for. Communities are also committed to some clearly defined set of values that guide their behaviour through allied social norms (Field, 2003). In the case of Mondragón, Bretos and Errasti (2017) found that these values and norms revolve around ideas of solidarity, co-operation, economic democracy and community participation, realized through action in the local institutions such as the co-operative university, the healthcare and social security system, the embedded participatory democratic governance structures and the mutual support between the co-operatives increasing economic resilience (see Chapter 12 of this volume).

In contrast, the PM is only now gaining confidence in its approach of prioritizing local procurement. And as it was shown, that is only one instance of many interrelated PM initiatives affecting vital sectors such as housing; funding for new worker-owned co-operatives and local SMEs; upskilling local labour; linking education and research to community and the market; widening community use of public assets, supporting the third sector and others, developed in Preston. Moreover, the PM seeks to foster co-operation, sustainable, resilient, environmentally sound economic growth and achieve better social outcomes in the area, in the face of a central government adverse to anything remotely 'collective', an aggressively competitive economic environment and, recently, a global pandemic, an energy and cost of living crisis, and an ongoing war in Ukraine. It is quite a high bar to clear, especially when the 'vessel' to clear it is a tenuous alliance between the local city council (with all the volatility and political baggage this brings), newfound co-operatives struggling to be financially successful and various anchor institutions, each with their own inherent priorities, constraints and imperatives. Additionally, any realistic hope of the further development of the PM in these early stages essentially demands the political commitment, backing, resources and direction provided by local authorities and the most influential anchors, thus 'leaving local communities behind'.

Thus, public awareness of CWB in Preston must be raised, more stable channels of communication and co-operation between anchors, social actors and co-operatives must be established, and innovative ways of including the voices of the wider Preston community, third sector practitioners and vulnerable social groups in the planning, and decision-making, must be discovered. It seems that just by generating wider participation, the tensions arising from the perception of the PM as a 'top-down' political plan primarily concerning the major local anchors could be overcome, and the goals for deeper social transformation based on cooperative values, can be achieved. For the PM, the long-term viability and sustainability of the intended socio-economic outcomes depends, not surprisingly, on true co-operation within the whole local community in all its diversity.

Neither the creation of more independent cooperative businesses – for all their potential benefits for local communities – nor the anchor institutions retaining more wealth and employment in the region are seemingly enough to achieve that, even if there are individual examples that managed to overcome the problems discussed in this section. These initiatives do not appear to be sufficient to develop a sustainable, new cooperative socio-economic strategy in Preston that would not only improve living standards and democratize the economy through worker-owned co-operatives, but would also shape the way people fundamentally think about democracy, co-operation, participation, economic growth, healthcare, the environment, social value, social justice and governance structures. For the PM to have a tangible impact on people's overall wellbeing, it is imperative that general attitudes towards what these concepts mean in the post-COVID-19 era change. Moreover, the question of how they can be realistically pursued in a globalized market economy also needs to be confronted.

Conclusion

Contemporary society demands more flexibility and choice in how organizations, businesses, communities and individuals access a range of opportunities (Castells, 2014). The emerging political economy of the PM is dedicated to achieving genuine social change, ecological stability and sustainable economic transformation (Cannon and Thorpe, 2020). I have argued that the PM has demonstrated through its early achievements and despite its stumbles that it is indeed able to create a beneficial framework and environment for enacting such broad change, eventually connecting democratic business ownership to participatory civic engagement and a cooperative social culture in Preston. The worker-owned co-operatives already formed, others that are being developed and the future establishment of the cooperative bank can become the backbone for a broader regenerative strategy, enhancing regional social cohesion and social justice and establishing a more democratic, resilient, sustainable, community-oriented local economy. Simultaneously, the massive range of different initiatives, social actors and social actions encompassed by the model in the context of CWB (environmental awareness, social value pursuit, community use of council assets, the living wage, prioritized recruitment of marginalized and vulnerable social groups by anchors, and so on) highlight its transferability and adaptability, and has inspired the development of similar efforts beyond Lancashire and the UK.

Thus, the impetus for the PM is to move beyond past dominant practices or minor stop-gap solutions like creating more cooperative corner shops. The challenge is to build a 'true cooperative ecosystem' by providing a range of locally developed mainstream and grassroots opportunities, and extended public, private and third sector-linking social value programmes, without relying predominantly on any one project, organization, social group, political authority or approach to deliver the intended economic and social outcomes. Including the local community in the decision-making and planning, focusing on the needs of the most vulnerable, while utilizing the resources and knowledge of anchor institutions and local authorities is crucial. And it is a hard balancing act. For this equilibrium to be achieved, the PM could benefit from the realization by all involved, that it is in this realm of dreams, expectations, aspirations and the power of simple human interaction forming social relationships in co-operation and identifying with a 'common cause' that its greatest advantage lies. Perhaps, it is by harnessing that organically growing force, like Mondragón, building on both this strong sense of belonging and identity that the PM can inspire and realize its potential; and it may well be that through its already significant contributions to local economic growth (Prinos and Manley, 2021), and its substantial efforts to link up with education, a genuinely cooperative and inclusive collective association can be solidified and grow in Preston, in a world where currently everything is shifting.

References

Aharpour, S. and Brown, R. (2002) 'Functions of group identification: An exploratory analysis', *Revue Internationale de Psychologie Sociale*, 15(3–4): 157–186.

Alperovitz, G., Williamson, T. and Howard, T. (2010) 'The Cleveland Model', *The Nation*, 1(1): 21–24.

Arando, S., Gago, M., Kato, T., Jones, D.C. and Freundlich, F. (2010) *Assessing Mondragon: Stability and Managed Change in the Face of Globalization.* Michigan: University of Michigan Press.

Bird, A., Conaty, P., Mangan, A., McKeown, M., Ross, C. and Taylor, S. (2021) 'Together we will stand: Trade unions, cooperatives, and the Preston Model'. In Manley, J. and Whyman, P. (eds) *The Preston Model and Community Wealth Building.* London: Routledge, pp 93–110.

Bretos, I. and Errasti, A. (2017) 'Challenges and opportunities for the regeneration of multinational worker cooperatives: Lessons from the Mondragon Corporation – a case study of the Fagor Ederlan Group', *Organization*, 24(2): 154–173.

Caldwell, N.D., Roehrich, J.K. and George, G. (2017) 'Social value creation and relational coordination in public-private collaborations', *Journal of Management Studies*, 54(6): 906–928.

Cannon, M. and Thorpe, J. (2020) 'Preston Model: Community wealth generation and a local cooperative economy'. Available from https://opendocs.ids.ac.uk/opendocs/handle/20.500.12413/15219 [Accessed on 15 March 2023].

Castells, M. (2014) *The Economic Crisis and American Society.* Princeton: Princeton University Press.

Castoriadis, C. (1987) *The Imaginary Institution of Society*, translated by Kathleen Blamey. Cambridge, MA: MIT Press.

Deller, S., Hoyt, A., Hueth, B. and Sundaram-Stukel, R. (2009) 'Research on the economic impact of cooperatives', *University of Wisconsin Center for Cooperatives*, 231(2209): 232–233.

Demos-PwC. (2018) 'Good growth for cities 2018'. Available from https://demos.co.uk/project/good-growth-for-cities-2018/ [Accessed on 15 March 2023].

Erdal, D. (2011) *Beyond the Corporation: Humanity Working.* London, Random House.

Field, J. (2003) *Social Capital.* London: Routledge.

Gilbert, A. (2020) 'Take back control: English new municipalism and the question of belonging', *Soundings*, 74(74): 68–85.

Hall, S. and Nevin, B. (1999) 'Continuity and change: A review of English regeneration policy in the 1990s', *Regional Studies*, 33(5): 477–482.

Hanna, T.M., Guinan, J. and Bilsborough, J. (2018) 'The "Preston Model" and the modern politics of municipal socialism', *Open Democracy*, 12.

Haskel, J. and Westlake, S. (2017) *Capitalism without Capital*. Princeton: Princeton University Press.

Heales, C., Hodgson, M. and Rich, H. (2017) *Humanity at Work: Mondragon, a Social Innovation Ecosystem Case Study*. London The Young Foundation.

Howard, T., Kuri, L. and Lee, I.P. (2010) 'The Evergreen Cooperative Initiative of Cleveland, Ohio'. White paper prepared for The Neighborhood Funders Group Annual Conference in Minneapolis, MN.

Imrie, R., Thomas, H. and Marshall, T. (1995) 'Business organisations, local dependence and the politics of urban renewal in Britain', *Urban Studies*, 32(1): 31–47.

LKS (2020) 'Analysis of Basque entrepreneurial initiatives: BBF, Gaztenpresa, Saiolan and ElkarLan to inspire the development of a Preston Cooperative entrepreneurial ecosystem' and 'Designing a cooperative entrepreneurship initiative for Preston: Challenges and strategic action lines'. Available from https://prestonmodel.net/ [Accessed on 10 March 2023].

Lockey, A. and Glover, B. (2019) 'The "Preston Model" and the new municipalism, demos, London'. Available from https://demos.co.uk/wp-content/uploads/2019/06/June-Final-Web.pdf [Accessed 8 December 2022].

Manley, J. (2017) 'Local democracy with attitude: The Preston Model and how it can reduce inequality', *British Politics and Policy* [Blog] 23 November, 2017. Available from https://blogs.lse.ac.uk/politicsandpolicy/local-democracy-with-attitude-the-preston-model/ [Accessed on 29 March 2022].

Manley, J. (2021) 'The Preston Model: From top-down to rhizomatic-up. How the Preston Model challenges the system'. In Manley, J.Y. and Whyman, P.B. (eds) *The Preston Model and Community Wealth Building: Creating a Socio-Economic Democracy for the Future*. London: Routledge, pp 17–31.

Manley, J. and Aiken, M. (2020) 'A socio-economic system for affect: Dreaming of cooperative relationships and affect in Bermuda, Preston, and Mondragón', *Organisational and Social Dynamics*, 20(2): 173–190.

Manley, J. and Froggett, L. (2016) 'Co-operative activity in Preston', Report written for Preston City Council by the Psychosocial Research Unit, UCLan, Preston. Available from www.academia.edu/75083620/Co_operative_Activity_in_Preston [Accessed on 15 March 2023].

Manley, J. and Whyman, P.B. (eds) (2021) *The Preston Model and Community Wealth Building: Creating a Socio-economic Democracy for the Future.* London: Routledge.

Novkovic, S. and Webb, T. (eds) (2014) *Co-operatives in a Post-growth Era.* London: Zed Books.

Prinos, I. (2021) 'The Preston Model and co-operative development: A glimpse of transformation through an alternative model of social and economic organisation'. In Manley, J.Y. and Whyman, P.B. (eds) *The Preston Model and Community Wealth Building: Creating a Socio-Economic Democracy for the Future.* London: Routledge, pp 32–47.

Prinos, I. and Manley, J.Y. (2021) 'The Preston Model: Economic democracy, cooperation and paradoxes in organisational and social identification'. *Sociological Research Online.* Available from https://journals.sagepub.com/doi/full/10.1177/13607804211069398 [Accessed on 15 March 2023].

Raco, M. (1999) 'Researching the new urban governance: an examination of closure, access and complexities of institutional research', *Area*, 31(3): 271–279.

Raworth, K. (2018) *Doughnut Economics.* London: Random House.

Thomas, H. and Logan, C. (2017) *Mondragon: An Economic Analysis.* London: Routledge.

Trebeck, K. and Williams, J. (2019) *The Economics of Arrival: Ideas for a Grown-up Economy.* London: Policy Press.

12

'Can a Leopard Change Its Spots?' How the Established Model of the Mondragon Co-operatives Struggles to Adapt to a Changing World

Julian Manley

The sign of vitality is not to last, but to renew and adapt.
Arizmendiarrieta, quoted in Isasti and Uribe, 2021, p 257

The co-operative must be reconstituted and renewed every day.
Arizmendiarrieta, 2013, p 116

Introduction

Despite claims made by theories of degeneration (Cornforth et al, 1988; Mellor et al, 1988; Pendleton, 2001), the co-operatives of Mondragón appear to both sustain themselves and continue to grow in different ways. This apparently contradicts theories of degeneration that suggest that co-operative businesses 'degenerate' in time and either collapse or become little different to the straightforward capitalist model businesses that they were originally attempting to challenge. As Bretos and colleagues (2019) explain, academic studies of co-operatives in a capitalist setting often condemn cooperative businesses to failure through 'degeneration', which suggests that co-operatives 'must adopt the same forms and priorities as capitalist firms if they are to survive in the market', and that they eventually degenerate into oligarchies (Bretos et al, 2019, p 436). The final conclusion of this process is an eventual transformation into capitalist firms. Cornforth (1995) and more recently Langmead (2017), an author in this edition (see Langmead and Webster, Chapter 4), and others (Paton, 1989; Spear and Voets, 1995; Storey et al, 2014), have argued against the degeneration thesis through studies of worker co-operatives, both in the UK and Mondragón. It is the Mondragón case that is the focus of this chapter, the biggest and longest-lived network of worker-owned co-operatives in the world. Arguably, the worker-owned co-operative is the starkest alternative challenge to the neoliberal status quo in business organizational structures, with the hierarchical pyramidal structure of the cooperative organization being completely inverted from that of traditional business (see, too, Kuznetsova and Kuznetsov, Chapter 8). However, this alternative is no longer an alternative when or if it becomes mainstream (Parker et al, 2014), as would be the case according to degeneration thesis. Therefore, many predicted the beginning of the end for the Mondragon co-operatives after the fall into bankruptcy of the largest and the founding co-operative, Fagor Electrodomesticos (FED) in 2013. The extent of this disaster for the Mondragon system is palpable upon reading Molina's 2012 eulogistic article on FED, ironically published just before the co-operative's rapid demise (Molina, 2012). Nevertheless, instead of this dramatic event becoming a harbinger of hopeless decline, the Mondragon Cooperative Corporation is alive and well. It is an extraordinary accomplishment, by any standards.

This chapter asks what lessons can be learnt about the development, adaptability, resilience and sustainability of the Mondragon co-operatives which are relevant for co-operative businesses elsewhere? To what extent do the Mondragon co-operatives manage to 'change their spots' while still maintaining their essential form? The chapter begins by considering the roots of the Mondragon experience to attempt to establish the qualities and characteristics of this essentiality. In other words, by reaching back in time, the chapter asks whether it is possible to identify those qualities that might be susceptible to adaptation or change today. This lays the foundations for an enquiry into the possibility of the adaptation of the cooperative model to changing circumstances, while still retaining whatever is essential to the Mondragon co-operative. Otherwise, adaptability risks morphing into conformity with the capitalist market, providing evidence, along the way, for the degeneration thesis. The chapter continues by considering this essential form, these qualities and characteristics, in the context of theories of social capital – while questioning some aspects of those theories – and concepts of solidarity, democracy and the meaning of what will be termed a form of 'secular spirituality' to define the relationships that bind people together in Mondragón. In continuation, the chapter brings in some feedback from interviews conducted in Mondragón that illuminate these questions before returning to and extending the metaphor in the title of this chapter, the question being, how can the leopard change its spots without becoming a different beast?

Catholic social action and the Mondragon co-operatives

According to Molina and Miguez (2008) not only was Don José Maria Arizmendiarrieta, the leader and inspiration of the Mondragon experience, a priest, he was perhaps even more importantly an individual who preached (literally) the values of his interpretation of Catholicism, what Molina and Miguez (p 291) call 'a sort of Catholic citizenship'. The values associated with this citizenship – 'equality, freedom, fraternity and reconciliation' (p 291) – could be aligned to an interpretation of Catholicism but ran opposed to the dictatorial regime of Franco's Spain. They go on to say that Arizmendiarrieta's methods 'bordered on the illegal' (p 291). The situation created in Mondragón was thus a strange one, where a political movement was accidentally created by an interpretation of religious doctrine that turned those values into revolutionary values, but with a base in Catholicism which, paradoxically, was supportive of the Spanish state at the time. It is surely because Arizemendiarrieta was an ordained priest that this 'illegality' was allowed to survive where any other form of political movement in this sense would very probably have been immediately and mercilessly crushed. Arizmendiarrieta was able to balance the politics which he openly cherished from the British Labour Party with his view of Catholicism. He 'equated the political ideals of the British Prime Minister [Clement Attlee] with those of Pope Pious XI: Labour ... will abolish the class distinctions that mostly arise from differences in education and will build a common educational base as a unifying factor for the community' (p 293). Maybe this is best summed up in Arizmendiarrieta's humanist theology as expressed in 'Let us not forget that all men, whatever their class or condition, carry a spark of divinity' (p 294). This unusual situation and the perception that accompanied it brought about a series of values that pre-dated cooperative values and were embedded in religious faith. The first series of guiding principles, therefore, that were drawn up for the first co-operative, ULGOR, in 1955, contained principles that in some cases consisted of conditions of morality and steadfastness that might be conjectured as going beyond currently accepted co-operative principles: 'cooperation, self-management, solidarity, hope, sacrifice, high personal standards, responsibility, authority and democracy' (p 297). All of these principles were conceived as expressions of the values embedded in Catholic social action such as 'enthusiasm for work, austerity in the social sphere, dedication and sacrifice for community ideals, faith in social initiatives, self- examination and personal integrity in collective tasks' (p 290). As a priest working within the framework of Catholic social action,

Arizmendiarrieta was expected to lead a life of personal sacrifice 'for the social redemption of the Christian community' (p 288), and to some extent, his followers would also be expected to follow this example.

It is important to emphasize this, since the quality, strength and depth of this commitment to this interpretation of Catholicism must not be confused with any kind of mild or vague religiosity. Of the first five worker co-operative founder members of ULGOR, three of them had been Presidents of 'Acción Católica' (Catholic Action), and one of these, Jose Maria Ormaetxea, has no hesitation in attributing their 'torrent' of enthusiasm and optimism to their religious faith (Isasti and Uribe, 2021 p 88). Furthermore, Ormaetxea makes no distinction between the inner spiritual qualities of the individual and the business and workplace of that individual: 'The company is a kind of emanation of oneself' (p 87). It is difficult to precisely evaluate the meaning behind these expressions of behaviour in individuals and for collectives at work precisely because these are aspects of being that are based around faith as opposed to objective norms or quantifiable advantages, which is ironic in the Mondragon context which is frequently presented to the outside world as based on business pragmatism (personal communications). In this sense, Ormaetxea was clear about the importance of these values to the development of the Mondragon co-operatives, and at the same time surprisingly pessimistic in his assessment of the future of co-operatives in Mondragón. By the time of his death in 2019, the role and presence of Catholicism in the social and community sphere had changed so dramatically since 1955 that he found it difficult to imagine how it could continue: 'many of the human values of solidarity and participation, which had a Christian root, and were present inside us as the protagonists of the Mondragon Experience, have been replaced by others which are dominated by individualism and competition. And this past won't ever return' (p 264, author's translation).

The values of Catholic social action as social capital: a secular spirituality

On the whole, definitions of social capital tend to take on a quantitative sense that may be something to do with the association of the word 'capital' with quantifiable economics. For example, one of the original definitions of 'social capital' comes from Bourdieu, and reads as follows: 'Social capital is the sum of the resources, actual or virtual, that accrue to an individual or a group by virtue of possessing a durable network of more or less institutionalized relationships of mutual acquaintance and recognition' (Bourdieu and Wacquant, 1992, p 119).

In some senses this does describe something about the cooperative structures in Mondragón, where resources of each co-operative are gathered and shared in the Mondragon Cooperative Corporation (a network co-operative of co-operatives) that is legally established and institutionalized as such. However, where Ormaetxea disagrees with Arizmendiarrieta (and this is a very rare disagreement) is in the lasting staying power of the institutions:

> D. José Maria Arizmendiarrieta had a theory: 'when the people disappear, the institutions remain', as if to say that the achievements go above and beyond individuals. In my opinion, this is an error. It's clear to me that the institutions come to an end along with the people who created them. (Isasti and Uribe, 2021, p 87)

For Ormaetxea, then, the sum of resources as provided by the institutionalized network of co-operatives is no guarantee of social capital or survival. Indeed, by Bourdieu's definition, there should be more social capital available today than in 1955, whereas Ormaetxea sees the reality as precisely the contrary to this thesis. It might be argued that the Catholic church was a powerful institution behind the first co-operative, but this argument would fail to recognize Catholic social action as the marginalized, anti-institutionalized expression of faith that it was. Even in this respect, there was little in the way of an institutionalized network in Mondragón in 1955. Many definitions of social capital – such as Coleman's 'forms of social capital' (1988, pp 101–105), that separates the 'human capital' of individuals with the 'social capital' of the functions of actors and their actions in relationships in networks, Nan Lin (2001) who emphasizes the importance of resources in social networks, or Portes (1998) who defines social capital as the benefits of membership of networks – tend to avoid exactly what Coleman himself describes as the move from physical capital that is 'wholly tangible' to social capital that is even less tangible than human capital (Coleman, 1988, pp 100–101). There is no space in this chapter to do these various perspectives on social capital justice. Suffice to say that none of them fully explain the unusual case of Mondragón. The question remains, therefore, both what kind of social capital created the Mondragon experience in the first place, but even more urgently, can we talk about the same social capital as persisting to the present day in Mondragón? If not, what kind of bonds or bridges, to use a well-known Putnam formula (Putnam, 2001), keep the Mondragon co-operatives surviving and thriving? As Ormaetxea himself pointed out, the origins of the Mondragon experience were solidly centred in the values of Catholic social action, to the almost miraculous extent that Ormaetxea points to the degree of ignorance about the basics of business and lack of what today would be regarded as basic business skills and resources (despite the best efforts of the education that was promoted by Arizmendiarrieta). It seems that business could be carried out almost exclusively relying on Catholic values:

Generally speaking, we began from zero in everything. There was no business experience – which is different from technical knowledge in production [which was what Arizmendiarrieta's Polytechnic provided] – the market was unknown, as was the demand, the number and relative importance of offers and opportunities; there were no personal financial resources, no industrial warehouses, no capital available for budgets to facilitate operations. (Isati and Uribe, 2021, p 103)

As has already been indicated, it seems that the bonds that made the Mondragon co-operatives a success in the beginning were rooted in the deep-seated religious convictions of Catholic social action, which nevertheless does not explain the continuing successes of Mondragon. Ormaetxea does continue to suggest that there may have been other bonding agents available to communities in Mondragón, for example the 'txikiteo', the social tradition of establishing contacts, conversations and interconnections between people by talking and wandering from bar to bar, eating and drinking on the way:

This provided a sense of participation among people, of any age and status, and depended on the character of people who were prepared to be open and trusting among neighbours, for whom a gesture was expressed in small deeds of support among themselves. These are the things that provided security and trust when confronting greater tasks, all of which brought meaning to their lives. (Isati and Uribe, 2021, p 90)

This distinctly secular activity is maybe meaningful as one of the social bonding agents in Mondragón. The interview feedback indicates a sense of community that is deeply felt. In the absence of a religious conduit, the bonds that knit communities together in Mondragón appear to be different but not radically so, maybe something akin to a 'secular spirituality'.

Interviewing co-operative worker-members in Mondragón

In 2016–2017, as part of a wider research project to investigate cooperative 'culture' in Mondragón, we conducted 15 in-depth interviews in Spanish and Euskera with members of Mondragon co-operatives (all translations are the author's). The interviews were conducted in conditions of strict anonymity, all names and references that might disturb this condition have been deleted. The research was inspired by the demise of FED, supported by the Mondragon Otalora Management and Cooperative Development Centre, and the felt need in Mondragón to better understand the nature of co-operative 'culture', in other words the qualities and aspects of working in co-operatives that distinguish such businesses in Mondragón from the standard company model, and what motivates and drives members of co-operatives to support such a system. The uneasiness that accompanied the Mondragon Corporation's withdrawing their support for FED brought with it a period of self-analysis and a questioning of the nature and value of the cooperative structures of Mondragon. In psychosocial terms, this might be considered the result of an overwhelming sense of collective guilt in allowing FED to collapse, leading to the need for reparation, short-term reparation – in the form of saving the jobs and livelihoods of the FED workers, through placements, training or early retirement schemes – and longer-term reparation in the form of an in-depth review of cooperative principles and values.

Needless to say, there is much in the literature about values, climate and culture at work (see, for example, a summary in Wallace et al, 1999, pp 551–554). The way these standard business values differ from co-operative values is immediately apparent in the following example (Table 12.1) quoted in Wallace, Hunt and Richards, side by side with the values of Mondragon (as distinct from the 'principles').

The values of the neoliberal view of world and work are remarkable for how, in many cases, and certainly in comparison to cooperative values, they might appear to be anti-values. This may well correspond to the view of such 'values' as being wholly misguided and framed within the overarching concept of the individual good being confused with the collective good within the neoliberal mindset, often referred to as the 'trickle down' idea.

Table 12.1: Business values in Wallace et al compared to Mondragon values

1. Power	Co-operation: owners and protagonists
2. Elitism	Participation: grassroots management
3. Reward	Corporate social responsibility: fair distribution of wealth
4. Effectiveness	Innovation: constant renewal
5. Efficiency	Self-motivation and shared responsibility
6. Economy	Inter co-operation
7. Fairness	Social transformation
8. Teamwork	Good corporate governance practices
9. Law and order	
10. Defence	
11. Competitiveness, and	
12. Opportunity	

Source: Business values adapted from Wallace et al (1999, p 553)

This view – that the wealth of the rich is justified because it eventually 'trickles down' to the poorer members of society, and that without this, the poor would be even poorer – provides a 'value' framework for wealth accumulation by a few successful individuals: the wealthier they are, the more value they give. Such a mind-bending idea very much fits in with what Hoggett has called 'perverse social structures', 'collusion' and organised self-deception' (Hoggett, 2010, p 58). This does not mean, however, that the worker-members of the co-operatives in Mondragón necessarily think differently, despite their stated values and principles. It would be difficult to imagine a Mondragón isolated from the world in which it operates. Indeed, this is one of the Ormaetxea's stated fears for the future of Mondragon, that he is 'concerned about to what extent we run the risk of converting ourselves into an archipelago' (Isati and Uribe, 2021, p 268). Indeed, there is a significant literature that criticizes Mondragon precisely for what some people consider to be its failure to be cooperative, therefore the failure to adhere to co-operative values and principles (see summary of this position in Heras-Saizarbitoria, 2014, pp 647–650). According to Heras-Saizarbitoria, the lack of interest and belief in cooperative values and principles in Mondragon is especially prevalent among the younger members. This was a factor that was recognized in Mondragon as part of their renewal of cooperative culture programme, and formed part of the present study. Within the conceptualization of the present study, the reason for the waning of commitment on the part of younger members may be due not to a degeneration thesis, but rather to the corresponding waning of interest and engagement with Catholicism and the virtual disappearance of Catholic social action, the drivers of the original values of Mondragon. The purpose of the interviews we conducted was, therefore, to find out to what extent the cooperative values of Mondragon were shared and lived values for its members, despite the significant decline of religious faith in Basque communities, as opposed to an institutional façade of a degenerating organization.

Responding to meaning and value

Democratic participation in governance, shared responsibility and motivation
Most of the interviewees agreed that participation was genuinely important in the governance of the co-operatives. The following extract demonstrates this very clearly, but adds, towards the end, the observation that participation is difficult to measure, and that some worker-members may be sceptical of the degree and quality of participation, simply as a result of this difficulty. That is to say, a position could be held that whatever participation there is will never be enough, and this might be especially the case in worker-members with no other experience of work than within co-operatives.

Decision-making was seen as closely aligned to the Mondragon value of 'participation: grassroots management':

'the way in which you have to take a decision, you have to analyse all the sensitivities, all the points of view, bearing in mind that we are human beings, with respect, and that it has to be done in a participative way, which has to reach consensus. In other words, in the style of working and the way of doing things, you realise that things are done in a participatory manner. Even though people think that they don't participate, I can say, compared to other companies that I have worked in, that the level of participation is definitely enormous.' (Interviewee A)

Such an emphatic approval of the value of participation bases its observation on a comparison with experiences elsewhere, which is not available to all in Mondragón, especially with the traditional passing on of work positions from parents to children, so that there is sometimes a sense of the co-operative at work being a mirror of the closest-knit community of all, the family, with all the dynamics that this could bring up. For another interviewee, this 'family' feel of working in a co-operative is a key binding element, where participation is a natural aspect of work and barely distinguished from life outside work: 'these family-like relationships in the co-operative I think are very much better than in a standard company. I'm referring to the ease of working together, the weaving together of working life and personal family life' (Interviewee D).

Whatever defines a family, it clearly is a small, intimate unit where members of the unit share responsibility for the whole. In this way, the comparison to family emphasizes another of the values of working in a co-operative. This is also linked by another interviewee to motivating factors and to the central social and economic necessity for co-operatives to create quality employment, a central pillar of the Mondragon mission: 'creating employment in the region … in the end this supports family life, reaching agreements, and all this is much, much better than in a standard company' (Interviewee F).

Inter co-operation

The demise of FED was traumatic for many. Many respondents referred to it both as an example of a lack of the value of inter co-operation and then, paradoxically, as an example of inter co-operation in action, which resonates with the guilt to reparation cycle mentioned previously:

'For example, in the case of FED, the way the co-operatives took action was completely praiseworthy, not only in [name of interviewee's co-operative]. Right now, we have about 45 workers relocated from

FED, and not only in [name of interviewee's co-operative], but in other co-operatives too, this terribly unpleasant situation has been absorbed into other co-operatives.' (Interviewee C)

This response exudes pride and solidarity and points to the degree of this inter co-operation in practice by citing the very elevated number of workers who were relocated into the interviewee's co-operative. In other words, this would seem to indicate an expression of solidarity beyond the merely symbolic.

Co-operation: owners and protagonists

As worker-owned co-operatives, the Mondragon co-operative places a special value on the co-operation that comes with being owners and therefore active members of the co-operative. The respondents to the interviews varied in their responses, with some reference to age differences being cited as reasons for this diversity. For the following interviewee, the structure of the co-operative is closely connected to the fact of being an owner and actively pursuing decision-making:

'For example, everything that we communicate to the Social Council and that is transmitted to the Governing Council gets a response, which can be sometimes good, satisfactory or unsatisfactory. But this attention exists, and following on from that, the request receives a proposal that offers a solution, trying things out … In some cases proposals are approved, in other cases not, but what this shows is that you are not alone, that you are in a co-operative within which there are other people who are valuing the ideas that you are proposing, and this is very important.' (Interviewee D)

As in any social situation, there were opinions contrary to this, indicating the struggle to maintain the written values and principles alive in a lived sense, and for the following interviewee, the only aspect of the co-operative structure that remained relevant was the General Assembly:

'We are cooperators, a co-operative. What is a co-operative? I think that we have lost a lot, the essence, everything that has been transmitted to us … In the end, what I see a lot of is that we come and do our own thing and we are aware of being cooperators because we attend the Assembly once a year, and not much else.' (Interviewee G)

As a person with over 30 years' experience at work the following respondent suggests that this lack of connection with cooperative values has something to do with the difference between the older members, who lived the values, and the younger members who know about but find it hard to relate to these values. Referring to a discussion about to what extent a worker should be counting and quantifying hours worked, and – in the context of a worker-owned co-operative, where the worker is as much a manager as an employee – to what extent the worker should take on a self-sacrificing position with a view to improving the chances of that person's own business, the following interviewee laments the loss of selfless sacrifice of the cooperative worker:

> 'In the thirty years I have been working in [name of co-operative] I have never counted the hours worked in my working life, and it makes me uncomfortable to say that here some people demand and ask for things and only remember their rights ... the statutes are there, but hardly anyone reads them. These types of comments, thoughts that people have mentioned to me, have forced me to re-evaluate our environment. In the co-operative there are people who have lived the experience differently, I don't know about better or worse or if they had become members today, in this situation, if they would have thought the same or in the way that others think, but for me, it has given me something to think about.' (Interviewee B)

Another respondent points to a similar dynamic, where the engaged cooperators have a long-standing post in the co-operatives, and also views great difference in the application of values at work, and blames this on a certain vagueness in those values:

> 'There are people who are very engaged and committed, and if it wasn't for them we wouldn't be where we are today, but there isn't a very clear culture or value set; everything is mixed up and it depends on the departments, depends on the day and even the same person may harbour contradictions.' (Interviewee A)

Overview

On the other hand, this same interviewee responds extremely positively to the cooperative experience, encapsulating the very contradictions that they have previously mentioned:

> 'it makes me feel good, it makes me feel like a better person, and even better because I have been in other companies where the objective has been to reduce costs, make people redundant, lowering salaries, company agreements with other objectives, all centred around costs.

That's not the case here. Here we look for genuine social peace and understanding. Over there, it's a social peace and understanding to prevent a strike ... Here, it's not like that, there is a way to deal with whatever opinion that is proposed by putting the person first, and the collective too. You can't be focussed only on the needs of a single person ... so whatever decision is taken places real value on the people and their needs and sensitivities, with empathy and by listening.' (Interviewee A)

The overall sense from these interviewees was one of positive support for cooperative values, with a degree of suspicion or concern that perhaps these values, which are acknowledged as the values that created and have sustained the Mondragon experience for over 60 years, are fading or less understood than before.

Paradoxes and contradictions

The conundrum facing the Mondragon co-operatives is, simply put, how to remain cooperative – meaning true to cooperative values – while competing in a globalized market which is less concerned about values and more about profit. Some believe that the entry into the global market has definitively destroyed the essence of Mondragon cooperativism (Errasti et al, 2003; Flecha and Ngai, 2014) As analysed by Flecha and Ngai (2014), the expansion of the Mondragon co-operatives abroad has been almost exclusively in the form of private companies, where the workers have no more rights than any other private company and work to serve the true owners and managers, that is to say the worker-owners in Mondragón. These rights are also social values and the root of social capital. They are identified by Flecha and Ngai as 'worker participation in ownership, capital and management' (Flecha and Ngai, 2014, p 671). It would be fair to add all the other values discussed in this chapter to that list and place a special emphasis on the lack of participation in democratic governance and decision-making. The argument made to explain this anomaly is that the barriers to cooperative development internationally – 'economic, legal, cultural and investment-related' (p 671) – are too great to overcome, and that this capitalist development is not due to a lack of willingness on the part of the original co-operatives in Mondragón. Whether this 'excuses' the Mondragon co-operatives from bearing the responsibility for this form of expansion is open to debate. Certainly, the Mondragon approach places survival above all else, even, maybe, strict adherence to cooperative values. This 'excuse' would fit in perfectly well with the Tavistock approach to an open systems view of organizational theory, that is to say that the primary task of any organization is to perform whatever tasks are necessary for survival (Zagier

Roberts, 2019). From this perspective, the Mondragon co-operatives have no choice but to do whatever they must to survive. This view of survival, however, is purely economic, and it has been argued that survival could be associated to the nurturing of social capital (Onyebuchi, 2018). What survives above all in Mondragon are the jobs of the worker-members, as demonstrated by the way the workers in FED were supported by the other co-operatives of the Mondragon group, a source of pride, as explained by Interviewee C, earlier.

It seems that social values are open to challenge in Mondragon, as long as this enables the cooperative businesses to survive and jobs to be created and/or protected. This is deeply cherished by the Mondragon system and forms the very basis of their existence as vaunted in their motto: Humanity at Work. Even Ormaetxea, from his privileged position as original founder member of the first Mondragon co-operative, and therefore presumably more deeply embedded in the values of Catholic social action, makes pragmatism of this kind the foundation of all other activity. According to Ormaetxea, a cooperative business is the preferred model, but the most important thing is to create quality jobs:

> Let's take the idea of a car to illustrate this point: the important thing is to have a car that works, and within certain parameters. The legal structure would be like the paint on the car. What does it matter if it's one colour or another! The most important thing is not to create trading societies [co-operatives], but to create new businesses. (Isasti and Uribe, 2021, p 280)

This approach, however, can only lead to a sense of constant agony and struggle that might even threaten the very existence of the co-operatives themselves, not as money-making ventures, but as businesses that adhere to co-operative principles and values. This, in part, explains the contradictions that seem to emerge from the findings and that seem to half resolve themselves in the universally agreed primary aim of the co-operative in Mondragón, which is to create and retain jobs. For the somewhat critical account of Mondragon espoused in Heras-Saizarbitoria (2014), this is, in fact, the only 'principle' that truly counts, and 'binds' together the worker-owners of the Mondragon co-operatives: 'We can call this attitude the principles of secure membership and employment, which is mainly what binds the worker-member owners to Mondragon, namely, job security' (p 656). Heras-Saizarbitoria's thesis is that this is the only binding agent of Mondragon, and other values are dismissed as being irrelevant, romanticized or outdated, a position that resonates with Interviewee G. However, between the reality of the importance of job security on the one hand and the 'romantic' version of cooperativism on the other, lie the mass of contradictions that emerge from the findings in this chapter. In the first place, the original co-operatives in Mondragón were not shy of a certain romanticism (if faith can be viewed as 'romantic' as opposed to 'reality'), and would not have considered this to be laughable or an object of derogation. It could even be argued, particularly from a neoliberal perspective, that cooperative values are in themselves 'romantic' or utopic. Yet for someone like Arizmendiarrieta (2013), values were the central 'unromantic' reality of the project from the beginning. He was able to argue both for values *and* against utopic ideas, once again bringing together what for many might appear to be paradoxes or contradictions: 'Solidarity and honesty are profitable in themselves' (p 80); 'We must guard ourselves from utopian aspirations, since those who can be qualified as such, although seemingly pleasing and attractive, are a disturbing element' (p 83).

Arizmendiarrieta's solidarity is precisely Interviewee A's 'genuine social peace and understanding'. Nevertheless, the same Interviewee can also say that there is no clear value system (no utopia), and that in the real, practical world of work 'even the same person may harbour contradictions'. For Heras-Saizarbitoria (2014, pp 658–660), these contradictions and paradoxes are evidence of a 'decoupling' of the formality of the Mondragon cooperative structure based on principles and values and the actual lived experience of the workforce. This implies a degeneration or erosion of authenticity. However, the apathy ('*rhetoric of abandonment* of the cooperative spirit and an *abstainer* stance', p 659 [italics at source]) that Heras-Saizarbitoria finds in their study is largely absent from the findings in this chapter. Contradictions abound, but as emerging contradictions that are not unusual in a human as opposed to a working context. There is a sense of hope and almost a blind faith in the lived experience that seems to resonate with the kind of religious interpretation of work which was explicit in the founder members. Once again, taking Ormaetxea's words as an example, he demonstrates this through the praising of the value of the 'soul' via a religious reference, as opposed to the pragmaticism of the car that functions: 'I'm reminded of Saint Ignacio de Loyola's question to Saint Francisco Javier, paraphrasing the words of Jesus in the Gospels: "Of what value is winning the world if you lose your soul?"' (Isasti and Uribe, 2021, p 283).

In today's largely secular environment, it would seem that something akin to secular spirituality has taken the place of religiosity. At first sight it may appear that a word such as 'spirituality' may be somewhat unnecessarily transcendental in the context of a description of the binding and bridging that Mondragon values bring to work and community, but it should be remembered that in this context, with the Mondragon project's background in Catholic social action, the 'spiritual' is one and the same with the 'social'. Therefore, many of the respondents in this study refer to the values in a general sense, not as elements that necessarily contribute to better productivity or economic performance of the business, but rather as spiritual achievements that make them 'feel good', that you are valued and 'not alone', where family life is supported, and where it seems that the 'the weaving together of working life and personal family life' is possible. More than values of business, these are values that still appear to have the sense of faith of the founders, and with these values, therefore, come a palpable emotional attachment and sensitivity that creates the 'weave' between work and community (for a discussion of affect in the Mondragon co-operatives, directly relevant to understanding the quality of the Mondragon values see Manley and Aiken, 2020).

Can the leopard change its spots?

To return to the metaphor of this chapter, the question is not so much can the Mondragon co-operative respond to change in order to continue being successful in today's business world – because it clearly has done so – but rather can it change and yet still remain identifiable as a cooperative business. The nature of the co-operative as a business which is distinct from a standard company is centred on its adherence to the core values and principles of cooperativism. In this chapter, the values that have emerged as important in this respect are deeply human values that are very difficult to measure. To some extent, therefore, an evaluation of the Mondragon co-operatives as sufficiently cooperative or not will be a question of taste or at least subject to differing criteria as to their success or otherwise. In this chapter, there is evidence to suggest that despite the bending and twisting of the model resulting from internationalization and pressures of the global market, there remains a good deal of 'faith' in the values of the cooperative system among the cooperative worker-owners. There is no doubt that there are tensions between the need for retaining a competitive edge in terms of business and this cooperative identity. There is no greater example of this than the story of the demise of FED (criticized as anti-cooperative by some of the worker-owners of FED, since some worker-owners interpreted this at the time as uncooperative abandonment), and the posterior relocation, training and early retirement plans brought to fruition by the Mondragon co-operatives as a whole. The former action is true to business sense, while the latter is true to cooperative values. Depending on circumstance and opinion, this story is one of solidarity on both accounts. If solidarity is a form of identification that both includes and excludes (Morgan and Pulignano, 2020), the former action is an expression of solidarity that includes the remaining Mondragon co-operatives and excludes FED; the latter action is an expression of solidarity that includes all worker-owners in Mondragón, including FED, and excludes others. This is why in , in times of economic shrinkage, it is the employees, both in Mondragon and abroad, who will be made redundant, not the worker-owners, which speaks to the absolute overarching principle of job security as identified by Heras-Saizarbitoria (2014).

Nevertheless, despite this apparent absolute emphasis on job security, even at the expense of others due to their status as employees, and, in this sense, a somewhat tainted view of solidarity and cooperative principles, there remains a tangible sense of a form of secular spirituality in the hopes, desires and aspirations of a significant number of cooperative workers in Mondragón. This resonates with the language of morality employed by the respondents in this chapter. According to Morgan and Pulignano (2020), the 'language of morality' is one of three sets of resources that enact solidarity (the others being political action and rituals and symbols): 'In this moral discourse, sharing binds us into relationships which go beyond individual calculation of benefits and costs. We engage in forms of solidarity because it is "right" to do so' (Morgan and Pulignano, 2020, p 21).

It may be, therefore, that the continuing success of the Mondragon co-operatives is not only due to sound economic decisions in the global capitalist market, but also to the binding agent that is solidarity glued into the Mondragon system in the form of a belief in the spiritual value of working in a co-operative. Ultimately, this leads to an essential difference between Mondragon and the external capitalist marketplace: Mondragon emphasizes the collective over the individual. As Interviewee A reminds us in this chapter, 'You can't be focussed only on the needs of a single person'. In terms of what can be learnt from this experience for other businesses and communities, it seems that Mondragon may be a precursor to the ways future businesses will have to change to survive. According to Snower and Wilson (2022), for example, the future of economic theory and therefore the way businesses are run, is in a refocusing on the collective as opposed to the individual, or at least a rebalancing of the collective and the individual. As part of re-imagining the collective, they discuss the centrality of moral values: 'An essential purpose of moral values is to promote intrinsic co-operation within groups and suppress destructive selfishness' (Snower and Wilson, 2022, p 37).

Although Snower and Wilson do not discuss the Mondragon co-operatives, their whole thesis resonates with the cooperative values and the move towards collectives as discussed in this chapter: 'The group can become the unit of selection when individuals – driven by internal mechanisms (such as moral values) and external mechanisms (such as institutions) – cooperate consistently in the pursuit of collective purposes' (Snower and Wilson, 2022, p 25).

Snower and Wilson set their analysis in the context of the evolution of natural systems. We may find that the old seeds of cooperativism of Mondragon still have a future flowering in the future of evolutionary economics.

Acknowledgements

The interviews cited in this article were conducted by Eva Alejo of the Otalora Centre in Mondragón as part of a research project into the 'culture' of Mondragon in 2016–17. Thanks to the Director, Yolanda Lekuona for her support of the project.

References

Arizmendiarrieta, J.-M. (2013) *Reflections*. Mondragon: Otalora.

Bourdieu, P. and Wacquant, L.J.D. (1992) *An Invitation to Reflexive Sociology*. Cambridge: Polity.

Bretos, I., Errasti, A. and Marcuello, C. (2019) 'Is there life after degeneration? The organizational life cycle of cooperatives under a "grow-or-die" dichotomy', *Annals of Public and Cooperative Economics*, 91(3): 435–458.

Coleman, J.S. (1988) 'Social capital in the creation of human capital', *The American Journal of Sociology*, 94, Supplement: Organizations and Institutions: Sociological and Economic Approaches to the Analysis of Social Structure: 95–120.

Cornforth, C. (1995) 'Patterns of co-operative management: Beyond the degeneration thesis', *Economic and Industrial Democracy*, 16(4): 487–523.

Cornforth, C., Thomas, A., Spear, R. and Lewis, J. (1988) *Developing Successful Worker Co-operatives*. London: SAGE.

Errasti, A.M., Hera, I., Bakaikoa, B. and Egoibar, P. (2003) 'The internationalisation of cooperatives: The case of the Mondragon Cooperative Corporation', *Annals of Public and Cooperative Economics*, 74(4): 553–584.

Flecha, R. and Ngai, P. (2014) 'The challenge for Mondragon: Searching for the cooperative values in times of internationalization', *Organization*, 21(95): 666–682.

Heras-Saizarbitoria, I. (2014) 'The ties that bind? Exploring the Basic principles of worker-owned organizations in practice', *Organization*, 21(5): 645–665.

Hoggett, P. (2010) 'Perverse social structures', *Journal of Psycho-Social Studies*, 4(1): 67–64.

Isasti, A. and Uribe, I. (2021) *Ormaetxea, De Principio a fin, toda una vida cooperative. Biografia dialogada*, Errenteria: Mondragon, Laboral Kutxa, Arizmendiarrietaren Lagunak Elkartea.

Langmead, K. (2017) 'Challenging the degeneration thesis: The role of democracy in worker cooperatives?' *Journal of Entrepreneurial and Organizational Diversity*, 5(1): 79–98.

Lin, N. (2001) *Social Capital: A Theory of Social Structure and Action*. Cambridge: Cambridge University Press.

Manley, J. and Aiken, M. (2020) 'A socio-economic system for affect: Dreaming of co-operative relationships and affect in Bermuda, Preston and Mondragón', *Organisational and Social Dynamics*, 20(2): 173–191.

Mellor, M. Hannah, J. and Stirling, J. (1988) *Worker Co-operatives in Theory and Practice*. Milton Keynes: Open University.

Molina, F. (2012) '*Fagor Electrodomesticos*: The multinationalisation of a Basque co-operative, 1955–2010', *Business History*, 54(6): 945–963.

Molina, F. and Miguez, A. (2008) 'The origins of Mondragon: Catholic co-operativism and social movement in a Basque valley (1941–59)', *Social History*, 33(3): 284–298

Mondragon Corporation (nd), 'About us'. Available from www.mondra gon-corporation.com/en/about-us/ [Accessed on 13 April 2022].

Morgan, G. and Pulignano, V. (2020) 'Solidarity at work: Concepts, levels and challenges', *Work, Employment and Society*, 34(1): 18–34.

Onyebuchi, O. (2018) 'Human capital development and organizational survival: A theoretical review', *International Journal of Management and Sustainability*, 7(4): 194–203.

Parker, M., Cheney, G., Fournier, V. and Land, C. (2014) 'The question of organization: A manifesto for alternatives', *Ephemera. Theory and Politics in Organization*, 14(4): 623–638.

Paton, R. (1989) *Reluctant Entrepreneurs*. Milton Keynes: Open University.

Pendleton, A. (2001) *Employee Ownership, Participation and Governance: A Study of ESOPS in the UK*. London: Routledge.

Portes, A. (1998) 'Social capital: Its origins and applications in modern sociology', *Annual Review of Sociology*, 24(1): 1–25.

Putnam, R.D. (2001) *Bowling Alone: The Collapse and Revival of American Community*. New York: Simon & Schuster.

Snower, D.J. and Wilson, D.S. (2022) 'Rethinking the theoretical foundations of economics', *Economics*. Discussion paper. Available from https://evonom ics.com/the-making-of-rethinking-the-theoretical-foundation-of-econom ics/ [Accessed on 1 July 2022].

Spear, R. and Voets, H. (1995) *Success and Enterprise*. Aldershot: Avebury.

Storey, J., Basterretxea, I. and Salaman, G. (2014) 'Managing and resisting "degeneration" in employee-owned businesses: A comparative study of two large retailers in Spain and the United Kingdom', *Organization*, 21(5): 626–644.

Wallace, J., Hunt, J. and Richards, C. (1999) 'The relationship between organisational culture, organisational climate and managerial values', *The International Journal of Public Sector Management*, 12(7): 548–564.

Zagier Roberts, V. (2019) 'The organization of work: Contribution from open systems theory'. In Obholzer, A. and Zagier Roberts, V. (eds) *The Unconscious at Work*. 2nd edn. Abingdon: Routledge, pp 28–38.

13

Possibilities and Challenges of the 'Sorachi Model': Learning from Preston's Attempts to Rebuild the Region

Hiroshi Sakai

Introduction

This chapter explores whether it is possible to revive the exhausted region of Sorachi (Sorachi, 2022), located in the centre of Hokkaido, an island in the northern part of the Japanese archipelago, by adopting insights from the Preston Model (Preston Model, 2022), a regional revitalization program currently underway in Preston, England. The aim is to evaluate the universal value and potential of the Preston Model to transcend regional and national boundaries.

The Preston Model, which has been attracting attention in the UK in recent years, is characterized by a simple mechanism to 'keep money circulating within the region and keep it from flowing out'. The concept of 'keeping the money circulating within the region' has already been advocated by many researchers, and some trial-and-error efforts have already begun to put it into practice, especially through the experiment of introducing local currencies, such as the Bristol pound (Johnson and Harvey-Wilson, 2018; Marshall and O'Neill, 2018). However, the Preston Model is groundbreaking and significant in that it has proposed and put into action a concrete place-making system firmly linked to cooperative values and visions (Manley and Whyman, 2021). As shown in Chapter 11 of this volume, key elements include persuading anchor institutions to buy services locally and in smaller contracts, as well as a concerted effort to promote the creation of local co-operatives to meet anchor institution need and other local demands.

Although the potential for this model is gaining traction in the UK, we need to consider the following question: Can this British model be applied to the regeneration of regions on the other side of the world, where the social environment is completely different? In other words, this is both a question and consideration of its universality and an exploration of the potential of cooperative place-making (Webster et al, 2021). If a version of the Preston Model were to be applied to the revitalization of a former coal-producing region in Japan such as Hokkaido which faces economic and social decline, various obstacles would be encountered. First, transferring a model designed to meet the needs of a locality in one part of the world to a place where the sociocultural environment is completely different will inevitably demand at the very least, considerable adaptation. Certainly any attempt to apply the Preston Model to the context of cooperative development in Japan will require serious research into local conditions. Key questions include not only the feasibility of adaptation, but also whether it could win strong popular consent. The market economy, driven as it is by the global mobility of investment to maximize shareholder returns, has neglected the interests of specific regions and communities. This is especially evident in the case of Sorachi and is one of the factors that has continued to divide the region and undermine the morale of its people. Of course, the market economy, with its competition, convenience and efficiency has shaped the region of Sorachi and the lives of its people. There is a prevailing belief that market generates growth, convenience, wealth and greater contentment for the mass of people. Notwithstanding the ubiquity of these beliefs about the market system, in reality many of the effects of the market have been negative for some regions and communities. Like in the UK, there is a widening gap between rich and poor, the collapse of local communities and a general sense of powerlessness in the face of seemingly unchallengeable, anonymous and remote economic forces and interests. Against this background, there exists a deep grassroots desire for change in which local communities and ordinary people can be empowered to address their own needs and shape their own future. There is a longing among many for the emergence of a new system that will create a change. Sorachi, in Hokkaido, Japan, is one such locality which might benefit from adopting the Preston Model, or aspects of it. How appropriate might it be?

Historical background: co-operatives in Japan

The history of co-operatives in Japan is long and deep. Their activities were first recorded in history some 100 years ago, when Toyohiko Kagawa, the father of Japan's co-operative movement, embarked on activities to help the needy in Japan. After the Second World War, much of Japan's urban infrastructure was destroyed, and rebuilding and recovery were top priorities for successive post-war Japanese governments. Co-operatives, with their emphasis upon member activism, egalitarian wealth distributing policies and serving the local community, held an especially strong attraction for both citizens and politicians. As a result, today, a total of 107 million people are members of co-operatives in Japan, with business revenues of 34.5 trillion yen. As the total number of cooperative members worldwide is estimated at 1 billion, one in ten is Japanese. The scale of business is also an astonishing achievement. Considering also that Japan's national budget is 114 trillion yen (in 2023), the importance of co-operatives to the national economy is clear.

Why have co-operatives become so important in Japan? An important factor may be linked to the mindset and culture of Japanese society. There is a long tradition of mutual aid, belief in contribution to the community and an emphasis on honest frugality. Of course, these traditional values have been challenged and even eroded by the expansion of the market economy; but they have proved robust tenets of Japanese life and they certainly came to the fore during Japan's post-war reconstruction. The rapid expansion of co-operatives is evidence of this. Moreover intellectual and academic interest in co-operatives in Japan has been very strong. Research on co-operatives in Japan has a history of nearly 100 years, and the country probably leads Asia in this field. In Tokyo, there is the 'Robert Owen Society', which upholds the values of Robert Owen (1771–1858), a social reformer who laid the foundations for co-operatives in the UK and elsewhere. There is also 'the Ruskin Library', which holds a large amount of material on John Ruskin (1819–1900), a social thinker whose ideas complemented those of Owen. All of these activities are based in prime locations in the centre of Tokyo, demonstrating just how strongly Japanese cooperators have been influenced by ideas and forms originating in the UK. Arguably, this augurs well for the transfer of the Preston Model to a Japanese context, as it would follow a well-established tradition.

Hokkaido and Sorachi: the need for regeneration
History and current situation

Hokkaido is an island in the northern part of the Japanese archipelago. It has an area of 83,000 square kilometres, almost a quarter of the total land area of Japan, and its population is 5.2 million. This is about the same size as Ireland. Because the population is relatively small for its size, it is not as densely populated as Japan's southern areas. Hokkaido has a cold climate similar to that of the north of England, and vast forests cover the entire island. The key industries are agriculture, fisheries and tourism. Currently, the island produces rice, dairy products, marine products and is a major supplier of the nation's food. Hokkaido's rich natural environment attracts many tourists from the rest of Japan and abroad. In the past, the island had to meet Japan's other needs. It was once a major supplier of coal, no small advantage in an industrial nation with few fossil fuel resources. However, in the 1960s and 1970s, cheap oil and coal imported from overseas forced the closure of many coal mines in Hokkaido. By the end of the 20th century, all of the coal mines had disappeared.

Located in the centre of Hokkaido, Sorachi covers an area of 5,800 square kilometres, or about 7 per cent of the island. The population is about 5.5 per cent of that of Hokkaido, or 282,000 (as of 2019). There are currently 24 municipalities with their own independent administrative functions in the Sorachi region. The FY2021 budget of Iwamizawa City (population 78,000), the most populous in Sorachi, was approximately $400 million. On the other hand, Urausu Town (population 1,700), the smallest in Sorachi, had a budget of $28 million. The difference in budget size is extremely large, almost 100 to 7 (FSMH, 2018).

Sorachi used to be a major energy supplier for Japan, with more than 100 coal mines. However, by 1995, due to a major shift in national energy policy, almost all the large mines were closed; the coal mines with their deep shafts had lost their competitive edge. In response, many municipalities in the Sorachi region switched to agriculture as their main economic activity, but they were no longer as prosperous as the days supported by the coal mine industry. The shift brought financial problems, depopulation, an ageing society with a declining birthrate, and an exodus of young people. Yubari City, which once boasted the largest coal output in Japan, went bankrupt in 2007, becoming the first municipality in Japan requiring national help to recover from its debts. There are other municipalities that are in a similar predicament. There is a serious concern as to a possible chance for a second or third Yubari in the region at any time. Population decline is very critical: Sorachi's population, which was 820,000 in 1960, fell to 280,000 by 2020. According to the National Research Institute, if the population continues to decline at this rate, all 24 municipalities in Sorachi could disappear by 2040 (Masuda, 2014).

Addressing the decline in Sorachi

This chapter will consider the combination of two potential strategies, inspired in the UK, for the revitalization of Sorachi. The first is the Preston Model, a systemic regional revitalization program being implemented in Preston, Lancashire, UK. The second is a cooperative initiative in a suburb of Manchester, UK: Unicorn, a grocery store (Unicorn, 2022).

In the summer of 2019, the author visited the University of Central Lancashire in Preston and Unicorn in Manchester. A number of key attributes were identified which have the potential for application in Sorachi. These will be outlined next.

Preston: a summary

Preston is a medium-sized city with a population of 120,000 in north-west England. In the past, the city thrived as a cotton cloth producer, powered by coal which was mined locally. However, as production bases shifted overseas during the 19th and 20th centuries, the spinning industry declined in many parts of the UK, including Preston. The socio-economic impact of declining industry between Preston and Sorachi is quite similar, with the same urgent need for economic regeneration.

The following is an itemized summary of the main features of the model as described in interview by Dr Julian Manley, a key figure in the development of the Preston Model:

- The Preston Model is a system that allows people to create their own local businesses and circulate money within the city, without relying on outside investors or major corporations.
- The model is supported by 'core members' and 'anchors' in the community.
- The core members of the model consist of Preston City Council and the University of Central Lancashire.
- The city is promoting community revitalization by providing land and buildings for citizens (especially young people) to start businesses.
- The university has established an on-campus business hub to help local people to develop business plans. Many students at the university take advantage of the hub, with a view to creating a career path after graduation, especially through the development of co-operatives.
- Anchors are institutions that support this model and are made up of organizations which are firmly located in Preston, such as the police, hospitals, schools and the university which possess large budgets and need to buy in a wide range of services (for example catering, building maintenance and so on).
- Anchors nurture local small businesses (especially coops) and prevent money from leaving the city by, for example, procuring services in small lots from local businesses.

Manley cited his own university as an example of a local organization that could have done more to support local economic activities in the past. He explained that there were a lot of events on campus every year which required catering services and that a decision to use out-of-town vendors or local ones can make a difference locally. The procurement of office and classroom furniture and fixtures is another case in point. Many of the 'anchors', including the university, replace their office and classroom furniture and some fixtures on a regular basis. At one point, there were no suppliers available in Preston, but efforts are now being made to develop local suppliers.

More generally, as Preston City Council and stakeholders in the city persuaded anchor organizations to cooperate, they managed to substantially increase their local procurement, keeping jobs and money in the city and in the county of Lancashire. In Lancashire as a whole, the amount of money flowing back into the region has increased by 80 per cent.

But more important than money is a change in attitude and morale within the city. It seems that the new localism and participatory democracy has brought a sense of pride and possibility among Prestonians. Manley concluded: 'The market economy, where shareholders and capitalists could do whatever they wanted without any restrictions, will soon come to an end.'

Sorachi: differences and similarities

The strength of the Preston Model is that it and associated networks are firmly located within the city of Preston. The core stakeholders, the City Council of Preston and the University of Central Lancashire, are within walking distance of each other. Anchor institutions are also concentrated in the city centre. Sorachi, on the other hand, is an aggregation of 24 municipalities in Hokkaido, and each municipality has its own administrative function, and each has a council composed of members elected by the local residents. The distance from the southern municipality to the northern municipality is nearly 100 km in a straight line.

In addition, there is little or no day-to-day co-ordination between the municipalities in the southern and northern parts of Sorachi. Under these geographical conditions, what kind of mechanisms might be put in place to unite the whole of Sorachi behind a revitalization programme? Is it realistically possible to establish a network of core members and anchor organizations in geographically dispersed Sorachi? To explore this, it is first necessary to assess the standing of potential interest groups in Sorachi.

With as many as 24 municipalities in Sorachi, it is not easy to form a core member group, as in Preston. Iwamizawa City, which has the largest population of all the municipalities, is home to the Sorachi Sub-prefecture Bureau, an agency of the Hokkaido government. This agency's role is to monitor developments in the entire Sorachi region, and report these to the Hokkaido government. But it is a limited role – it is not expected to take the initiative in mobilizing and organizing local governmental or private interests to stimulate reform and change. There are many public facilities and businesses that have their roots in each municipality. Although small-scale, most of the 24 municipalities have their own independent facilities such as city halls, schools, libraries, hospitals and police stations. The question is whether these might be harnessed in a Sorachi-wide regeneration strategy. The success of any project will depend on this. The following section examines the most likely candidates to become anchor institutions.

Anchor institutions in Sorachi

Schools form a particularly strong group of potential anchor institutions. There are 100 elementary and junior high schools in 24 municipalities, with approximately 16,000 students. There are 21 high schools in 14 municipalities, with approximately 5,600 students. There is also one small university in each of the three municipalities, with 1,700 students enrolled. The elementary and junior high schools are financed by the local governments, and most of the high schools are financed by the Hokkaido government. There are one national university and two private universities.

Hospitals also constitute potential Anchor institutions. There are three, one each in Iwamizawa, Sunagawa and Fukagawa. All are operated by their respective municipalities and have a total of 1,250 beds. In addition to these three hospitals, many other municipalities maintain hospitals with inpatient facilities ranging from a few dozen to around 100 beds. One of the reasons why this area has such a good medical system for a depopulated area is that there used to be many coal mines in the area, and medical facilities were needed to deal with many associated accidents. This legacy of Sorachi's industrial past is a fortunate asset in a Preston Model-type regeneration programme. The case of harnessing the hospitals as part of the Sorachi Model also resonates with work in Cleveland, Ohio, and the Evergreen co-operatives, a system that in turn influenced the Preston Model (Democracy Collaborative).

There are other public facilities in the municipalities such as gymnasiums, libraries, museums, children's centres and community centres – all with the potential to become important anchor institutions. In terms of local government participation, authorities in the region offer both challenges and opportunities. It is not easy to form a network of core members and anchor organizations in Sorachi, given both the size of the region and its administrative division into so many centres of power, many jealously defending their independent ability to shape local conditions. On the other hand, the fact that there is such a large number of public facilities and businesses means that the large budgets they command offers very substantial purchasing power which could be directed to local procurement and co-operatives.

Sorachi's patchwork of small municipalities has led to concerns that there might be a great deal of duplication of services, and that greater efficiencies could be achieved by co-operation in terms of various procurement, enabling the achievement of greater economies of scale. Such partnerships might help overcome some of the political rivalries and administrative duplication which could obstruct a Preston-style strategy for the region.

However, there is more to revitalizing Sorachi than just the anchors. As with Preston, to address problems of decline and social inequality, new forms of enterprise, geared to generate employment and spread wealth more evenly, are needed. In this sense there is a necessity for a microeconomic dimension to any plan – in the same way that the Preston Model envisages a flourishing of local co-operatives. What would a cooperative Sorachi look like? For the revitalization of Sorachi, a cooperative model is needed which allows local residents to take the initiative. The workers cooperative model seems the most appropriate, but are there any specific models which might be ideal?

Unicorn: a UK case study

During the author's visit to the UK, he was able to gain insights into the workings of the Unicorn Grocery Workers' Cooperative in Manchester. The store is widely known in the UK as a successful workers' cooperative grocery store and might provide an ideal template for cooperative development in Sorachi. Visiting the store created a strong impression. The selection of organic vegetables is rich, and the format of the store is attractive and inviting. The co-operative is professionally run and constantly implements improvements. A processing factory is located in the back of the store, where a range of preparatory activities take place, sorting large quantities of flour, rice grains, nuts, and so on, into small bags, and the processing and cooking of fresh foods. On a blackboard near the cash register was a price comparison chart with some major supermarkets, revealing a strong awareness that Unicorn must compete on price. One of the great strengths of Unicorn is the pervasive sense of commitment of its worker-members. Unicorn has 70 members, all have a say in management, and they make decisions by consensus. Their salaries are all almost the same. On the wall of the staircase leading up to the office on the second floor, there are snapshots of all the members. The lively expressions on each person's face convey pride, passion, and confidence in their work.

How is commitment and enthusiasm for the co-operative sustained among members? Interviews with members reveal several compelling reasons. One interviewee attributed the success of the grocery store in which he worked to a strong sense of camaraderie: 'I enjoy my work and the pay is not bad. I am blessed with good friends, and my days are fulfilling.'

But it is clear that the work was not easy, and that there was a formalized system of worker 'mutual evaluation' to create a culture of continuous improvement. As the interviewee stressed, this was challenging: 'In fact, it can be hard … Unicorn has a system where we regularly evaluate each other's work performance. In a few days, the day for submitting the mutual evaluation report arrives. This is the hardest part.'

Mutual evaluation is a key strategy of Unicorn to improve its operations and sustain morale. Worker-members motivate each other to improve, and this does seem to have played an important part in Unicorn's success. At the same time, mutual evaluation can be a painful and difficult practice. The people you normally trust with your work are now having a hard look at your daily work and pressing you to do better. As one member confided:

'The pressure of this mutual evaluation system is too much for us ... some of my colleagues have left the company because they could not bear the pressure of this mutual evaluation system ... It's much easier to be warned by the boss. It is quite hard when colleagues, with whom you normally feel comfortable, make various suggestions about your work performance.'

It is a system which therefore depends upon a high degree of trust and solidarity. But it does make real the maxim that 'everyone is responsible for the management of the company'. It seems that Unicorn and its methods might provide the micro-enterprise model required for Sorachi. But mutual evaluation might have to be amended to account for Japanese sociocultural differences, where mutual evaluation among peers can be seen as demoralizing and even humiliating, thereby reducing rather than strengthening the motivation to work. Japanese workers tend to value social harmony, and can be intimidated by confrontation. They therefore might find the rigours and confrontational potential of mutual evaluation demotivating. Clearly this is a system which would need considerable adjustment to meet the needs of the local culture.

Adapting the Preston Model to Sorachi

Plainly the Preston and Unicorn models would need to be adapted to meet the particular circumstances of Sorachi. The most significant of these are local geographical conditions.

To overcome the challenges of distance and diversity, a base facility would be needed to serve as a nucleus of the project, and from which the project could be directed and led. This would be best located in Bibai City, which is near the geographical centre of Sorachi. The facility to be established could be based on an existing *Michi-no-Eki* (CERI, 2018), which has the advantage of being linked to a government's system of such centres. Bibai City (Bibai, 2022) is less than an hour's drive from Sapporo, the capital city of Hokkaido. However, like other municipalities, it has not been able to stop the exodus of young people and the declining birth rate and ageing population. What then are the *Michin-no-Eki*?

Michin-no-Eki: *a vision for a cooperative future*

Michin-no-Eki or a 'roadside station' could play a central role in a Sorachi scheme based on Preston/Unicorn. Michi-no-Eki are facilities which exist all over Japan with three main objectives: (1) to provide road users with a place to rest, (2) to enable local communities to interact with road users and promote local development and (3) to serve as a base for disseminating a variety of local information to road users. Local authorities are responsible for the establishment of these facilities, and the Ministry of Land, Infrastructure, Transport and Tourism (MLIT) certifies them. Since the introduction of the scheme in 1993, over 1,193 have been established in various parts of Japan. More than 100 of these have been established in Hokkaido. Hokkaido is a *Michi-no-Eki* kingdom, so to speak. A *Michi-no-Eki* must have four main facilities: a main building with a rest area, a restaurant, a store, a terrace or an observation facility; restrooms; parking; and a plaza or a square. However, there are no strong restrictions on the additional facilities. Rather, each municipality is encouraged to develop its own unique ideas – implicit then is the potential for the development of a central facility to co-ordinate the application of the new model. The operational details of the *Michi-no-Eki* provide sufficient flexibility for it to become a major centre for the regeneration project. The MLIT envisages three main operational pillars: public services, revenue-generating businesses, and tourism business. The public services focus on providing comfortable rest stops, providing information, offering support to local activities and events, and providing relief in case of disasters. The profit-making businesses devise ways to sell locally produced goods, provide food and beverages, and develop uniquely local products. The tourism business provides information on local spots of interest and accommodation, conducting tours, and developing tourism products.

The management of these facilities is frequently provided through the 'Designated Management Method', using a subcontractor who manages the facility on behalf of the municipality. Usually, the subcontract goes to private companies or a public interest organizations funded by the municipalities. The *Michi-no-Eki* in Bibai City would function both as a base for activities to promote the revitalization of Sorachi and as a 'Unicorn-like' food and general merchandise outlet. As an activity base, it could unite core members and anchor organizations. The facility would house the secretariat of the regional regeneration organization, which would include both local government and university representation. In addition to co-ordinating the creation and relationships between organizations, the facility would also disseminate information both domestically and internationally about Sorachi, especially information to encourage the inward immigration of young people, businesses and tourists.

Participation and consensus

The biggest challenge in creating the organization would be building consensus among core members and 'anchors'. For this, it is essential to not only have a compelling vision for the future, but also a forum for ongoing discussion of it, enabling the emergence of a commonly agreed view and plan. Advice from Preston, which has much experience in building consensus, would be invaluable. In order to develop the concept, university and city officials from Preston would be invited to Sorachi, providing them with opportunities to discuss ideas with local residents and administrative agencies. Another challenge would be to create a new micro-enterprise cooperative model amenable to Japanese workers. At the Bibai City centre, a facility to sell food products and sundries could symbolize revival of Sorachi in a tangible form. It could also provide a model for similar co-operatives across the region.

The sales facility would be a workers' co-operative. With advice from Unicorn, a variety of food-related activities could be promoted. Specifically, the co-operative would promote and expand production of organic vegetables and build a reputation for Sorachi as the home of organic food. The co-operative would be advised and guided on production methods and organization by Unicorn. In addition to promoting healthy eating habits, the co-operative could supply safe boxed school lunches using organic vegetables, as well as delivering boxed lunches to the homes of the elderly. There is already a strong precedent for home delivery. Coop Sapporo, a leading retail co-operative in Hokkaido, already reaches out to all parts of the island in supplying households – a facility which proved invaluable during the COVID-19 pandemic (Mori, 2011). When making home deliveries, the co-operative could cover the entire Sorachi area using drones. Unicorn is volunteering its support activities to spread their efforts domestically and internationally. Therefore, as well as experts from Preston, core members of Unicorn could be invited to Sorachi, with a view to collaborating with them as partners in the creation of the *Michi-no-Eki* in Bibai.

Leadership culture: leading and managing workers co-operatives in Sorachi

As mentioned, there may be difficulties in persuading Japanese workers to respond positively to frank evaluations by their close associates. How might a form of evaluation that is more appropriate for Japanese culture and values be designed (Pilla and Kuriansky, 2018)? Japanese culture values highly collective endeavours. Diligence is also a powerful ingredient of the Japanese work culture. This is encapsulated by the Japanese word kaizen, literally 'improvement'. Japanese people prefer to work together with their peers to achieve higher performance through collective effort and ingenuity. Japanese people tend to be very concerned about what others think of them. Therefore, children and adults alike are extremely sensitive about their relationships at school and work and the impression they make on those around them. Many people fall prey to mental illness because they are too concerned about what others think of them. Given this, what kind of leadership and organizational culture would be most appropriate? In considering leadership in workplaces in Japan, Kawai's work is instructive as described in 'The Hollow Structure in the Depths of Japan' (Kawai, 1982). Kawai contends that Japanese society is 'hollow at the centre', implying that leadership in Japan is not envisaged in the same way as in the West. Where Western societies stress dynamism and decisiveness as key leadership qualities, in Japanese society a leader is seen as a 'caretaker'. The caretaker's job is not to lead the organization through self-assertion and direction, but rather to build a consensus. Even if a caretaker has superior power and ability, he or she should never show it, and ideally, should do little. If there is a role, Kawai points out, it is to maintain balance in the organization. Interestingly, this is a cultural trait which could lend itself very successfully to democratically controlled businesses like co-operatives, many of which depend upon consensus building to reach decisions.

By leaving the centre empty, Japanese culture tolerates conflicts and contradictions within the organization, and does not seek to eliminate them. Under this system, even if one side gains power, a place or a haven is provided for the opposing side. According to Kawai, leaving the centre empty allows conflicts and contradictions to coexist, ensuring balance and stability. In light of this, it would be appropriate for co-operatives to have a 'caretaker' in the post of a leader. The caretaker usually spends his or her time in passive observation. Their only role is to keep an eye on the entire organization and to occasionally talk to individual members and encourage them. However, if a problem arises within the organization, he or she formally takes responsibility for it, but responsibility is ultimately diffused throughout the organization and is eventually resolved. Progress, therefore, is achieved through the power of the group, encouraging each other to reach greater heights. While it is capable of following orders from above, the true strength of an organization comes when it finds and overcomes its own challenges through group harmony. This is indeed a key cooperative approach.

Leadership and systems of evaluation

The caretaker needs to have a set of guiding principles all the participants of the Sorachi Model can agree upon. The mutual evaluation as exercised at Unicorn could harm the self-esteem of some members. In Japan, there would have to be boundaries, such as not criticizing the personality or character of any member. The evaluation has to be action-focused. Positive encouragement for the purpose of improvement should be used.

Leading the central organizing body for the regeneration project will be no easy task, seeking to unite as it does 24 cities and towns. But the assertive command-style leadership of the western model is unlikely to be successful. The stress should be on team building and team working, which are best suited to Japanese culture. Therefore, what kind of evaluation tools might be needed to maximize efficiency and how might the mutual evaluation system adopted by Unicorn be reworked in a Japanese style? A kind of organization Sorachi should aim for is a team that tackles challenges with a collective effort that overcomes inadequacies through teamwork. The most natural way to evaluate the performance of individual members in the Japanese context is not to mutually evaluate each other to show improvements, but to unite as a team and support each other so that better results can be achieved. It may be that the hollow centre of Japanese organizations is connected with cooperative activity in Japan. We might hypothesize that the ambiguity of responsibility itself has supported the growth of co-operatives in Japan. In other words, the 'hollow structure' of Japanese society may have resonated with the basic philosophy of leaderless co-operatives and supported co-operative activities in the region.

Towards a 'Sorachi Model'

What then, are the principal components of a 'Sorachi Model'? First, a base facility to lead and co-ordinate the project is essential. Bibai City, at the centre of Sorachi would be ideal. The existing state provision for a *Michi-no-Eki* (Roadside Station), could be utilized to enable the base to bring together the 24 municipalities in the region. Important core members of the Sorachi Model would be universities and local authorities. In addition to the three national and private universities in Sorachi, a wider coalition of universities could be formed by calling on neighbouring universities. Building a coalition of local authorities, preoccupied with local problems, is likely to be more challenging. One way forward would be for the Bibai City centre to take the lead and start with projects that are relatively easy to realize, accumulate small achievements and attract the interest and support of the neighbouring municipalities.

Bringing on board anchor institutions would be another key component. The region is rich in possibilities. Each municipality in Sorachi has its own police station, city and town hall, hospital, school and library. Therefore, procuring fixtures alone would generate a huge demand which might be met locally by new cooperative producers. Preston's experience in persuading anchors to procure locally from small local companies and co-operatives is invaluable here, not least in facilitating smaller orders which smaller organizations can meet. A huge challenge is to persuade Anchor institutions to break with existing practice which frequently favours large and distant providers. It will be essential to present a persuasive vision for the future to the anchors. The Sorachi Model would be led by a caretaker who would maintain overall balance between the vested interests involved, aiming to maximize group harmony, watching over and encouraging the efforts of each member organization. A Sorachi Model would operate a 'mutual support system', a Japanese adaptation of the Unicorn's mutual evaluation system.

Ultimately, however, the Sorachi Model will depend on winning the hearts and minds of local residents in the region. They must be convinced that the model not only offers the prospect of economic improvement, but also a sense that control over their own lives is being restored. In this respect the Sorachi Model, as with Preston, is about building community.

Overseas expansion?

The utilization of the *Michi-no-Eki* opens the possibility that the model might be exported across Japan and even further afield. The 'Roadside Stations' are highly regarded overseas as a regional development idea and have been established in a total of more than a dozen locations in Central America, the Caribbean, and other countries. Meanwhile, Japan's International Co-operation Agency (JICA, 2022) has recently been teaching the operational know-how of *Michi-no-Eki* to engineers from Central Asia who are coming to Japan to learn the technology. This therefore offers the opportunity of using the *Michi-no-Eki* to replicate the Sorachi model elsewhere.

JICA leaves it to the local communities to make their own decisions as to the use of the *Michi- no-Eki*. This is a stance that respects the autonomy of local communities. However, if the principles of dissemination activities are not clear, they may become an extension of conventional development assistance programs, which may divide local communities and assert the rule of the market economy. Adoption of the Preston/Sorachi Model by the international *Michi-no-Eki* offers the prospect of spreading a much more equitable system of local regeneration. In this way, maybe an idea originating in the UK can revitalize communities around the world via Japan's overseas development strategy.

Conclusion: find a style that fits the society

Incorporating the Preston Model into a Japanese context certainly appears to be a challenge. But adaptation to Japanese culture does not seem impossible. The Preston Model could be transformed into the Sorachi Model, which blends Preston (and Unicorn) principles with ones better suited to the Japanese context. No matter how good an idea is, when the country or region changes, it must be adapted to suit that region. Ideas must be decisively modified in order to support the communities and lives of the local people.

Of course, problems are likely to arise. Can co-operatives without a clear leader be effective in regenerating Japan's former coal-producing areas? But there is room for optimism. Japanese institutions have always been ambiguous about where responsibility lies, but this is an accepted trait and there seems no pressing reason why this cannot be accommodated in the hybrid Sorachi model. No matter what kind of experiment you start, the environment and conditions will naturally change as the geography changes. Experiments such as those in Preston and the example of Unicorn can be integrated into the lives of people in different parts of the world through bold evolution. If this is seen to happen, such an experiment might evolve from a local to a global idea.

Post-conclusion, a final word and personal reflection

The author is not a researcher specializing in regional revitalization, but rather worked for 30 years as a reporter for a Japanese newspaper company before moving to a university. His specialty is not regional economics, but media ethics. It was a conversation with a student that led him to encounter the Preston Model and to adapt it to the needs of Japan. About ten years ago, a student in my seminar came to my laboratory one day and said, 'I have been thinking about the homeless life as a theme for my graduation research.' I agreed, and together with her, we worked on a project on the lives of homeless people in Sapporo City. I went with her to a homeless hangout in Sapporo. There were several homeless people lying on benches, passing the time idly. When I approached them, five or six of them agreed to be interviewed. They were all kind-hearted people. The story of how they became homeless after falling out of various competitions or facing a series of misfortunes was like a drama. Such a downfall can happen to anyone. After the interview, I said to the student, 'You picked up valuable information from the interviews. I am sure your research will be worthwhile.' She gave me a surprising answer: 'I can't work on this theme,' she said. She was an excellent student. She had studied hard since she was a child, and her grades were always above average. She was instructed by her parents that the path to happiness was to enter a reputable junior high school, high school and then university, get a job at a secure company, find a husband with a good enough income, and raise a peaceful family. It was not possible for her to empathize with the homeless interviewees who spent their days idly wandering around parks and offtrack betting offices while there is plenty of work available. She could sympathize with them, but could not empathize with them. In her view, she did not think it was sincere to pretend to empathize with them in order to write her thesis. It was a revelation that pierced my heart.

The exchange with her led me to ask myself whether a shift from a competitive society to a symbiotic society was really possible. In my classes,

I have often stressed the preciousness of symbiosis to my students. In reality, however, I myself am one of those who has negotiated through a competitive society. Was I being a hypocrite? I am sure many students can see through me. From then on, every time I uttered the word 'symbiosis' I would feel a choking sensation in my throat. Soon after I had these thoughts, a horrific incident occurred at a facility for the physically challenged near the centre of Tokyo, where a young man in his 20s stabbed to death a total of 19 severely handicapped people. The arrested youth declared, 'Severely disabled people do not deserve to live'. While being escorted in a police car, he even had a smirk on his face. Japanese society perceived him as a madman. But to me, his words and actions seemed like the end result of our competitive society.

When I was a reporter, I had the experience of interviewing many severely disabled people who had been abandoned by their families, ending up in institutions. It is easy to lament the cold treatment of their families. However, not many people understand the painful realities of the daily lives of the families who take care of severely disabled people in Japan. And the hardship of the facilities that take care of such severely disabled people is also rarely understood. This is the reality of welfare in Japan. Can we steer the course from the competitive market economy filled with inequity toward a society of symbiosis? My visit to Preston was to find an answer to such a question. It was also a journey to confront my own inadequacies, for which I could only give a vague response to a student who had so earnestly revealed her heart in front of me. Perhaps I was searching for a better answer to give to the student working through the issue of community revitalization.

After graduation, the student went on to work for a major insurance company in Japan, where she proved competitive among her peers, achieved top class results, and was featured prominently in a public relations magazine.

References

CERI (2018) 'Michi no Eki' (Roadside station). Available from https://scenic.ceri.go.jp/michi_no_eki_handbook/pdf/michi-no-eki-handbook202002en.pdf [Accessed on 10 June 2022].

FSMH (2018) 'Financial status of municipalities in Hokkaido'. Available from www.sorachi.pref.hokkaido.lg.jp/ts/tss/gyouzaisei.html [Accessed on 10 June 2022].

JICA (2022) 'JICA (Japan International Cooperation Agency): Cultivating character around the world'. Available from www.jica.go.jp/english/index.html [Accessed on 10 June 2022].

Johnson, S. and Harvey-Wilson, H. (2018) 'Local currency adoption and use: Insights from a realist evaluation of the Bristol Pound', *Bath Papers in International Development and Wellbeing, No. 56*, University of Bath, Centre for Development Studies, Bath.

Kawai (1982) 'The Center-Empty Structure: The Deep Structure of Japan (「中空構造日本の深層」)', Hayao Kawai, Chuo Koronsha, pp 57–63.

Manley, J. and Whyman, P.B. (eds) (2021) *The Preston Model and Community Wealth Building: Creating a Socio-Economic Democracy for the Future.* London: Routledge.

Marshall, A.P. and O'Neill, D.W. (2018) 'The Bristol pound: A tool for localisation?', *Ecological Economics*, 146: 273–281.

Masuda (2014) 'The disappearance of rural areas: The rapid decline in population caused by the concentration of people in Tokyo (「地方消滅〜東京一極集中が招く人口急減」)', Hiroya Masuda, Chuko Shinsho, pp 208–210.

Pilla and Kuriansky (2018) 'Mental health in Japan: Intersecting risks in the workplace', *Journal of Student Research Review Articles*, 7(2): 38–41.

Preston (2022) 'Preston Model'. Available from https://thenextsystem.org/the-preston-model [Accessed on 10 June 2022].

Sorachi (2022) 'Sorachi Subprefecture'. Available from https://en.wikipedia.org/wiki/Sorachi_Subprefecture [Accessed on 10 June 2022].

Unicorn (2022) 'Unicorn'. Available from www.unicorn-grocery.coop [Accessed on 10 June 2022].

Webster, A., Kuznetsova, O., Ross, C., Berranger, C., Booth M., Eseonu, T. and Golan, Y. (2021) 'Local regeneration and community wealth building–place making: Co-operatives as agents of change', *Journal of Place Management and Development*, 14(4): 446–461.

14

Conclusion: Clues to a Co-operative Future?

Julian Manley, Olga Kuznetsova and Anthony Webster

The three sections of this book move from local case studies of cooperativism to examples of systemic designs, especially in the form of CWB, that incorporate co-operation in the widest sense of the word. The Preston Model and its budding offshoot in Japan are just two examples of a changing mindset in how life, space and work can be organized, with human beings taking centre stage. The Preston Model is highlighted in this book because of recent attention to its successes and influence and its focus on co-operation. The Preston Model has captured the imagination and ignited hopes and desires for change. We do not claim that the Preston Model is uniquely innovative. Not only does it have its roots in Cleveland and Mondragón, but there are many versions of CWB or the social economy dotted around the world, each with its local touch. Some are recent, as in Barcelona or Cincinnati, and others have been established for several decades, as is the case of the 'Chantier' system of social and economic innovation in Quebec (Mendell, 2009). It does seem, however, that the development of the Preston Model is uniquely situated at a moment of social and economic change in the UK with significant outreach and influence – as in the national economies of Scotland and Wales – that is not common to all such systemic innovations.

It is no longer incontestably accepted that the neoliberal modality of the capitalist system based squarely on competition and hierarchical structures of reward can solve its own problems in a world beset by multiplying and recurring crises. This is why a growing number of academics and public intellectuals argue in favour of market plurality and many endorse the cooperative model of organizing as a promising alternative to market orthodoxy, capable of advancing more socially balanced and participatory practices (Stiglitz, 2002; Porritt, 2007; Restakis, 2010; Birchall, 2013). The authors of this book align with this thinking and have engaged with the task of outlining thoughts of an exciting future of co-operation as a force that can counteract the failures and shortcomings of the neoliberal way of engaging the market and the competition that accompanies it.

In addition to this, co-operation, even beyond or apart from the governance demanded of actual cooperative organization, appears to be emerging as some form of alternative to a system based solely or largely on competition. Co-operation offers a different way, format and value sets for running a business based on the internationally agreed and recognized seven cooperative principles (ICA, nd). However, such principles, in a general way, are also relevant for a life based on and promoting equality, justice and a kind of democracy that goes beyond the occasional vote in an election every few years. Cooperative principles, therefore, can be thought of as a guide for living and working differently, not just at work, but in community (Ridley, 2021).

Thus, a sense of participation, equality and democracy that underpin the Preston Model, and co-operation between different entities and stakeholders in Preston is at the core to its success (Manley and Whyman, 2021). Importantly, when the cooperative principles are translated into ways of being, in a more general sense, what is being encouraged is attitudinal and behavioural change. Stakeholders in the Preston Model make the shift from a disconnecting competition to co-operation as an affective choice, unlegislated and subject to persuasion rather than bound by obligation (Manley and Aiken, 2020; Prinos and Manley, 2022). Co-operation of this kind is relational and it might be understood through the use of different terminology. For instance, in the example of Preston, there is a growing focus on recognizing social value as a legitimate and necessary constituent of economic value. Such an emphasis on social value is not just a wish, it is a practical reality, as demonstrated in the creation of the *Social Value Network* in Preston and Lancashire (Our Central Lancashire, nd; Manley et al, 2023). Whatever the definition of social value, specifics of which may vary from one application to the next, the important universal change in terms of what social value means for cooperative community wealth building projects such as the Preston Model, is in the understanding of a value which is not uniquely based on financial rewards. It is something that is of a benefit to a system of co-operation and community and not principally to a business (which might be the interpretation of corporate social responsibility (Manley et al, 2023)). For the cooperative system the social element in value is intrinsic to cooperative Principle 7: 'Concern for community'.

As mentioned in Introduction to this book, there is currently a plethora of literature, both academic and popular, that attempts to look to a future beyond stagnating, wasteful, uninspiring and self-serving capitalism. In the most daring and critical outlooks and versions of these reassessments, it is possible to find new concepts such as 'degrowth' (Vandeventer and Lloveras, 2021) or 'post-growth' (Banerjee et al, 2021; Pansera and Fressoli, 2021). Webb and Novkovic, for example, explicitly link the ideas of 'post-growth' with a cooperative society. In this cooperative post-growth context, they reject 'both the state socialist and capitalist models of the twentieth century' (Webb and Novkovic, 2014, p 1). In this rejection, they seek an alternative which paves the way towards a cooperative society of the future rather than one based on the past roots of co-operation and the 20th-century tussle between state and market forces.

One of the questions of the present edition is how to go from the localized cooperative examples exemplified in Part I to the systemic change implied through illustrations in Part III. One way, we suggest, is through the channels of knowledge production and delivering education. It is striking to note how embedded the capitalist system is in people's minds, almost as if 'there is no alternative', as Margaret Thatcher was fond of saying. Similarly, it is equally striking to point out that very significant numbers of the general population have no understanding of what a cooperative organization is, and in our research fieldwork the idea of 'cooperative' was frequently equated with the Coop supermarket or the Coop funeral service, as if these were brands rather than ways of working (Manley and Froggett, 2016). Education, as Wright and Manley (2021) have previously discussed, was fundamental to the beginnings and continued success of the Mondragón co-operatives and is embedded in Principle 5 of the ICA cooperative principles. This theme is picked up in Chapters 7 and 8 of this book, where cooperative education and education about cooperative economy is looked at in the light of community development on the one hand and formal university education on the other. The importance of education, training and dissemination is also fundamental to Mondragón and to the 'Chantier' in Quebec, where the Community-University Research Alliance (CURA) has been long-established and respected as a sustainable source of research for innovation and policy. According to Mendell (2009) 'the broad circulation of material [deriving from CURA] and the organization of numerous public events have been critical to generating a dynamic policy dialogue within Quebec and *across the country*' (p 202, our italics).

However, apart from direct education and research as imparting knowledge and skills, it seems that there is a lot to be said in how participation in cooperative ventures as described in Part I of this book can offer ways of experiential learning, that is to say learning by doing and participating. This kind of learning can be identified with communitarian concepts of learning as knowledge which is self-organizing and understood through authentic acts of living. Empowerment through action is a vital feature of cooperative democratic participatory governance that might support the idea that co-operation is not to be limited to the cooperative venture or business, but can provide a general template for the way society as a whole can function. Polletta points to this possibility by connecting Boggs' coining of the term 'prefigurative' to 'describe attempts to enact a radically egalitarian society in the lived practices of the movement [leftist movements that embraced participatory democracy]' (Polletta, 2014, p 81). It is by participating in democracy that attitudes and behaviours can begin to change and the 'no alternative' mindset may find its alternative. This resonates with Stewart (Chapter 6 in this book), where an alternative way of collectively owning a football club becomes reality. In this case the prefigurement of society is mirrored in the participatory and democratic structure of ownership of the club. It is a structure that leads to more than simply organizational change, because the football club in question is embedded in the culture, identity and pride of place.

There appears to be something of a rebirth in participatory democratic movements from the 1960s and 1970s which resonate with the ideas emerging from this book. It has been suggested that this may have something to do with the connectivity of online communities among young people (Polletta, 2014). Similarly, in this book, Wallers (Chapter 2) connects the participation of past movements to new cooperative cultural movements. Mannan (Chapter 5) also considers the joining of cooperativism and the interconnectivity of platform co-operatives. As Polletta (2014) asserts, in a discussion of participatory democracy, participating is not only participating, but being in a position to decide, which is a theme that is echoed in Langmead and Webster's chapter in this book. In other words, there appears to be a growing awareness of the need to define work, community and society through interconnectivity and through the nurturing of relationships. In a similar vein, it is possible to understand Deblangy's chapter on environmental commitment of co-operatives as a development of Bookchin's 'social ecology' (Bookchin, 2005): a theory and movement with its roots in the 1960s and 1970s that seems to be finding a new form in the 21st century.

Another defining feature of 21st-century cooperativism may be in its ability to join the dots of past movements into coherent wholes. What is emerging from the chapters in this book is a sense, as described in depth in Meyers and Vallas (2016), that co-operatives may enable an efficient means of holistically gathering together what may in the past have been different progressive threads or choices of how to work and live. Meyers and Vallas argue that the phenomena of 'employee participation' and 'diversity management' are areas of work that have been traditionally studied in isolation. These two apparently separate topics are in fact intrinsically connected. Since this connection encourages collective thinking as opposed to individualistic positions, such a connection is inherent in a cooperative structure. Webster's chapter in this regard may suggest how it is a conservative political position in the UK to promote individualism as opposed to the collective and embracing nature of cooperative enterprises that has in part prevented political backing for cooperative development. This may be why the joined-up features of systems such as the Preston Model are so firmly rooted in the local, since national policy is unsupportive. Even though the Preston Model is identified with 'Corbynomics' (Manley, 2018), it is also frequently described as 'common sense' (Manley, 2021; Webster et al, 2021), in other words depoliticized. Chapter 10 of this book describes the attempt by the CCIN to depoliticize the network of cooperative councils in the UK.

Where there is a lack of national identity, so important in Scotland and Wales in the UK, the CCIN is an example of networking an identity where none previously existed. This contributes to the sensation of inevitable change seeping into the system and reflected in this book. The changes are neither consistent nor necessarily durable, as Prinos relates in his chapter, but the Mondragón example described in Chapter 12 demonstrates the potential for durable change.

The final chapter of the book contributes to the evolving research theme and a field of conversations between practitioners and academics on the transferability and richness of the cooperative organizational formats (Webster et al, 2021). If co-operation is centred on social and human values, then this may be an ethical opportunity for Europe to learn from and absorb all the best achievements of co-operation around the world, and eventually to mainstream cooperativism and its humanistic spirit into a dominant entrepreneurial model. Such a humanistic spirit, identified as a 'cooperative difference', is the subject of a very recently published book by Novkovic and colleagues (2023). Such synergetic coincidences perhaps indicate a certain prescience or inevitability for future cooperative socio-economic transformation that is the central theme of our book.

This book has also identified challenges which cooperativism continues to face. Perhaps the most intractable of these is a cultural one, which in many ways reflects half a century of pronounced individualism and neoliberal ideology. Prinos stresses the difficulty of building not just an understanding of co-operation but also an emotional commitment to it. In a chapter on Mondragón, Manley identifies a similar problem, citing the need for strategies to regularly 'refresh' support for cooperative values as new generations of members are inducted into the consortium. The need for a kind of 'secular spiritual' belief in co-operation is crucial to ensure that the movement endures. Manley and Eseonu further extend this thinking in the context of local authority commitments to co-operatives values, citing the importance of 'cooperative character' attributes in guiding local government policies to promote co-operatives. Deblangy argues that an important opportunity to win hearts and minds for cooperative organization is provided by the capacity for workplace democracy to enable cooperative members to exert influence over issues beyond the workplace, especially in the field of protecting the environment and strengthening local communities. Langmead and Webster also allude to this, adding the opportunities co-operatives offer for the development of fulfilling 'meaningful' work. The role of education in building this belief in and enthusiasm for co-operation is demonstrated by Noble, but Kuznetsov and Kuznetsova demonstrate that there is still a way to go in building the apparatus to support this in higher education. Their criticisms of the Business School echo the long-standing and influential work of Parker, who calls for an end to traditional management-orientated business education in HE and makes a plea for alternatives and regeneration (Parker, 2023). Our book proposes that the cooperative alternative can and should be part of this transformation. Parker's 'provisional manifesto' for a 'School of Organizing' is replete with references to ethically sound practices (implying their lack in the corporate business world). Co-operatives and cooperative ecosystem designs can provide this ethical turn. Nevertheless, we could ask at this juncture, is this a 'chicken-and-egg' situation: does the education come before the culture change or vice versa?

The foundations of cultural change are also potentially undermined by those problems which have all too frequently confronted co-operatives in the past: a shortage of capital, a lack of institutional support from the state and hostility arising from ideological scepticism. To overcome these obstacles, a change in political attitudes as well as state policy is necessary, and in this respect, the Preston Model is instructive, at least in terms of political attitudes. Perhaps even more urgent is a willingness and mechanisms for co-operatives to work together both commercially and politically to establish more robust, self-supportive and integrated systems, as evident in Mondragón and the Trentino. As Webster shows, despite the efforts in Preston, also in evidence in isolated pockets elsewhere in the UK, this is lamentably absent in the British case.

The development of systems of co-operation studied in this book brings up questions of localism in the context of globalism (sometimes referred to as *glocalization*), with Sakai's chapter suggesting a way to join the two. The area of study in Sakai's chapter, Hokkaido, has its own cooperative tradition and success (Kurimoto, forthcoming), but Sakai demonstrates the desire for the transferability of a cooperative ecodesign system based on Preston that goes beyond individual cooperative achievements. In this sense, the local in Hokkaido can become global. The issue related to local/global is a dilemma that is especially prominent in the 21st century, where high speed travel and virtual connectivity provide a means of being present elsewhere while still coming from somewhere. Crises lead to changes, as we can see in the reactions to the pandemic and changes in work practices from the workplace to the homespace. The nature of place in an interconnected world, especially in a post-COVID-19 and virtually connected world, brings up unresolved dilemmas of community, place and co-operation. The gaps in the literature that need addressing are related to problems of identification by citizens of place and space and therefore what it means to participate. Future research is needed to understand the potential impact of local cooperative development and emerging modern-day social movements in addressing social crises which are often global and yet felt locally. Community wealth building, local economies and regional regeneration are now intrinsically linked to macro-level emergencies, including climate change and environmental activism, inclusivity, diversity, participatory democracy, social justice and their opposites in present-day tensions with extremist reactionary positions manifested around the world.

By combining theory and practice, the authors of this book are pointing towards a rebalancing of society based on using insights and guidance from the cooperative principles and values. In doing so, this book contributes to the development of visions on 'post-growth era' that appreciate and endorse the relevance of cooperative form of organizing and governance, as discussed in Novkovic and Webb's forward-looking publication *Co-operatives in a Post-Growth Era* (Novkovic and Webb, 2014). By bringing co-operatives to the fore as a possible solution to the multiple crises facing humanity today, our book on co-operation in 21st-century Europe suggests a way forward. 'Solution' is maybe too simplistic a word to describe such a process. Accordingly, this book also emphasizes the complexity and difficulties of such a venture. A cooperative future, if there is one, will not be a quick fix, but rather a transitional period of change and adaptation to circumstances involving a wider engagement with the cooperative principles and the philosophy of co-operation and participation by all groups of economic agents. The interconnectivity of the micro-meso-macro components that constitute life on this planet have been well illustrated in Raworth's 'doughnut' model (Raworth, 2017) that shows a fundamental interdependence of the macro elements of global and ecological limits to life and the social limits and needs to live a fulfilled life at a local level. The difficulty in sustainably balancing macro and micro, global and local, societal and individual is in the *how* in terms of the organizational forms. We hope that this book goes some way to suggesting some answers to this challenge and that a new socio-economic era might be organized in a more compassionate, collective and cooperative way.

References
Banerjee, S.B., City, M., Jermier, J.M., Peredo, A.M., Perey, R. and Reichel, A. (2021) 'Theoretical perspectives on organizations and organizing in a post-growth era', *Organization*, 28(3): 337–357.
Birchall, J. (2013) 'The potential of co-operatives during the current recession: Theorizing comparative advantage', *Journal of Entrepreneurial and Organizational Diversity*, 2(1): 1–22.

Bookchin, M. (2005) *The Ecology of Freedom* Edinburgh: AK Press.

ICA (nd) 'Cooperative identity, values and principles'. Available from www.ica.coop/en/cooperatives/cooperative-identity [Accessed on 26 August 2022].

Kurimoto, A. 'Strategic renewal and financial crises: Case of Co-op Sapporo'. In Wilson, J.F., Ekberg, E. and Skurnik, S. (eds) *Strategic Renewal in the Consumer Co-operative Sector: An International Study*. Routledge (forthcoming).

Manley, J. (2018) 'Preston changed its fortunes with "Corbynomics": Now other cities are doing the same', *The Conversation*. Available from https://theconversation.com/preston-changed-its-fortunes-with-corbynomics-now-other-cities-are-doing-the-same-106293 [Accessed on 29 August 2022].

Manley, J. (2021) 'The Preston Model: From top-down to rhizomatic-up: How the Preston Model challenges the system'. In Manley, J. and Whyman, P.B. (eds) *The Preston Model and Community Wealth Building, Creating a Socio-economic Democracy for the Future*. London: Routledge, pp 17–32.

Manley, J. and Froggett, L. (2016) 'Co-operative activity in Preston', University of Central Lancashire. Available from https://clok.uclan.ac.uk/14526/1/Co-operative%20activity%20PrestonREPORT%20copy.pdf [Accessed on 26 June 2023].

Manley, J. and Aiken, M. (2020) 'A socio-economic system for affect: Dreaming of co-operative relationships and affect in Bermuda, Preston and Mondragón', *Organisational and Social Dynamics*, 20(2): 173–191.

Manley, J. and Whyman, P.B. (eds) (2021) *The Preston Model and Community Wealth Building, Creating a Socio-Economic Democracy for the Future*. London: Routledge.

Manley, J., Garner, C., Halliday, E., Lee, J., Mattinson, L., McKeown, M., Prinos, I., Smyth, K. and Wood, J. (2023) 'Saving lives and minds: Understanding social value and the role of anchor institutions in supporting community and public health before and after COVID-19'. In Idowu, S.O., Idowu, M.T. and Idowu, A.O. (eds) *Corporate Social Responsibility in the Health Sector: CSR and COVID-19 in Global Health Service Institutions*. Cham: Springer.

Mendell, M. (2009) 'The three pillars of the social economy: The Quebec experience'. In Amin, A. (ed) *The Social Economy. International Perspectives on Economic Solidarity*. London: Zed Books, pp 176–208.

Meyers, J.S.M. and Vallas, S.P. (2016) 'Diversity regimes in worker co-operatives: Workplace inequality under conditions of worker control', *The Sociological Quarterly*, 57(1): 98–128.

Novkovic, S. and Webb, T. (eds) (2014) *Co-operatives in a Post-Growth Era*. London: Zed.

Novkovic, S., Miner, K. and McMahon, C. (eds) (2023) *Humanistic Governance in Democratic Organizations: The Cooperative Difference.* Cham: Palgrave Macmillan.

Our Central Lancashire (nd). Available from www.healthierlsc.co.uk/cent ral-lancs [Accessed on 26 August 2022].

Pansera, M. and Fressoli, M. (2021) 'Innovation without growth: Frameworks for understanding technological change in a postgrowth era', *Organization,* 28(3): 380–404.

Parker, M. (2023) 'Against management: Auto-critique'. *Organization,* 30(2): 407–415.

Polletta, F. (2014) 'Participatory democracy's moment', *Journal of International Affairs,* 68(1): 79–92.

Porritt, J. (2007). *Capitalism as if the World Matters.* London: Earthscan.

Prinos, I. and Manley, J. (2022) 'The Preston Model: Economic Democracy, Cooperation and Paradoxes in Organisational and Social Identification', *Sociological Research Online.* https://doi.org/10.1177/13607804211069398

Raworth, K. (2017) *Doughnut Economics: Seven Ways to Think Like a 21st-Century Economist.* Vermont: Chelsea Green.

Restakis, J. (2010) *Humanizing the Economy: Co-operatives in the Age of Capital.* Gabriola Island: New Society Publishers.

Ridley, J. (2021) 'Community and co-operatives: A Preston perspective'. In Manley, J. and Whyman, P.B. (eds) *The Preston Model and Community Wealth Building: Creating a Socio-economic Democracy for the Future.* London: Routledge, pp 64–79.

Stiglitz, J.E. (2002). *Globalization and Its Discontents.* New York: W.W. Norton & Company.

Vandeventer, J.S. and Lloveras, J. (2021) 'Organizing degrowth: The ontological politics of enacting degrowth in OMS', *Organization,* 28(3): 358–379.

Webster, A., Kuznetsova, O., Ross, C., Berranger, C., Booth, M., Eseonu, T. and Golan, Y. (2021) 'Local regeneration and community wealth building place making: Co-operatives as agents of change', *Journal of Place Management and Development,* 14(4): 446–461.

Wright, S. and Manley, J. (2021) 'Co-operative education: From Mondragon and Bilbao to Preston'. In Manley, J. and Whyman, P.B. (eds) *The Preston Model and Community Wealth Building, Creating a Socio-Economic Democracy for the Future.* London: Routledge, pp 48–64.

Index

References to endnotes show both the page number and the note number (36n1).

Printed and bound by CPI Group (UK) Ltd, Croydon, CR0 4YY

23/04/2025

14661024-0004